The Leader F

CW00350775

Fiasco Or Triumph?

Kevin Robertson

The Leader Project

Fiasco Or Triumph?

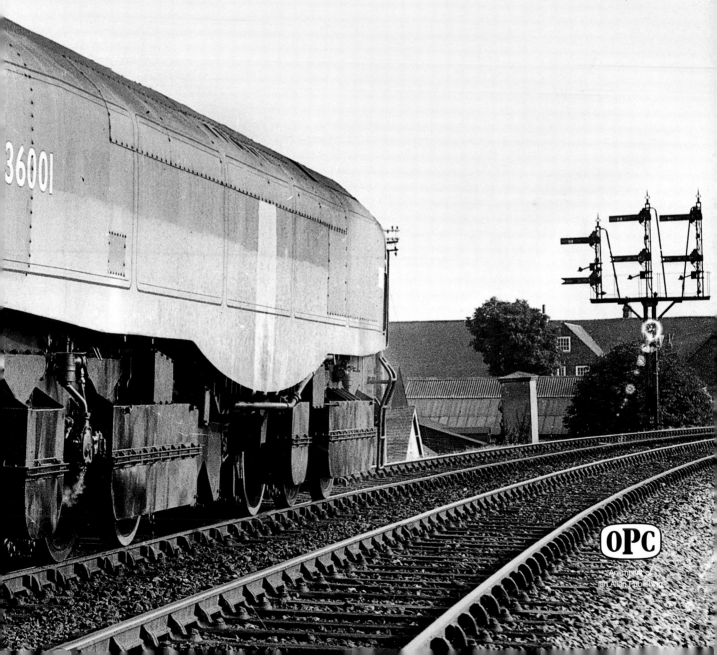

36001

OPC

An imprint of
Ian Allan Publishing

Contents

Front cover: **No 36001 and her test train heading back towards Eastleigh past Winchester Junction.** From a painting by Craig Tiley (www.craigtiley.co.uk).

Left: The almost complete second 'Leader', No 36002, in store at New Cross shed in the early summer of 1951. Shortly after this view was taken the engine – complete except for the addition of covers to the springs, minor pipework, and cab windows – was towed to Brighton and dismantled. Chalked on the side is what appear to be the words 'Property of the British Taxpayer', proof if it were needed that feelings over both the 'Leader' project and Nationalisation were generally still running high three years after a change to public ownership.
A. C. Sterndale

First published 2007 in hardback
First published 2009 in paperback

ISBN 978 0 86093 628 2

Published by Ian Allan Publishing

an imprint of Ian Allan Publishing Ltd, Hersham, Surrey KT12 4RG.
Printed in England by Ian Allan Printing Ltd, Hersham, Surrey KT12 4RG.

Code: 0901/B

Visit the Ian Allan Publishing website at www.ianallanpublishing.com

Acknowledgements and Bibliography

'Leader' has always fascinated me. Indeed, as is recounted in the text, it was comments made by others that made me want to discover for myself if there was actually more to tell. That quest for knowledge about the single prototype has now spanned two decades, during which I have had the privilege of meeting a number of individuals who had a similar fascination for the project. Not all expressed the same opinions – some I could agree with, others not – but I do thank you all.

So what is different this time? Well, for a start, some material that was deliberately left out 20 years ago can now be included – material that it would not have been appropriate to include for what will be seen to be obvious reasons. No criticism is intended – everyone is entitled to different views, and who is to say who is right and who is wrong? That surely depends on the principles that are being applied.

Unfortunately time has taken its toll on those who were personally involved in our story. Individuals like Stephen Townroe, John Click, Don Bradley and Les Warnett are no longer able to contribute. Stephen Townroe especially was a source of continued inspiration for me; indeed, at times when the going was getting a bit rough, it was he who persuaded me to carry on. I hope therefore that at long last I can do justice to a project such as 'Leader' – how dearly would I have loved to know what it sounded like as well!

Accordingly I can do no more than list those individuals whom I have had the privilege to contact for assistance. Gentlemen – and Ladies – I thank you all:

Hugh Abbinnett, Mike Arlott, Mike Arscott at 'Markits', Charles Attwell, H. W. Attwell, C. Banks, John Bell, Eric Best, W. Bishop, C. P. Boocock, D. L. Bradley, E. Bramble, E. Branch, Don Broughton, H. A. P. Browne, H. A. V. Bulleid, D. Callender, H. C. Casserley, Derek Clayton, John Click, Terry Cole, Barry and Joe Curl, Brian Davis, Ken Dobson, Peter Dunk, W. Durban, R. Eagle, Les Elsey, John Fairman, Ted Forder, Harry Frith, John Fry, Geoff Gardiner, Jack Gardner, W. Gilburt, David Fereday Glenn, Roger Hardingham, Graham Hawkins, C. C. B. Herbert, Dave Heulin, J. T. Howard-Turner, P. Ineson, The Institution of Mechanical Engineers (especially S. G. Morrison), Bill Jackson, Phil Kelley, Mike King, Graham Long, Ron Manley, Henry Meyer, Max Millard, Tony Molyneaux, B. Musgrave, S. C. Nash, The National Newspaper Library, The National Railway Museum (especially Phil Atkins and John Edgington), G. L. Nicholson, The Patents Office, Reg Randell, R. C. Riley, John Rooney, Reg Roude, The Science Museum, John Scott-Morgan, John Scrace, Tony Sedgwick, Ian Shawyer, Ernie Shepherd, Pursey Short, R. C. Simmonds, Roger Simmonds, Alf Smith, The Stephenson Locomotive Society, A. C. Sterndale, Richard Stumpf, Mrs Talbot, Arthur Tayler, Mike Thorp, Craig Tiley (www.craigtiley.co.uk) Dennis Tillman, The Times Photographic Library, S. C. Townroe, Mike Turner, Fred Waller, Les Warnett, George Wheeler, D. W. Winkworth, Les Wright, Doug Yarney and Chris Youett.

The following works have been quoted from or consulted:

Allen, G. Freeman *The Southern Since 1948* (Ian Allan, 1987)
Bradley, D. L. *Locomotives of the Southern Railway Part 2* (RCTS, 1976)
Bulleid, H. A. V. *Bulleid of the Southern* (Ian Allan, 1977)
Carter, Ernest F. *Unusual Locomotives* (Frederick Muller Ltd, 1960)
Chacksfield, J. E. *Ron Jarvis: From Midland Compound to HST* (Oakwood Press, 2004)
Chapelon, André *La Locomotive à Vapeur* (Camden Miniature Steam Services; English translation of original 1950 edition, updated and revised 2000)
Cook, A. F. *Trains Annual 1952* (Ian Allan)
Cox, E. S. *Locomotive Panorama Vol 1* (Ian Allan, 1965)
Day-Lewis, Sean Bulleid: *Last Giant of Steam* (Allen & Unwin, 1964)
Fryer, Charles *Experiments With Steam* (Patrick Stephens Ltd, 1990)
Jones, Kevin P. *Steam Locomotive Development* (Library Association, 1969)
Nock, O. S. *Southern Steam* (David & Charles, 1966 and 1972)
Rimmer, Alan *Testing Times at Derby* (Oakwood Press, 2004)
Robertson, Kevin *Leader: Steam's Last Chance* (Alan Sutton Publishing, 1988)
Leader and Southern Experimental Steam (Alan Sutton Publishing, 1990)
Rogers, Col H. C. B. *Chapelon: Genius of French Steam* (Ian Allan, 1972)
Shepherd, Ernie *Bulleid and the Turfburner* (KRB Publications, 2004)
Townroe, S. C. *'Arthurs', 'Nelsons' and 'Schools' At Work* (Ian Allan, 1973, revised 1983)
Tufnell, Robert *Prototype Locomotives* (David & Charles, 1985)

Backtrack – various issues, including November 2005
Journal of the Stephenson Locomotive Society, in particular No 483, October 1965, article by J. M. Dunn and 'A.F.C.' (J. M. Dunn refers briefly again to the design in his autobiography *Reflections on a Railway Career: LNWR to BR* (Ian Allan, 1966))
The Railway Gazette – various issues, but in particular that of 19 November 1948

Introduction

What, another book on 'Leader'? Surely there have been three already? Yes, and yes, and yes to the present writer having been the author of all three. To be fair, the third was an amalgamation of the first two, while the second did not cover the story in detail, but instead provided readers with what was a new collection of photographs of the engine unavailable at the time of the original work. So that really means that there has just been a single previous book, and one in which I recounted, to the best of my ability, the true story of the 'Leader' project – some indeed might say 'fiasco', hence the 'tongue in cheek' play on words in the present title.

Prior to the previous books, a number of authors had touched on the subject, but none in detail and most with little more than a passing reference. Indeed, I well recall the late O. S. Nock in his volume *Southern Steam* concluding a single paragraph on the engine with the words, '… I feel it is still too early to give a reasoned appraisal of an experiment which can only be described as fully in keeping with the personality and career of the designer.' Even that doyen of Southern locomotive history, the late Don Bradley, failed to refer to the engine in any of his books, although it has since been rumoured that he had intended to produce a further work that would have included 'Leader' as well as the Southern electric and diesel locomotives. Indeed, when I began a correspondence with Don Bradley concerning the project before he sadly died, he never mentioned he was doing another book himself! However, O. S. Nock and others had done their job well, and my curiosity had been stirred, my appetite whetted.

In every work prior to 1988 the same few facts were repeated, and sometimes elaborated or expounded upon, often resulting in inaccurate, though well-intended, inferences. My first book in 1988 was therefore intended to set the record straight, the full information to do so only then being available. A visit to the NRM on a totally separate issue had resulted in a chance conversation with Phil Atkins, then the Librarian, who was only too happy to produce all the necessary files, evidently only just released under what was the '30-year rule'.

This was an opportunity not to be missed, and I was personally gratified when the finished work proved as popular as it did. However, the project was not without its difficulties. I believe the fear at the time was that I would condemn Bulleid – as indeed some others had done – not just for 'Leader' but also for other aspects of his work.

No 36001 appears to be in almost a silver grey livery outside the front of Eastleigh Works on what is either 26 or 27 June 1949. At this stage she was awaiting number and BR insignia decals and inspection by 'the great and the good'. S. C. Townroe/Colour-Rail

I did not do so then, and I will not do so now (although ironically others have since!).

Perhaps what I still find sad is that despite factual information having been placed into the public domain at York in the 1980s *and* made accessible by me to a wider audience through the 1988 book, inaccuracies have been perpetuated in subsequent publications by other authors.

So, who am I to make such a critically bold statement, perhaps – some might say – an accusation? Well, I am not a mechanical engineer – I actually trained in electronics before deciding on a different career path – but does one need to be a mechanical engineer to recount every political and operational detail? If building a steam engine from scratch, such a qualification would be a distinct advantage – but my remit was different both then and now. I want to set out the facts. Not just supposition, conjecture or opinion masquerading as fact, but the true facts themselves, then let the reader form his or her own opinion. Inevitably, to supplement those facts a degree of supposition, conjecture and opinion is necessary – indeed, that was the very remit with which I approached the present publisher and for which approval was subsequently given to proceed – but where details are given that are not confirmed as fact, I have ensured that I have stated as much. Thus I am hoping – for the second time, and with far more detail than previously – to put the record straight. Much of what is recounted this time could not have been said 20 years ago. 'Leader' deserves a fair hearing, rather than to be condemned or defended without all the facts being recorded. If you have read thus far, I trust you will similarly continue with an open mind. What follows is still as full and as accurate an account as I have been able to compile of the events that led up to the building, trial running and demise of what I genuinely believe was the ultimate British-built steam engine.

As regards the players, foremost among them must be Bulleid himself. Nowhere will you find in these pages, nor in any of my previous works, any condemnation of the man by me. Who am I to criticise such an august individual? And I say that not through fear of legal retribution, but because there is no justification to criticise the designer. Bulleid did what he no doubt perceived was right at the time. This may not have seemed right to other contemporary players, and I have carefully and accurately – without taking phrases out of context – included quotes and comments of others where necessary. (The word 'carefully' is also used in a dual sense – the quotes I use can be borne out as necessary.)

Perhaps the biggest danger now – more than half a century after the period in question, and approaching 20 years since I first put pen to paper on the subject – is to apply 21st-century ideals to a mid-20th-century project. Times have changed both socially and economically. Thus I have tried to refrain from the oft-used 'with hindsight' viewpoint as far as possible. This book is an account of what actually took place at the time, and most conclusions and reflections 'with hindsight' are left for the last chapter – but please don't skip through and read the last chapter first, or you will simply end up with a distorted view, as indeed others have in the past.

What follows may seem radical to some – yes, it is. Controversial – yes, it certainly is. (You may find some well-known engineers portrayed in a different light from usual.) Topical – yes, it is that as well, certainly if you were around at the time (I was born the year the thing was scrapped). Thought-provoking – I do hope so, but not as far as to openly encourage anyone to try and build a full-size engine today!

I think I can say that, with nearly 50 railway books under my own name or written jointly with others, the 'Leader' project is still very high among my favourite topics (everyone has to earn a crust somehow...). I think it is regrettable that the available facts on the 'Leader' project have been so distorted. Have an opinion by all means, but base it on fact, not inaccurate hearsay. And if this also sounds controversial, it is meant to be.

However, stepping down from the soapbox I must at this stage also record my heartfelt gratitude to friends old and new – indeed, all those who have assisted my quest both originally and since. Accordingly I feel it no more than appropriate to repeat in the Acknowledgements the names of those who assisted first time round. As this is by no means a reprint, some of the material those individuals provided may not have been used, but it all goes to make up the complete picture. Sadly, as time passes, the list of living contributors reduces ever further. None of what follows would have been possible without them; we may not have always agreed, but I respect and thank you all. Above all, I must thank O. V. S. Bulleid himself. We never met, nor corresponded, but an especial thankyou to an inspirational man – and for giving me something to write about!

Kevin Robertson
January 2006

CHAPTER ONE

The Why is Important

There have been two biographies of Bulleid, the first by Sean Day-Lewis in 1964 and the second by Bulleid's son, H. A. V. (Anthony) Bulleid some years later. I recall devouring the first at an early age – indeed, it was one of the first railway books I recall actually reading from cover to cover, and one that I can also say put me on the track – apologies for the cliché – of a quest for the unusual. (At one time I had designs on writing about a number of the various experimental locomotives – the LMS 'Turbomotive', Gresley's 'Hush-Hush', the Beyer-Ljungström, etc – but I leave such essays to others should anyone be so inclined.)

The difficulty for those who write biographies is that by their very nature they have to place every event chronologically and in context, while at the same time attempting to conjoin matters into a cohesive account. In this work, however, I can intentionally take just one aspect, 'Bulleid the Engineer', and concentrate on just one aspect of that theme; I can leave discourse on his other achievements – and achievements they were – outside these pages.

To start with it is necessary to make some bold statements. First, Bulleid was a competent, clever, innovative and skilful engineer. If proof were needed, one only has to consider briefly his intellectual ability, professional qualifications, and rapid rise within the Great Northern Railway. Subsequently he advanced still further to the high position of Principal Assistant to Nigel Gresley on the LNER, then to the top job as CME of the Southern Railway, and finally to a similar role on Córas Iompair Eireann (CIE) in Ireland.

It is during his time with the LNER that we must first consider his engineering prowess. To begin with let it be said that there is no evidence to suggest that Gresley and Bulleid had anything other than an excellent working relationship. Gresley was six years older than Bulleid, and the age difference may perhaps have enabled him to control his assistant carefully. What exactly Bulleid's activities were under Gresley is not completely clear. We know his formal role from the title 'Principal Assistant', but what did that actually mean in effect, and how much influence, if any, did Bulleid have on Gresley's locomotive designs? This is a vitally important point, for apart from reference to Bulleid having been involved in aspects of carriage design and the introduction of welding techniques, there are really only two known definite features of the Gresley steam types that may have had more than a passing connection to Bulleid himself.

The first was the use of Poppet valves[1] as fitted to the first of the Gresley 'P2' 2-8-2s, and the second the addition of the side fairings on the streamlined 'A4s'. The latter were really little more than a cosmetic interlude, while the former was not carried over to his days on the Southern. Day-Lewis regards the Gresley-Bulleid combination as unmatched, with Gresley sitting in firm judgement over Bulleid, the ideas man; perhaps somewhat puzzlingly, Day-Lewis does not elaborate further on the 'ideas' topic.

The difficulty also arises that, in general, the output of the Chief Mechanical Engineer's department would, out of courtesy, be attributable to the man at the top. Of course, this was physically just not possible: a veritable army of skilled individuals within the drawing office produced either the designs suggested by the master, or suggested ideas that were considered, and possibly approved, for development.

So where does Bulleid fit in on the LNER? The answer is that we just cannot be sure. What little we do know is

Oliver Vaughan Snell Bulleid MIMechE CBE. A genius without doubt, but sadly perhaps working in the wrong location at the wrong time.

Top and above: **Wartime experimentation from an agile and astute mind at the instigation of the Ministry of Transport: in an attempt to disperse steam to the atmosphere more quickly and with less visible effect, Bulleid instigated a series of experiments at Eastleigh on the Southern Railway using 'King Arthur' No 783 *Sir Gillemere*, with at first three, then two chimneys, then additional plates between the smoke deflectors. These experiments were undertaken between November 1940 and February 1941, at a time when the exhaust from a steam engine increased its visibility. No 783 only ran in the form seen here for a time, the best results being obtained from the two-chimney version, although the driver's forward view was also obscured. A side-effect was the dislodging of soot from the underside of a large number of bridges as for the first time the exhaust was directed at them from different angles (see also the illustration on page 29). Neither fitment did much for the aesthetics.**

that he was a strong advocate of the use of welding whenever possible, which was utilised in various aspects of Gresley coach designs, no doubt at the instigation of Bulleid. This goes to show how the man at the top is thus credited but the next in line forgotten. Certainly there is no evidence to suggest that welding was used to any great degree, if at all, in any of the Gresley steam designs. Equally it is interesting to consider for a moment how LNER policy might have developed had Bulleid returned to take over from Gresley in 1941 – was there even discussion within the LNER Board as to recalling him from Waterloo? This is possibly unlikely, as there were a number of well-qualified individuals ready to assume the role. The fact that Gresley's successor, Edward Thompson, acted the way he did may have been due to a number of reasons: wartime, a genuine belief, or even a personal vendetta. We can never be exactly sure as to his intent.

However, to return to Bulleid and in particular his involvement with the Gresley design principles, Bulleid must have been aware of the locomotive designs produced at Doncaster. Accordingly he will have been equally aware of the production of the first five 'A3' Pacifics to be coupled to the new corridor tenders in 1928. He must also have been aware that the first test run with one of the new corridor tenders revealed a bearing running hot and that subsequently all such corridor tenders were fitted with counterweights on the corridor side and below the actual corridor to act as a balance against the otherwise asymmetrical load distribution. This counterbalance

10

'N' class 2-6-0 No A816 is seen at Eastleigh c1933, when it had been experimentally converted with the Holcroft/Anderson heat conservation system. These experiments were prior to Bulleid's tenure on the Southern – indeed, by the time of his arrival at Waterloo No A816 had already reverted to conventional form in 1935. But the legacy continued, and one of the original aims of the 'Leader' project was to utilise the exhaust from the rear bogie to operate a heat exchanger with the feed water in similar fashion to that fitted to No A816. Likewise the fan draughting arrangements as fitted to No A816 were another feature that later, in 1950, he would 'commend to young engineers as worthy of investigation' (see page 120). When he moved to Waterloo, Bulleid must have been aware of previous experimentation work; any senior mechanical engineer would clearly make it his task to ensure that he was fully conversant with both current and previous engineering practice. This makes his failure to do other than copy the weaknesses of the earlier Paget design all the more surprising. Did he really believe he could resolve or hide the difficulties of the past by adding more complications? What is even more surprising is that no one around him seemed able to dissuade him.

added just over 6 tons to the weight of the tender, but with a fully laden weight of 62 tons 8 cwt this was not a problem when distributed across four axles. There is no subsequent record of excess heating of any of the bearings on these tenders beyond the normal level. (According to Alan Rimmer in his book *Testing Times at Derby*, the LMS also possessed a single corridor tender that was used for test purpose only. Don Broughton of Leeds confirms that this was built during Stanier's time, and the corridor could be used by the dynamometer car crews to reach the locomotive footplate if required. There is no information available as to any balance or weight distribution difficulties that might have been encountered.)

But why this emphasis on the LNER corridor tender design and the important fact that it was necessary to balance the load and increase the all-up weight? Simply because later, with 'Leader', Bulleid would place the boiler away from the centre line, yet the original design did not incorporate any form of counterbalance. As a result, bearings ran hot and it is suggested by some, but not Townroe, that this unequal weight distribution contributed to the later crank axle failure on the No 1 (smokebox-end) bogie. The corridor in the 'Leader' continued past the fireman's compartment to the rear driving cab, so there was also a weight imbalance at that end of the machine.

Did Bulleid ignore, forget, or choose to ignore what even to the layman might have appeared obvious? Why also did his very able drawing office staff likewise not comment on the issue? Leaving these questions deliberately 'hanging' for a few moments, let us consider further.

It must be said that Bulleid, as a member of the Institution of Mechanical Engineers, would in the course of his professional life on the railway have absorbed vast amounts of information on both the contemporary and the historical development of the steam engine. This must surely have included reference to the Paget engine of 1908, which was the first (and indeed believed to have been the only) time that sleeve valves, together with a dry-back firebox, had been used in a railway locomotive. Paget's engine was basically a failure. It is unnecessary to repeat the story here, but suffice to say that difficulties in both the area of the valves and the firebox, allied to political manipulation behind the scenes, resulted in neither innovation being pursued – that is until Bulleid came to the Southern.[2]

On the LNER, Bulleid's chief was himself an innovator. It was Gresley who sent Bulleid to France (Bulleid was fluent in the language) with the first of the 'P2' 2-8-2 engines, so did Bulleid even then have ideas more radical than Gresley's, and if so did Gresley chose not to allow them to develop? We can only guess, as there is absolutely no evidence to support the suggestion either way. Indeed, outside the higher echelons of railway management, and likewise mechanical engineering circles, the name of Bulleid was at the time little known. As already stated, it is a sad but true fact that the person at the top took the credit, with his second in command and those who translated his ideas into practical reality generally receiving little acclaim or acknowledgement.

That said, we have no evidence to suggest that Bulleid was unhappy or unsettled with Gresley. Born in 1882, Bulleid was 54 when he was approached by the Southern

to consider the top job at Waterloo, and it seems to have come as a bit of a shock. Did Waterloo see him as a man who would not 'rock the boat', especially as the company's avowed intention was still towards wholesale electrification? Perhaps he was indeed seen as a safe bet – but how wrong they were to be. Possibly something in the appointment allowed an otherwise latent flame to burst into life. As I said in my previous books, Bulleid had a lifetime of ideals to compress into a few short years. His time in office would also be seriously affected by world conflict and, nearer to home, political interference in the form of nationalisation. Time would not be kind to Bulleid, although what he would achieve in that time and under those circumstances was without equal on any railway, certainly in the UK.

[1] Poppet valves (often to the Lentz design) had been used to great effect in both the USA and in several European railways, although it must be said in the latter case usually on compound steam types. Either single or twin inlet and exhaust valves might be provided, with the usual method of operation via an oscillating shaft or rotating cam. The advantages of the poppet valve were that far less lubrication was required compared with a piston valve, while there was also a consequential weight reduction and the physical movement of the valve off its seat necessary for admission (or exhaust) of steam was also less. There was also a reduction in 'throttling' of steam and consequently increased free running. As with any change, the advantages had to be weighed against the disadvantage of increased complexity and therefore maintenance.

[2] Paget's engine is ably described in a booklet produced by the *Railway Gazette* in 1945. A brief description is also given as Appendix A in *Leader: Steam's Last Chance*, and a further good description is given by Charles Fryer in his work *Experiments With Steam*, details of which are given in the Bibliography. Mr Fryer sets out to describe a number of locomotives within the experimental category, including 'Leader', although his description of the latter is unfortunately not completely accurate.

As a means of experimentation with sleeve valves, Bulleid selected former LBSCR Atlantic No 2039 as a guinea-pig, his original choice of a 'King Arthur' being rejected by the operating department. In this unusual view, Atlantic No 2039 *Hartland Point*, experimentally fitted with sleeve valves, smaller bogie wheels and stovepipe chimney, is seen in company with sister engine No 2038 *Portland Bill* in original form at Brighton on 24 July 1948. Among the operating authorities there was apparently some resentment that No 2039 had been selected as both it and No 2038 were regarded as good engines. The opposite applied to No 2037, which by December 1948 was described by a correspondent to the *Railway Observer* after a visit to Brighton as '...the most decrepit Atlantic of the lot, a fact that is adequately reflected in its outward appearance'. (No 2037 *Selsey Bill* would eventually make a final works visit to Brighton in February 1949, when it received a replacement boiler. It would survive, on paper at least although not necessarily in continual usage, until July 1951.) T. C. Cole

CHAPTER TWO

How? From an Ideal to an Abomination

Make no mistake about it, in 'Leader' Bulleid set out to produce a steam engine technically more efficient than any other. There were limitations, of course, principal among these being time and available resources.

Unlike other designers, who may have had a basic precept on which to base their ideal, this time there was nothing that was sacrosanct. The same had of course applied with his original Pacific classes and the 'Q1s'. It was normal to produce an approximate design on paper, which would be subject to approval. Once approval was given the minutiae would be resolved. There was no reason to believe that the same would not apply to 'Leader' – or was there? Minutiae was hardly the appropriate word applicable here.

One of the problems facing Bulleid was that of time, not just from the pending nationalisation and with it the loss of local control, but from an industry and society slowly attempting to rebuild themselves after years of conflict. Socially, as with the 1914-18 war, working men were becoming less inclined to accept the dictates of management, which in turn led to the ever-increasing power of the trade unions allied to a call for better working conditions and wages. Such political, social and economic change did not of course occur overnight. But there were milestones, the most obvious of these being the 1946 General Election, which in turn led to nationalisation of the railways in 1948.

Bulleid was therefore faced with several dilemmas when it came to his new design. The Southern Railway required a suitable machine capable of working empty stock trains from Waterloo to Clapham Junction and the like, while at the same time able to keep out of the way of both electric suburban and main-line steam services. At the time the 'M7s' principally operated in this role, and were the smallest and oldest engines used by any of the pre-nationalisation railways for similar work in and out of the London termini.

With hindsight a large tank engine of the 2-6-4T or 2-6-2T design would have been ideal, but, as is well known, the memory of the Southern management stretched back a long way, in particular to the Sevenoaks disaster of 1927, which, while principally attributable to the tank engine involved, was also contributed to by the state of the ballasting on what was a main passenger route. Briefly, the Sevenoaks accident resulted in the rebuilding of the 'River' class tank engines to 'U' class tender engines, and restrictions were placed on the duties of the only other modern tank design possessed by the Southern, the 'W' class. Again with hindsight, such a reaction was very

Stages in the evolution of 'Leader'. The main 'fish-belly' frames for the first of the 'Leader' class are laid out at Brighton on 24 July 1948. In front is a partial view of the monocoque side frames for a 'Leader' bogie, while on the ground is a cylinder block, possibly at this stage still awaiting machining. Bearing in mind that construction of 'Leader' is thought to have commenced around the end of 1946 or early 1947, progress appears to have been slow, having taken 18 months to get to this stage – and the first boiler has yet to arrive from Eastleigh. However, it must be remembered that progress was rather a 'two steps forward, one step back' situation, with some ideas still not finalised and designs being altered piecemeal. Work was continuing on the trials with Atlantic No 2039, and although there is no evidence to support the suggestion, it may even have been that work on 'Leader' was deliberately not hurried in order to incorporate any lessons from *Hartland Point*. H. C. Casserley

much 'knee-jerk', for while there could well have been justification for the rebuilding of the 'River' tanks, there was absolutely no reason why a 'W' or similar tank engine could not have been successfully used in place of the 'M7s'.

Whether Bulleid first experimented on the drawing-board with a conventional tank engine (the word 'conventional' being used with caution) is not certain, but what emerged was an idea that, while commendable on paper, almost seemed to feed on itself, resulting in a design that was nothing like what had been requested by Waterloo or what the management had good reason to expect from its CME. Indeed, the design that resulted was the opposite: neither a tank engine nor a tender engine, something untried, something unknown, and which in physical size alone was hardly suitable for carriage

Above: **On 1 October 1948 the bogie frames are held in a rotating jig, where the various components, including the cylinder blocks and stretchers, can be added and welded in place. Welding was used to a great extent in 'Leader', with the advantage that, should a change of design occur, the affected part could be easily burned off and a substitute added. The disadvantage of this almost 'ad hoc' system was that the prepared drawings either displayed little resemblance to the actual machine or were so heavily modified as to be almost unreadable and impossible to work from. It was also later suggested that a localised heat build-up in consequence of welding the cylinder blocks in place may even have distorted the bores of the cylinders, adding to the sleeve failures. However, such a theory does not explain why sleeve-valve breakages and seizures also occurred with No 2039, where no such welding had taken place.** Don Broughton collection

shunting duties, being the length of a coach itself. Somewhere Bulleid seems to have forgotten the physical constraints of the London termini, or had he deliberately forgotten and others were too wary to remind him?

The original order passed by the board, and which resulted in 'Leader', was for 'six tank engines of unspecified design'. How this was passed without question is in itself surprising. Costs were set, a timescale was set, but in approving the project without apparently any further detail, the Board, or certain factions of it, were seemingly taken in by Bulleid or were simply unconcerned with the day-to-day practicalities of railway operation.

The next question concerns the working relationship between Bulleid, his drawing office and the other senior colleagues within his department. Here again we have to draw conclusions based on little definite fact. What is known is that, apart from a draughtsman, Clifford S.

Five months later, on 19 March 1949, progress has continued to be painfully slow. Still the wheels and boiler have to be added, although all of these, certainly for at least the first engine, were already on hand – see the later views. What is particularly interesting in the photograph is the view of the bunker assembly now almost complete and welded to the main frames. Without the outer skin of the engine in place it is possible to view the access ladder leading from what would become No 2 cab to the roof-top water filler point, as well as the crew cupboard. The offset position of the bunker will be noted – it was not even as if the bunker and boiler were offset to opposite sides of the frames. What is not clear and has never been established is that if the far side of the bunker actually took on the curve of the outer skin, was a further skin added around it? T. C. Cole

A fascinating view of five wheel and axle sets for 'Leader' at Brighton on 1 October 1948. That nearest the camera would appear to be the only one of the set with a crank axle, clearly showing the design's 'three-throw' crank. Viewed from this position one can only tend to agree with the comment made by J. M. Dunn, and discussed in the final chapter, that the crank axle does indeed look 'strangely weak'. However, as stated in the Introduction, care must be taken to ensure that comments are not taken out of context, and no one else has ever referred to this as a possible reason for later failure. Notice that while the journals have already been machined, they are protected 'in transit' by sacking. Don Broughton collection

Cocks, he did not take anyone with him from the LNER, so took over a regime previously operating under Maunsell that was very much in the doldrums as far as new development was concerned.

Many of the staff were also senior in years, and it was for this reason that the Southern management looked beyond its own personnel when it came to replacing Maunsell. How they must have reacted when Bulleid produced his visions and eventual designs for the Pacific and 'Q1' classes can only be guessed at. As professional men they would no doubt have kept any private views to themselves, but as time went on and their Southern Railway began to be seen as striking out in developing new designs more adventurous and radical than anywhere else, there must have also been an amount of pride. Forget the difficulties that were experienced by the operating and running staff, and the fact that the Pacific burned more coal than earlier designs – it could pull twice as much. The fact that a beleaguered operating department could not accommodate such services was irrelevant.

It is against this background that 'Leader' took shape. Everything Bulleid had touched so far had turned to gold (well, gold-plate, perhaps), and there was no reason to believe that his new design would not do likewise.

But despite the euphoria it is known that there were also some words of caution. Bulleid, well aware of the limited time left to him before nationalisation, needed to get his new design either running or sufficiently far

advanced for it to be accepted by the new British Railways regime. A project based on paper alone had every chance of being cancelled. It appears therefore that he was all for pressing ahead with the building of 'Leader' straight off the drawing-board, and it was his senior staff who actually persuaded him to try as many of his more radical suggestions elsewhere before the new design was too far advanced.

Enter into the arena the former Brighton Atlantic No 2039 *Hartland Point*. Even in 1947 the Atlantic design was considered obsolete, and as such it was an ideal vehicle in which to try his sleeve valve ideas. (It was said that the idea for the use of the sleeve valve had come from their use in a Sabre-engined fighter aircraft flown by his son during World War II). Bulleid also believed that he could solve the seizure problems that had beset the earlier Paget engine by imparting a degree of axial rotation to the valve, which would thereby not only slide back and forth – dependent upon the setting of the cut-off – but would also rotate through something like 25% either side of the horizontal axis. (This type of axial rotation was then commonplace when sleeve valves were used in an internal combustion engine.) Also, by increasing the supply and volume of oil

Seen from the opposite end on the same day is a plain axle set complete with wheels, roller bearings, dashpots and final drive sprockets. Part of the chalk mark visible on the wheel clearly reads '00' and may reasonable be taken to imply that these were destined for No 36001. Similarly, the letters 'LT' could well mean 'left-trailing', two axle sets being so marked as there were two identical bogies. Some idea of the scale of the final drive chains can also be gauged from the size of the sprockets; it is also very important to note that the final drive was non-symmetrical in that the chains were attached 'centre-to-front' and 'centre-to-rear' on opposite sides, sprockets being attached only to the axle ends where required. The wheelsets themselves were assembled at Eastleigh and transhipped to Brighton; some of the protective wooden packaging provided for the journey and safeguarding the exposed components is also visible. Don Broughton collection

and ensuring that it reached every possible area, he reduced the chance of seizure through lack of lubrication.

Bulleid's attempt to utilise sleeve valves was perfectly valid. This type of valve had the advantage of very accurate steam admission and release allied to the provision of a circular warming steam jacket around the actual cylinder. It would therefore afford an increase in thermal efficiency by ensuring that steam was used both more efficiently and also at a higher temperature. In theory at least there was an advantage to be gained. But as with all attempts to increase steam engine efficiency, at what cost would it be achieved, especially in terms of both expense and complexity in construction and maintenance?

Chronicling what would eventually be the birth of No 36001 and her sisters is not easy. In attempting to unravel the background negotiations and wrangling that was going on, some aspects might be recorded slightly out of context, but with no loss of accuracy.

It would appear that some time in 1944, probably with the success of D-Day confirmed, Bulleid's fertile imagination began to consider the prospects for the future. Still to come of course were the first of what would become the Light Pacific classes, but that work was very much in the hands of the drawing office, while Bulleid, it seems, was more 'mentally unemployed'. It appears that he set himself a brief as only he might.

Wheelsets at Brighton, with a part complete engine behind, clearly showing that sprockets were attached only to the centre and one other axle end. The wheels were the same diameter as those of a 'Q1' – 5ft 1in – but without a crankpin, and, as would be expected, of the 'BFB' (Bulleid-Firth-Brown) type. (Did any of the Bulleid-designed engines have spoked wheels? There is a rumour that some of the BR Standard Class 4 tank engines built at Brighton were to have 'BFB'- design wheels, but for whatever reason this was not proceeded with.) Wheels of similar design were extensively used on many of the larger American steam designs. The part-built 'Leader' in the background could almost be said to look conventional with its boiler and bunker in normal positions; the flat top to the smokebox will be noted.
National Railway Museum/J. G. Click

In the same way that he had set himself the task of providing the 'Merchant Navy' class with greater power than the traffic department had requested, so this time he set himself a further goal of encapsulating into a steam design the advantage of total adhesion and as many as possible of the potential advantages of contemporary early diesel and electric locomotives as then existed. (According to 'A.F.C.' in the SLS *Journal* for October 1965, Bulleid intended the new design to equal the performance of the SR electric locomotives, later BR Nos 20001/2; this is referred to later in a similar though not identical fashion by E. S. Cox.)

Top: **On 2 May 1949 sleeves have been inserted and oscillating gear added to what would be the front bogie of No 36001,** then just over six weeks from completion. The view is interesting as, with the front cover not yet fitted over the oscillating gear, some idea of the complexities involved in the design of this particular component can be appreciated. (The reader is also referred to the accompanying series of 'stills', where stages in the actual operation of the oscillating gear can be seen.) What is also interesting is that the bogie appears to be supported on timber baulks, yet is complete with wheelsets. This must therefore have been very close to the time when the 8psi steam test was carried out, **resulting in the buckled rods.** Don Broughton collection

Left: **Work in progress at Brighton: a bogie is now on its wheels** while the cab and mainframes of a member of the class are just visible to the right. It is 10 November 1949, which means that the visible parts were destined for No 36003. Unfortunately, just nine days later instructions would come down from Marylebone that work was to cease, by which time the bogies were actually under the engine. Like its so nearly complete sister, No 36003 would never run under its own power. Don Broughton collection

Below left: **A close-up of what was destined to be the rear (No 2) bogie for No 36002,** seen at Brighton on 4 October 1949. This is in a far more complete state than that in the previous view, although it still awaits final drive chains, spring and chain covers, and brake-gear. Painting has also been undertaken. This bogie would be complete and under No 36002 at the time the order came for the cessation of work. Don Broughton collection

These stills are from the only known film footage of the engine while No 1 bogie was on stationary steam test at Brighton. The views show the oscillating and reciprocal gear at the end of the sleeves, which as well as moving from side to side also moved in and out with the movement of the sleeves. Transport Video Publishing: *Reflections on Southern Steam*

His choice of timescale is also of interest. It cannot be believed that such ideas – perhaps it might be fairer to call it inspiration – would have appeared overnight. It is more likely that what Bulleid had in mind was the culmination of a lifetime of ideals, a vision of steam for the future. Now was probably the very first time he had dared to allow these ideas to develop. For as long as there are steam enthusiasts, so will there be debate as to how he managed to get not only the Southern Railway Board but also the Ministry of Supply to agree to the construction of what were clearly express engines in 1940/41. Forget the suggestion that with a wheel diameter of just 6ft 2in the 'Merchant Navy' class was intended for mixed traffic – rubbish! This was an express design exactly as Bulleid had envisaged the Southern Railway required to operate its peacetime boat trains and similar workings. Had wartime restrictions not interfered, the valves of the 'Merchant Navy' class might well have been very different, but such

Viewed from the opposite side a few weeks later, on 13 June 1949, this is thought to be the same bogie. Extra detail in the form of the ladder that will be used to access the driver's cab has also been added. However, the lifting shackles were a temporary addition and would be removed before the engine was completed. Don Broughton collection

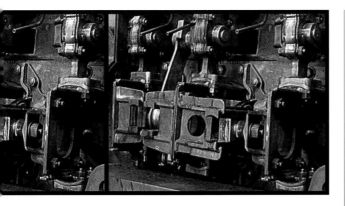

conjecture has been well covered already by others elsewhere and it is not necessary to repeat the history of that class here.

Suffice to say that he set his drawing office, under Clifford S. Cocks, the task of translating his radical thoughts on to paper. (As already mentioned, Cocks had come with Bulleid from the LNER to the Southern, where he held the role of Chief Locomotive Designer. He is not to be confused with C. M. Cock, who from 1945 was appointed the SR's Electrical Engineer. C. S. Cocks was eventually replaced at Brighton by Ron Jarvis in 1949.) Under Cocks several schemes emerged for both the Pacifics and 'Leader', amongst others, a number of which were reproduced in the now long out of print volume by H. A. V. Bulleid, *Bulleid of the Southern*. It is therefore appropriate to include the relevant 'Leader' drawings here.

From a perusal of the following sketches it can easily be understood how and why the vast majority were quickly rejected on the grounds of excessive novelty, although despite this Bulleid was often regarded as 'rather clever' by certain members of the SR Board as well as a number of other senior non-technical officers. He also had a staunch ally in the form of Sir Eustace Missenden, the Southern's General Manager.

According to the SR Board minutes, the project (which would eventually culminate in 'Leader') appears to have

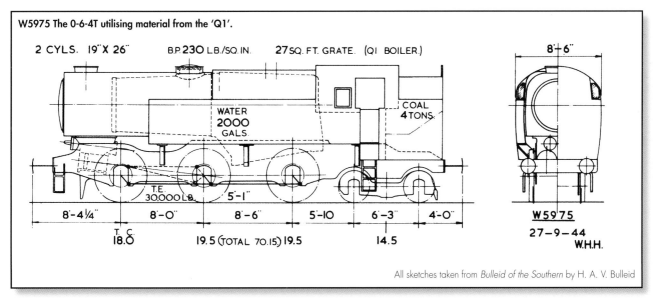

W5975 The 0-6-4T utilising material from the 'Q1'.

2 CYLS. 19" X 26"   B.P. 230 LB./SQ. IN.   27 SQ. FT. GRATE. (Q1 BOILER.)

WATER 2000 GALS.

COAL 4 TONS.

T.E. 30,000 LB.   5'-1"

8'-4¼"   8'-0"   8'-6"   5'-10   6'-3"   4'-0"

T.C. 18.0   19.5 (TOTAL 70.15) 19.5   14.5

8'-6"

W5975
27-9-44
W.H.H.

All sketches taken from *Bulleid of the Southern* by H. A. V. Bulleid

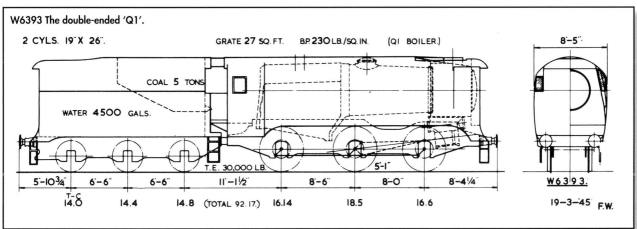

W6393 The double-ended 'Q1'.

2 CYLS. 19" X 26".   GRATE 27 SQ. FT.   B.P. 230 LB./SQ. IN.   (Q1 BOILER.)

COAL 5 TONS

WATER 4500 GALS.

T.E. 30,000 LB.   5'-1"

5'-10¾"   6'-6"   6'-6"   11'-1½"   8'-6"   8'-0"   8'-4¼"

T-C 14.0   14.4   14.8 (TOTAL 92.17)   16.14   18.5   16.6

8'-5"

W6393.

19-3-45 F.W.

19

first been raised at Board level in December 1944, although as stated above, a great deal of behind-the-scenes work had been going on before then. Not unnaturally, Bulleid would have wished to ensure that as clear a proposal as possible was both available and thus presented at this time. That is what he might have wished, but even then the whole concept appears slightly muddled and it is likely what was actually approved was an agreement to built a number of engines, possibly the volume and type not actually specified at that time. If it appears muddled to us now, think how it must have appeared then. Once more Bulleid's charisma shines through – here was the man

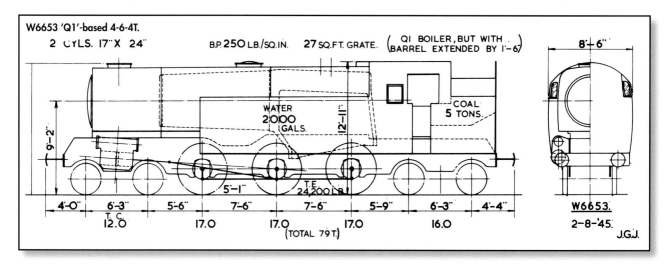

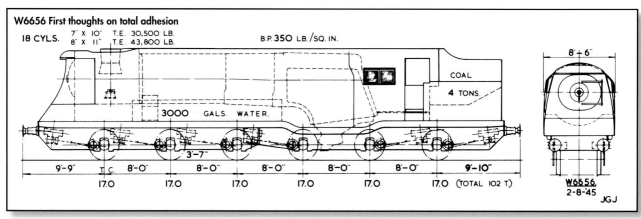

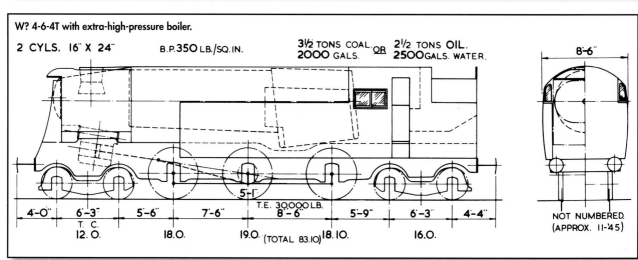

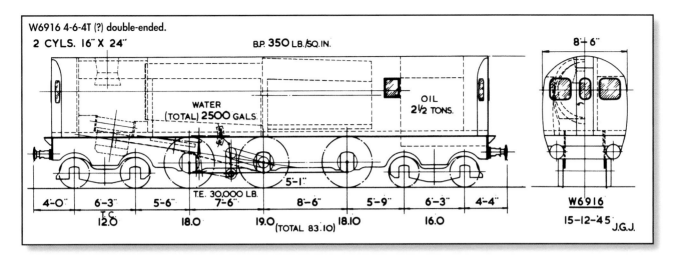

W6916 4-6-4T (?) double-ended.

2 CYLS. 16" X 24"   B.P. 350 LB./SQ.IN.

WATER (TOTAL) 2500 GALS.

OIL 2½ TONS.

8'-6"

T.E. 30,000 LB.

5'-1"

| 4'-0" | 6'-3" | 5'-6" | 7'-6" | 8'-6" | 5'-9" | 6'-3" | 4'-4" |

T.C. 12.0   18.0   19.0 (TOTAL 83.10)   18.10   16.0

W6916

15-12-45   J.G.J.

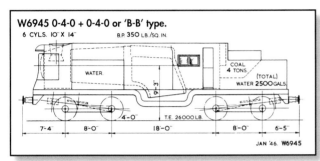

W6945 0-4-0 + 0-4-0 or 'B-B' type.

6 CYLS. 10" X 14"   B.P. 350 LB./SQ.IN.

WATER.

COAL 4 TONS.

(TOTAL) WATER 2500 GALS.

T.E. 26000 LB.

4'-0"

| 7'-4" | 8'-0" | 18'-0" | 8'-0" | 6'-5" |

JAN '46. W6945

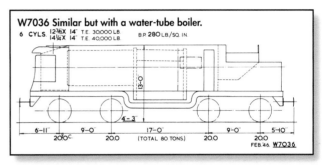

W7036 Similar but with a water-tube boiler.

6 CYLS. 12⅜X 14" T.E. 30,000 LB. 14¼X 14" T.E. 40,000 LB.   B.P. 280 LB./SQ.IN.

13'-0"

4'-3"

| 6'-11" | 9'-0" | 17'-0" | 9'-0" | 5'-10" |

20.0 C   20.0   (TOTAL 80 TONS)   20.0   20.0

FEB.'46. W7036

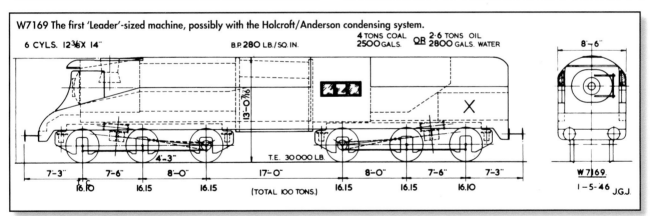

W7169 The first 'Leader'-sized machine, possibly with the Holcroft/Anderson condensing system.

6 CYLS. 12⅜X 14"   B.P. 280 LB./SQ.IN.   4 TONS COAL 2500 GALS. OR 2·6 TONS OIL 2800 GALS. WATER

8'-6"

13'-0 7/16"

4'-3"

T.E. 30 000 LB.

| 7'-3" | 7'-6" | 8'-0" | 17'-0" | 8'-0" | 7'-6" | 7'-3" |

16.10   16.15   16.15   (TOTAL 100 TONS.)   16.15   16.15   16.10

W7169.

1-5-46   J.G.J.

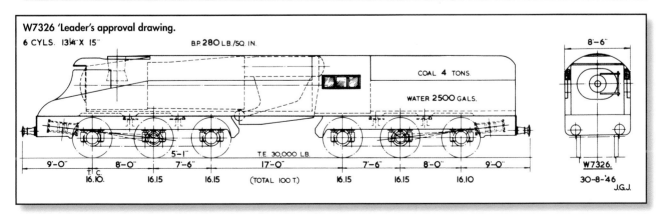

W7326 'Leader's approval drawing.

6 CYLS. 13¼"X 15"   B.P. 280 LB./SQ.IN.

COAL 4 TONS.

WATER 2500 GALS.

8'-6"

5'-1"

T.E. 30,000 LB.

| 9'-0" | 8'-0" | 7'-6" | 17'-0" | 7'-6" | 8'-0" | 9'-0" |

T.C. 16.10   16.15   16.15   (TOTAL 100 T.)   16.15   16.15   16.10

W7326.

30-8-46   J.G.J.

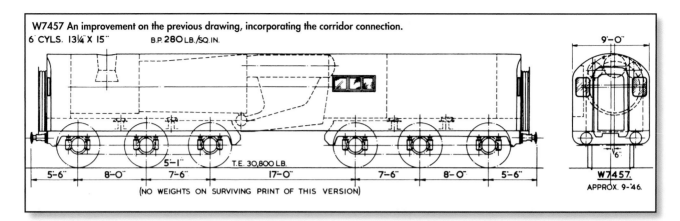

W7457 An improvement on the previous drawing, incorporating the corridor connection.
6 CYLS. 13¼ X 15"   B.P. 280 LB./SQ. IN.

9'-0"

5'-1"   T.E. 30,800 LB.

5'-6"   8'-0"   7'-6"   17'-0"   7'-6"   8'-0"   5'-6"

(NO WEIGHTS ON SURVIVING PRINT OF THIS VERSION)

W7457
APPROX. 9-'46.

who had already given the Southern the 'Merchant Navy' class), a design that on the surface could rival anything on any of the other railways. There had of course not yet been any comparative trials to prove or disprove efficiency or economy; all that was known to date was that these prodigious machines were hauling loads far in excess of anything previously dealt with by a single engine,

providing a saving in locomotive mileage, locomotive crews, coal, line occupancy and the like. The fact that they cost more to maintain than an equivalent machine, were not universally popular, and the traffic department could not handle the loads the engines could haul was perhaps not mentioned. Bulleid had put the Southern back on the map, and from an engineering perspective the company was up

Below: **In order to test the valve events of certain of his various classes, notably the 'Merchant Navy' and 'Leader' designs, Bulleid had wooden mock-ups prepared. This is believed to be the quarter-scale model used to assess the use of sleeve valves for Nos 2039 and 36001 and was produced by pattern-maker Dick Martin.**
National Railway Museum/J. G. Click

Left: **The rear end of a power bogie shows the pair of brake cylinders, one pair being fitted to each bogie. This was part of the superb braking system fitted to 'Leader', which operated in conjunction with reservoirs mounted horizontally above the smokebox (as described further in Chapter 4). In the background is 'West Country' Pacific No 34017 *Ilfracombe*, which, as it is carrying a BR cabside number, dates the view to at least May 1948, probably some time later. At least one 'Leader'-type boiler is also just visible ahead of the Pacific.**
National Railway Museum/J. G. Click

Above: **A power bogie is seen from above, complete with the cylinder block in place. The three sleeve valves have also been slid into place, but the axial rotating gear has yet to be added. The main steam pipe was constructed to allow for a 2-inch lengthways expansion when heated, and included the use of an exterior asbestos lining referred to as 'bestobel'. The pipe itself had a maximum diameter of 8 inches. Of interest also is the conspicuous use of welding – not a rivet to be seen – while the generous number of oil pipes and feeds are yet to be added.**
National Railway Museum/J. G. Click

with the others again. To some, including certain factions within the operating department, Bulleid could do little that was wrong.

The December 1944 board meeting was, however, not completely clear as regards the 'Passenger Tank Engines'. But behind the scenes a meeting is known to have taken place between the Traffic Manager, R. M. T. Richards, Sir Eustace Missenden and Bulleid. Whether this preceded the Board meeting is not clear; what is known is that it was one of the regular senior officers' meetings, and among the items discussed was the projected 1946 locomotive building programme, out of which two items of particular note emerged. The first was a request by Richards for a replacement for the 'M7' tank engines, which were even then considered out of date for branch,

secondary and empty stock duties, the latter mainly between Waterloo and Clapham Junction. Richards's comments on the 'M7' class could almost be said to be the impetus for Bulleid to push ahead with the 'Leader' concept, for according to the Traffic Manager they were

'...completely out of date and inefficient by modern standard, ... their continued existence prevents any improvement of the services they operate.'

To be fair, of course, such a criticism could well be applied to any number of the pre-Grouping small tank engine designs inherited by the SR, which at that time included a large number that were still operating. Interestingly, Richards makes no mention of a larger tank engine being more suitable – which it clearly would have been. The Southern already had several large tank engine designs, notable the 15 members of the 'W' class, and yet, as referred to previously, there was still the melancholy spectre of the Sevenoaks disaster haunting the corridors at Waterloo, which precluded the use of large tank engines on fast services anywhere unless absolutely necessary. This was to Bulleid's advantage, and he would not be slow to capitalise upon it.

The outcome of the meeting between Richards, Missenden and Bulleid was, however, somewhat strange, for it was agreed that the projected locomotive building programme would now include a further 25 of the 'Q1' class 0-6-0 tender engines, Bulleid seemingly having got his colleagues to agree that these would be a better alternative to the existing 'M7s'.

It is very likely that Richards left the meeting far from happy with the outcome; either that or he had second thoughts shortly afterwards, for a note from him to Bulleid

Left: **Having looked at the bogies, we now turn our attention to the boilers. The first of the batch is known to have been in the course of construction, in a fairly advanced state, on 26 June 1948. All the boilers were built at Eastleigh, made of all-welded construction and with at least that destined for No 36001 subjected to X-ray examination in the area of the seam – the others may not have been (again, see the final chapter). Five boilers were ordered, and that seen here is probably the first to be delivered, which had arrived at Brighton by 6 September 1948, although it would be a further nine months before it was steamed again. The initial batch of 'Leader' class engines to order No W7326 was for five examples, but it cannot be confirmed if all five boilers were actually completed. Three certainly were, but it is possible that Eastleigh may not have finished all five before November 1949.**
Don Broughton collection

dated 15 December 1944 has survived, and clearly indicates his lack of agreement to the use of 'Q1s' on 'M7'-type duties:

'With regard to your suggestion that the material already available for the construction of Q1 engines should still be used for this type instead of for passenger tanks, an opportunity has been taken of inspecting locomotive No C1 and the conclusion has been arrived at that the lookout facilities provided on this engine are not suitable for regular tender-first running. The rear lookout on the driver's side does not give a sufficient wide range of vision, and the absence of a lookout on the fireman's side is a serious drawback, having regard to the fact that it is

Left: **The following day, 7 September 1948, inside Brighton Works, the boiler has been unloaded and propped ready to be added when necessary. Leaving aside any comments concerning the dry-back firebox and the use of welding alone – notice the seam along the horizontal axis and also the first weld ring – this boiler can only be described as Bulleid's masterpiece. No figures are available to confirm its evaporation abilities, but it is known to have been able to raise steam faster than a 'Terrier', while its ability to generate steam on the later tests, when the sleeve valves were wasting almost as much, was never suitably commented upon. Interestingly, it is not tapered on the underside as was Bulleid's preference. Structurally it contained 36 large and 283 small tubes, and as would be expected, all the tubes were welded in place at both the firebox and smokebox ends. The completed boiler is seen here painted in grey primer, in which form it was recorded by the official railway photographer. (Compared to the heating surface of the Bulleid Pacifics, that of the 'Leader' boiler was between that of a 'Merchant Navy' and a 'West Country'. In terms of superheater area though, 'Leader' was by far the smallest of the three – 'MN' 822, 'WC' 545, 'L' 454 – as applicable to the unrebuilt Pacific design.**
Don Broughton collection

Right: **This completed boiler was possibly recorded at Eastleigh. Two of the four thermic siphons are clearly visible, together with their associated wash-out plugs. The other two were on either side, and one is just visible. It is not believed that the boiler fitted to No 36001 was ever washed out during its 17 months of spasmodic running, due to the presence of the TIA water treatment. Even so, periodic blow-downs would undoubtedly have been undertaken.** Herbert Browne

necessary for the fireman to assist in looking out for signals when not otherwise engaged and this is particularly important having regard to the fact that the normal position for signals is on the left-hand side. Unless, therefore, the observation condition, tender-first, can be materially improved, I am afraid they will not be suitable to traffic requirements. Another point I would like to raise is to whether you are satisfied that these engines are suitable for maintaining the necessary speeds running tender-first when light in coal and water.'

Richards might well have been guided by others in his reply, while Bulleid's response, although not recorded, might well be guessed at! But Bulleid was a shrewd individual and it appears that his suggestion of additional 'Q1' class engines was probably playing for time. Possibly he already knew even then that the 'Q1' was indeed unsuitable for anything but its originally intended freight role, but in making the suggestion for extra engines of the type he was thus allowing an alternative to be suggested by others – 'his new design'. Even so, the next stage shows that Bulleid was perhaps even 'hedging his bets', for a series of trials were undertaken between Ashford and Maidstone with No C36 attached to a Pacific tender. Unfortunately no results have been discovered, while it is interesting to note also that no similar test was made using a 'Q1' on empty stock from Waterloo. Indeed, it was rare to see a member of the class at Waterloo at all. Notwithstanding the trials, the drawing office was instructed to see if there might be a means of duplicating the driving controls of a 'Q1' on the tender; this would have to be done by mechanical means, so it is not surprising that the drawing office was unable to come up with a workable solution. (It is perhaps interesting to speculate for a moment that if such a duplication of

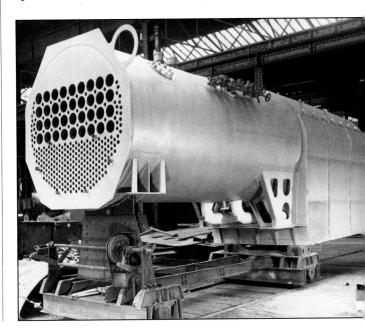

The boiler and frames are now united, with the fabricated smokebox also added. As this latter item would be hidden from view by the casing, no attempt at symmetrical aesthetics was made and it remained purely functional. Accordingly the opportunity was taken to mount the vacuum reservoirs on the top. Purely coincidentally, when viewed from the front the flattened top of the smokebox was strikingly similar to that of an LNER 'A4' with the streamlined casing open.
Don Broughton collection

controls had been satisfactorily achieved, would 'Leader' ever have materialised? Possibly it might have delayed the design somewhat, while the 'Q1s' ran around 'in all directions'. It seems likely, however, that Bulleid would soon have tired of what was really a double-ended tender engine produced as an afterthought, and would probably still have wished to continue with a 'Leader'-type project, but one specifically designed as such. By that stage, though, time would have been against him, with the onset of nationalisation.)

It is clear that Bulleid and Richards resolved any differences that might have existed between them, for the next step was a joint approach to Missenden with a suggestion for a total of 60 new engines to be included in the 1946 building programme, including 25 of the 'Passenger Tank' type. (The others were 10 shunters and 25 'West Country' class; the shunters would eventually appear as the 14 0-6-0Ts brought in from the Ministry of

Supply as the 'USA' class, whilst 32 'West Country'/'Battle of Britain' engines would eventually be built in 1946, numbered 21C121 to 21C152.)

As General Manager, Missenden had to work not only with his senior officers but also the Board of Directors, which in turn had to obtain authority from the Ministry of Supply for the release of necessary materials, notably steel. Accordingly, and no doubt with this in mind, Missenden wrote to both Richards and Bulleid as follows:

'...I think we might, pending a decision being reached on the question of the passenger tank engines, indicate at the next M & E [Mechanical and Engineering] Committee that our building programme will be 25 mixed traffic, 25 freight and 10 shunting engines. Later on when I have received your recommendation as to whether passenger tank engines are required or not (which I should like to have before the end of February), the programme can be adjusted as necessary.'

This was a very strange response from Missenden, and without any further information to clarify it there are a number of possible alternatives to consider. Certainly on the face of it, Missenden was taking Bulleid's side, with the 25 freight engines seemingly implying a return to the suggested building of 25 more 'Q1s'. Or was Missenden being rather clever in formally putting through a proposal

Navy' was unveiled at Eastleigh, simply saying, 'My dear Oliver – Well done, Yours ever, E J M'), could it be that the General Manager now privately harboured some doubts over the Chief Mechanical Engineer's ability to not behave in too radical or drastic a fashion? All this must be supposition, and in case the reader is tempted to form a definite conclusion at this stage let it also be said that the SR Board had had plenty of opportunities to forestall the progress of Bulleid had it wished.[1]

So, within the drawing office of the Chief Mechanical Engineer work now began on a project with a conclusion that few could have envisaged.

Utilising the basic parts – boiler and wheels – of a 'Q1', a series of drawings were produced for almost every variant of a six-wheeled tank engine, viz 0-6-2T, 2-6-2T, 0-6-4T, 2-6-2T, 2-6-4T, and 4-6-4T. (Seemingly about the only ones not to have been tried were a 2-6-0T and 4-6-0T!) Some among Bulleid's staff, including apparently Cocks, were in favour of stopping there – after all, a tank engine based on the 'Q1', with either pony and trailing trucks or perhaps with carrying wheels at the bunker end only, would certainly be a theoretical improvement on an 'M7', and at least twice as powerful. But it appears that Bulleid saw all of these types as 'stodgy' and old-fashioned, and weight would be carried that was not being used for adhesion, although there was an advantage that any guiding wheels in the form of a bogie or pony truck would theoretically assist in 'steering' the engine around curves. That was the avowed belief at the time, although

Above: **Seen from an unusual side angle, this view is looking forward from alongside the firing compartment and with the lagged boiler in position – 'Idaglass' was used for the lagging, a variant on present day 'fibreglass'. Above the main frames and nearest the camera, the slab-sided section is part of the additional water space, referred to as the 'mantle-tank'.** National Railway Museum/J. G. Click

Right: **At this stage the framework to support the exterior skin is beginning to be put in place, and we are now looking from ground level into what will become the 'central' firing compartment. Note the offset firehole door, to which Bulleid-type steam-operated 'butterfly' doors will later be added. Visible protruding upwards from the floor are three of the four steam and water controls for the injectors, which were located underneath the engine close to this point. The opening section to the right of the picture is an inspection/access hatch into the fuel bunker. Note also the 'mantle-tank' continuing around the lower part of the 'firebox' area. Above this is the crown of the boiler, to which are attached the two water gauges and blower control. Within the glass case is the boiler pressure gauge, although at this stage much in the way of pipework connections still remains to be made.** National Railway Museum/J. G. Click

that he knew would be more likely to succeed with Government? Did even he have doubts about Bulleid's ability to stay 'on the straight and narrow'? Certainly, while back in 1941 Bulleid had Missenden as an ally (Bulleid received a letter from the General Manager on 11 March 1941, the day after the very first 'Merchant

This remarkable view is from alongside the smokebox looking back along the corridor towards the firing compartment, then further still past the bunker to the rear cab. At this stage parts of the floor still remain to be added. Notice the clack valves along the side – just at head height and designed to catch the unwary! Actually moving through this corridor while the engine was in motion must have been formidable – the cramped space, assorted obstructions, the heat and, of course, the associated movement would have hardly made it viable. Of course, modern-day traction has been built with a corridor of sorts on either side of the power unit, but these *access corridors* were never intended for regular use while the locomotive is in motion, and are usually accessed only by maintenance staff.
National Railway Museum/J. G. Click

interestingly, as smaller wheels have become the norm on various types of traction in more recent years, guiding wheels have never been considered so necessary.

Accordingly the tank engine designs were consigned to the files and instead Bulleid instructed his staff to approach the design from a more radical aspect. No doubt at this stage it was Bulleid who was leading from the front, having the ideas and quashing suggestions offered to him as being too conventional.

Aesthetically the drawings for all the tank engines, which were in effect simple weight diagrams, display an 'Austerity'-type appearance; it must be said that aesthetics may not have been Bulleid's strongest point.

Meanwhile, other areas of the drawing office were still working on variations of the 'Q1' class, as a sketch of an 0-6-0 appears with Pacific-type cowlings at both the front of the engine and rear of the tender. It is not clear whether these drawings were being undertaken at the same time as work on the duplication of controls mentioned earlier, or had some relatively successful means of duplicating the controls even now been achieved?

However, any success with a back-to-front 'Q1' was now shelved, and instead matters progressed through the first of what would be the double-bogie ideas. The concept at this stage owed much externally to the styling of the 'West Country' class, but there the similarity ended, for at this stage it was designs of a multi-cylinder type that predominated, with many engineering problems unanswered. Interestingly, the boiler pressure was shown as to be as high as 350psi.

With too many unanswered engineering problems remaining, it was back to a 4-6-4T, this time at the suggestion of Cocks, who probably incorporated the same 350psi boiler, maybe in the hope that this alone would be of sufficient novelty. What Cocks could not disguise, however, was the obvious waste of adhesive weight suffered by the 4-6-4 wheel arrangement; indeed, the proposal included an unacceptable 28 tons on the carrying wheels, representing slightly more than a third of the total weight. It is therefore likely that such a design would display a marked propensity to slip when starting away in either direction as the weight transferred itself to the bogie and away from the driving wheels.

Viewed from above, this 'Leader' – it could well be No 36002 – displays its 'upper innards' to the camera. The lens is looking from the No 1 (smokebox) end backwards, the chimney opening visible (slightly offset to the left, of course) behind the sheeting of the cab. (Presumably, with the chimney offset from the centre line of the locomotive, an awful lot of soot must have been dislodged as No 36001 blasted its way under bridges and through tunnels. Surprisingly this is not mentioned in any report or by any observer.) Moving further back, the safety valves can be made out, while further back still is the opening on the top for the bunker. National Railway Museum/J. G. Click

Another variant of the double-ended steam design now emerged, with inside cylinders and enclosed motion. A variant on the conventional boiler was also shown, this one being welded throughout and with vertical tubes either side of the firebox welded into two headers behind the main barrel – similar in some respects to contemporary Sentinel designs.

At this stage there were also a number of designs showing coal and oil as alternative fuels, which has given rise to conjecture concerning the intended fuel for No 36001. What the formal intention was is not totally clear – Bulleid and the drawing office were probably keeping their options open, especially since it was not then clear which way the fuel situation within Britain would develop.

What would appear to have been the case is that at some stage something gelled in the mind of the designer to produce an engine with the advantages of diesel and electric locomotives, whereby it could be driven from either end, thus incorporating excellent visibility.

Certain of the tank designs were possibly submitted for approval, although each was understandably rejected by either the Chief Civil Engineer or possibly the Traffic Manager. Bulleid must have been aware that this was likely, and again was probably rather cleverly ensuring that when the time came, the two men would both eventually play straight into his hands in approving the unconventional. Both the CCE and Traffic departments were still acutely aware of Sevenoaks, and it would be the successor to the Southern Railway, the Southern Region of British Railways, that would eventually accede to the need for large tank engines, with a number of both LMS and later BR types later being built at Brighton. Could it be that if one of the tank engine designs *had* been accepted, 'Leader' might never have been built?

Turning away from the Southern briefly, at this stage the plot definitely thickens! In 1945 Bulleid presented a paper entitled 'Locomotives I have known' (the same title

was used by the late J. H. Maskelyn in a totally unrelated book) to the Institution of Mechanical Engineers. Its content was summarised by K. P. Jones as 'An unusual paper in that it selects a number of locomotive types for detailed consideration. Three are obvious – "Lord Nelson" modifications, "Merchant Navy" and Q1 classes – in that

Below: **The body is almost complete, with the centre external casing added – well, almost. Notice the trestles – a single pair were specially built to support the main frames complete with boiler. Minor visible additions are the driver's seat and regulator handle. At this stage, in the late 1940s, some 600 men were employed at Brighton Works, although this did include technical and design staff. In charge of the erecting shop during the 'Leader' project was Foreman Harry Ede. Recalled as a strict disciplinarian, together with most of the staff he was proud of what they were creating.** National Railway Museum/J. G. Click

Below right: **Almost complete: below the frames the final drive chains have been added, although together with the axlebox springs they still await their oil-bath covers. This is the No 2 (bunker) end where the cab, due to the presence of the bunker, was much more restricted in size, being no more than about 4 feet deep. The oscillating gear has been temporarily protected with what appears to be cloth.** National Railway Museum/J. G. Click

they were his own designs. The others considered were the Gresley A1, A4, O1 and P2 designs, the Ivatt Atlantics and a French design. From the choice of LNER types it would appear then that Bulleid agreed with much of Gresley's design policy.'

In public at least it would appear that Bulleid was a man who was not only justifiably proud of his own achievements but also appeared to admire the work of his former chiefs. The paper also contained nothing unknown – radicalism, it would appear, was not yet ready to be made public.

Probably at Bulleid's suggestion thoughts now returned to this most radical of proposals – radical, that is, for a UK railway – of a steam engine carried on two powered bogies, thus combining the advantages of tank and tender engines with, for the present at least, some of the advantages of the contemporary diesel and electric locomotive. (There were as yet no main-line diesel locomotives operating in the UK, but electric locomotives had been at work on the Southern since 1941.)

Again, basic weight diagrams survive, but with a number of vital yet unanswered engineering questions. On the first few of these weight diagrams a machine with

no fewer than 18 cylinders is proposed, but with apparently no room for the necessary steam and exhaust pipes. Likewise the boiler was unlikely to be able to supply all the steam required by such a multitude of cylinders, while available water capacity would seemingly restrict the range to just 50 miles.

While Bulleid was thus perhaps just getting into his stride and going further and further into the unknown, there were those among his more senior subordinates who were far more cautious. One of these was Clifford Cocks. According to Day-Lewis, Cocks is described as '...loyal and admirable...', but with reservations regarding the manner in which Bulleid was determined to get his ideas through. To quote Day-Lewis:

'Bulleid's attitude to his professional staff was rather different. The workmen received the courtesy and consideration due to outsiders, his [professional] staff he treated more roughly as though they were his brothers: and with the departure of Holcroft, younger brothers. His ideas were sufficiently revolutionary to give offence to the more conventional of his own department as well as the professional employees of other departments, and as an

individualist he found it impossible to work with some of the men he inherited from Maunsell. But he was respected by all and inspired a fanatical enthusiasm in many. If greatness can be measured by the reaction set up in those who meet it, then Bulleid was, with Gresley, the greatest British locomotive engineer of the century.

"It got so that nobody thought he could do any wrong, particularly himself. I think we would have given him square wheels if he had asked for them," dryly commented one such admirer.

The Brighton drawing office, whatever it did to Bulleid's locomotives after his departure, remembers his regime with gratitude and glowing pleasure. Many of his notions seemed outrageous and they sometimes came to nothing, but the effect was to keep the staff constantly on the alert. They learnt that everything should be constantly re-examined and nothing done simply because it was the traditional practice of the past.

"We never knew when he might call. Sometimes he would be on the phone asking for some drawings to be ready by 9.30pm. And we happily worked through the evening for him."

His confidence was boundless, but he was never satisfied with anything. No two locomotives were exactly the same and even an order for twenty-five coaches might be stopped half-way through because some improvement

Above: **In the Erecting Shop of Brighton Works on Wednesday 17 August 1949, to the left work progresses on the second of the 'Leader' class, No 36002, while just discernible in the background is another 'Leader' boiler, no doubt destined for No 36003. Other 'Leader' components are also visible, including a cylinder block.** Don Broughton collection

Below: **Components are all in position on No 36001 on 22 June 1949, brand new from the works. This is the centre section of the locomotive under the main frames on the right-hand side – No 1 end to the left. Visible is the steam cylinder operating the reversing gear together with its associated transfer gearbox. The ashpan discharge ducts can also be identified, together with the brake cylinders at the ends of each bogie.** Don Broughton collection

This view is similar to the previous one, but is included to show the complicated arrangements necessary for the transfer of valve events simultaneously to both bogies; the inclusion of the various universal joints was essential when the engine was on curved track. All these necessary additions created more opportunities for inaccuracy in the valve events and could well have added to the later experience of the steam reversing cylinder – seen both here and in the previous view – being just not able to handle the required task. Notice too the massive casings enclosing both the final drive and also the stub axle.
National Railway Museum/J. G. Click

had suddenly come to mind. This gave much discomfort to his Works Managers at Eastleigh and Brighton, A. E. W. Turbett and L. J. Granshaw, and when the first "Leader" class locomotive was nearing completion new ideas were being welded on right up to the first test, and after.

Sometimes it seemed that Bulleid would never come to the point of saying: "Yes, go ahead." He was restless and impatient, but if his Chief Locomotive Designer, the loyal and admirable Clifford Cocks, turned down a proposition as completely unworkable he was quite capable of waiting until that official had gone on holiday and then getting his deputy to work out a plan.'

Such then was Bulleid the Engineer, and, equally important in this instance, Bulleid the Manager. And if a further example of the admiration he courted were needed, the late Reg Curl, when photographed in his office at Eastleigh before he retired, was seen to have a number of photographs on his office wall, including one of 'Leader'.

At another of the regular meetings attended by Bulleid and Richards, the subject of suitable locomotives for the cross-London freight workings was discussed. At the time these were ably handled by Maunsell's 'W' class tank engines, a further batch of which would no doubt have sufficed. But Bulleid, fresh from his work with the drawing office team, was insistent that a more flexible approach was required, and, after apparently listening to the request in silence, is reported to have exclaimed:

'...you don't really want them, because they are confined to one class of duty. What you keep is a substantially more powerful mixed traffic tank locomotive with full route availability.'

(In practice, and according to Townroe, the cross-London freight turns were a nightmare for the operators. Any engine diagrammed for the duty would spend much of its time waiting either for pathways or loads to be made up. It was very unlikely in the 1940s and 1950s railway scene that such engines could practically have been used for much else.)

Despite any perceived opposition to what was quickly evolving into a most radical project, Bulleid continued apace. The next step was an official request to Richards with a view to finding out exactly what the Traffic Department required from a new design (a replacement for the 'M7s'?), which resulted in the first of what were the two famous memoranda often quoted as setting out the criteria upon which 'Leader' would be based.

From Richards:

'Routes and weights to be hauled:
Plymouth to Tavistock or Okehampton – 256 tons
Okehampton Halwill Junction and Bude – 256 tons
Barnstaple and Ilfracombe – 325 tons
Exeter and Exmouth – 384 tons
Bournemouth and Swanage – 320 tons
Brookwood (or similar outlying stabling grounds) to Waterloo – 450 tons
Speed of trains – 50 to 60mph
Distances to be run between taking water and coal –
60 miles for water and 120 miles for coal.'

These criteria were certainly not what the 'M7s' were currently capable of, so it appears that Richards might even have set out a proposal that he knew was unachievable in the hope Bulleid would 'see sense'. Indeed, such requirements were probably never truly achieved by any one single steam type.

But if Richards had hoped to set an impossible target, the opposite effect was achieved. Armed with information with which he could then indeed challenge the General Manager if necessary, on 11 July 1945 Bulleid wrote to Missenden with the second of the famous notes, and in so doing responded to the Richards criteria:

'In order to meet these requirements within the limits imposed by the Chief Civil Engineer as regards permanent way and bridges, I propose a locomotive in accordance with the enclosed diagram [shown on page 21]. The engine will have a maximum speed of 90mph, will be able to work goods trains which are normally taken by the Q1, and passenger trains equal to the "West Country" engines, and will carry at least sufficient water and coal to run 80 miles between taking water and 150 miles without taking coal. The engine weights are so distributed as to enable it to run over the whole of the Company's lines with the following exceptions: Wenford Bridge line, Hayling Island Branch, Bere Alston and Callington Line, Rye Harbour Branch, Newhaven Swing Bridge, Dover Prince of Wales Pier,

Axminster and Lyme Regis Branch, Isle of Wight Lines, none of which is important. It is estimated that, if a batch of 25 engines of this class were built, cost per engine would be £17,000. If one prototype was built, the cost would obviously be greater, dependent upon the development work found to be necessary during construction, and might reach £25,000. With reference to the conversation at the Progress Meeting on the 28th June 1946, I hope it will be possible to hold the proposed meeting soon as I am anxious to put in hand without delay the construction of the prototype in order to complete it by June 1947.'

Interestingly perhaps, nowhere is there a mention of axle weights, although it would be reasonable to assume that they would have to be restricted to around 18 tons. Likewise it is not known whether anyone had the courage to challenge any of the comments made by Bulleid at this time. Neither does it appear that any were subsequently challenged, even though almost every objective criterion set by the designer at this time would unfortunately not be

With just a week to go, on 14 June 1949, No 36001 stands amongst the clutter of a busy workshop at Brighton, seemingly almost complete. Bulleid is reported as preferring to refer to engineering dimensions in larger fractions of an inch rather than thousandths.
Don Broughton collection

met. In some respects one gets the impression that Bulleid was riding roughshod over the Traffic Department. Seniority is not mentioned here, although it is probable that the CME was in a more powerful position with the Board – and possibly even character-wise – than the beleaguered Traffic man.

The stage was now set for design work to begin for the production of a locomotive akin to the specified criteria. As before, with Bulleid nothing was sacrosanct. As an example he set one of his senior drawing office staff, W. H. (Joe) Hutchinson, to investigate the possible use of sleeve valves as a means to save space on what he doubtless already saw as a potential multi-cylinder design.

At this stage a brief foray into sleeve valves themselves might be appropriate, and while the present work is in no way intended to be an engineering thesis, it should be mentioned that in theory at least the sleeve valve was far more efficient than the piston valve. The use of the sleeve valve was then fashionable in a number of engine types, notably the stationary steam engine, and, after being fitted to the prototype Napier 'Sabre' engine in 1935, was used extensively in the 24-valve Hawker 'Typhoon' aircraft, which had a 24-cylinder 'Sabre' engine. On the railway, however, the type has only been traced to a single use anywhere in the world, in the solitary Paget engine of the Midland Railway.

Bulleid had an ally in this field in the person of Sir Henry Ricardo, whose company, Ricardo Engineering, based at Shoreham, just 6 miles from Brighton, was ideally placed from a technical point of view. Bulleid and Ricardo were destined to maintain a long-lasting relationship that continued after the former had left British shores and was working for CIE at Inchicore.

If on the LNER Bulleid had been the ideas man and Gresley the power to control and direct the ideas so as to keep them within the bounds of possibility, the reverse now applied on the Southern. It appears that Cocks was beginning to be seriously concerned at how the new project was developing, and accordingly attempted to steer his chief back towards more conventional thinking. In so doing it is possible that the November 1945 proposal for a 4-6-4T may have been a revision of earlier ideas, and at the instigation of the assistant rather than the master. As before, there were definite shades of the unconventional – the 350psi boiler pressure and two cylinders – but without any indication as to the type of valves that would be fitted. (Exactly where and how this particular design emerged is interesting, as the very high boiler pressure is beyond what was then and still is today the accepted 300psi maximum for a conventional steam boiler.)

Certain CMEs would have been content to allow the drawing office free rein with ideas, having previously set the basic criteria. However, this was not Bulleid's way, so the type of design that would probably have evolved under Cocks – possibly the 'Q1' boiler but built into a tank engine – was not proceeded with. Instead, matters appear to have become ever more far-reaching, and for the first time there appears a locomotive unit contained on a frame – albeit reminiscent of a 'well-wagon' – and having a pair of powered bogies. This design itself went through various stages of development, including one version with a water-tube boiler. Both were of the 0-4-4-0 (or should it be B-B?) type, but herein lay a difficulty as the proposed axle weight was now 20 tons, so this proposal was rejected.

With his mind ever racing ahead, it seems that Bulleid did not take the all-important step of liaison with the men who would actually be the operators of the machines – the Motive Power and Traffic departments. This is perhaps slightly strange as beforehand he had been known to take great pains to ensure that the Pacifics in particular were as comfortable as possible. (Townroe elaborates on this point in the final chapter.) Plug-in electric lights for the driver to carry round, steam-operated fire doors for the fireman, a comfy draught-free cab, and controls grouped on either side of the cab are all examples of his previous care and attention to detail, together with the oil baths that were intended to reduce maintenance to a minimum between works visits. The fact that some of these did not work well in practice, or were not used as had been intended, was not always the fault of the designer.

Having now set the criterion of a locomotive on powered bogies, it was but a simple step to provide six-wheeled bogies that would thus reduce the axle loading. By

lengthening the whole assembly, a suitably sized boiler, firebox and bunker could also be accommodated. The disadvantage was that the length of the proposed engine was now 62ft 6in, akin to most coaches. While this additional size might not have mattered everywhere, certain of the restricted platform lengths at Waterloo could well have caused operational difficulties.

At this stage the design was still in many respects conventional, with a traditional 280psi boiler and firebox placed centrally on the frames. A single central cab would be provided, and the wheel diameter was set at 4ft 1in. However, even this would be not unusual enough for Bulleid, who went one stage further by including a possible condensing apparatus to the Holcroft/Anderson design. Accordingly it was proposed that only the front bogie would exhaust direct to the atmosphere, while the exhaust from the rear bogie would be used as a feed-water heater. This was similar, but not identical, to that used in the experiment on No A816 a decade earlier. Oil-firing was also suggested but not confirmed, although the ramifications of this would later re-emerge as the fireman's compartment of 'Leader' was small, with limited space to swing a shovel, compounded by the offset firehole door (it has been suggested by outside observers – but interestingly not commented upon by Ted Forder, Alf Smith, or in the official report – that due to the restricted space a somewhat dextrous 'flick of the wrist' was needed to avoid removing lumps of skin from the fireman's knuckles). This was one of the very few occasions at that time when oil-firing was mentioned, maybe arising from the fact that oil was being seen as a potential major fuel for railway use in the very near future. Large supplies of heavy fuel oil were then available following the end of the war, while the best-quality coal was being exported as much as possible in order to accrue necessary foreign currency.

There now being an almost workable proposal, it was up to the Board to sanction the project. It is known that a Board meeting was held in either July or August 1946, yet tantalisingly for us, and frustratingly for Bulleid, no approval was given for the new design. Yet despite this and the perceived pressure over timescales, especially with the countdown to nationalisation already having begun, Bulleid was if anything now more enthusiastic than ever. The new design evolved into one with a dry-back firebox, thermic siphons, and the definite inclusion of sleeve valves. This in itself was so unusual that Bulleid applied for a patent to cover the new boiler design. (In the event the patent was not issued until 21 January 1949, as No 616.445, covering 'Improvements relating to locomotive and like steam boilers'.)

Hutchinson's work with the sleeve valves was also complete, an added complexity being at the suggestion of Sir Harry Ricardo, who advocated the inclusion of the aforementioned degree of axle rotation to the sleeve in addition to its fore and aft movement; it was believed that this would prevent any likelihood of seizure in use.

Stages in the abortive painting of No 36001, which seems to have been moved to a different location within the erecting shop. BR deemed that the 'Leader' class would fall within the 'mixed-traffic' power category and accordingly the designated livery would have been lined black. Certainly it would appear this instruction was in part carried out as the engine is seen with what appears to be black undercoat, then a black top-coat and varnish applied. Of course at this stage there would have been no requirement for yellow warning panels at the ends – what a thought! More seriously, though, is the situation seen in the final view, where No 36001 is seen almost complete – numberplates and the steam heating pipe from the body to the bogie are awaited. The date is recorded as 21 June 1949, yet this was also the very day that she was noted – in grey – outside the works and complete. Why then the rapid repaint? Probably because at the time the official photographs had yet to be taken, and as these were traditionally still taken with an engine in 'photographic grey' it may well be that the intention was to take the views, then apply the lined black livery before entering traffic. Analysis would indicate that someone was simply a bit too eager with the paint-pot. However, black – clean black, that is – suited the engine well. It was also reported that on 20 June an attempt was made to persuade No 36001 to leave the works, but she became stuck in a door, so the prospect of her being seen outside in black was thus very close.
National Railway Museum/J. G. Click (2), Don Broughton collection (1)

37

The design was also evolving aesthetically: a rounded cowl appeared, like a cross between the front end of a Pacific and contemporary French styling, while the length had increased further to 66 feet, dictated in part by the inclusion of what were long and thin sleeve valves.

The proposed design was sufficiently advanced for a number of drawings to be made available to the Rolling Stock (Repair & Renewals) Progress Committee at a meeting held at Waterloo on 4 September. It is not clear if Bulleid himself was present, although he had personally prepared a descriptive memorandum: notwithstanding the fact that his description had already been superseded in places by the development of the design.

'LEADING CLASS SHUNTING ENGINE C-C TYPE

The principal features of the new engine are as follows:

This design of engine makes full and complete use of the total weight for adhesive purposes and braking. The type of bogie is similar to that introduced on the electric locomotive, the riding of which has been found to be satisfactory. The springs and gear will be above the axleboxes and under continuous lubrication. The whole of the moving parts will be enclosed and fitted with automatic lubrication, so that it will not be necessary for the driver to lubricate any part of the machine. Each engine will have three "simple" cylinders driving the intermediate axle. The load is transmitted to the leading and trailing axles by chain drive in an oil-tight casing. Roller bearing boxes will be fitted to all axles and will receive force feed lubrication. The axleboxes will be contained in an oil bath. Each axlebox guide is fitted with a "Silentbloc" bearing. The leading engine will exhaust to atmosphere, by way of the blastpipe in the smokebox, so as to provide the necessary draught in the boiler, but exhaust from the trailing engine will be used to heat the water in the tank, the hot water being pumped to the boiler by suitable hot water pumps. The boiler is a new design which will obviate the maintenance inherent in the normal type of locomotive boiler. The engine will also be fitted with feed water treatment incorporated in the tender. The controls of the engine will be such that both men will be able to carry out their duties seated and will be duplicated where necessary, so that they can drive in either direction. The weight of water and fuel indicated should be ample for the normal requirements of the Southern Railway, especially as by condensing steam from one engine, the water consumption should be appreciably reduced. The engine is fitted with 5ft 1in wheels and this, in conjunction with the short stroke, will allow the engine to run at speeds up to 90 mph, without exceeding the normal piston speed. The engine will not be air-smoothed in any sense of the word, but the front end will be based on that successfully introduced on the "West Country" class engines, in order that the steam, when the engine is working lightly, is carried out of the cab.'

For the first time reference is made to the 'Leading' class of locomotive. Where exactly this term had arisen is not totally certain: it may have been Bulleid himself, or even the publicity department at Waterloo. From here, though, it was but a simple step to the name 'Leader', which is also used in official records from now on.

There are a number of obvious anomalies in Bulleid's description. 'Both men will be able to carry out their duties seated' – but how? Was the engine still intended to be oil-fired? That would surely be the only explanation. But oil-firing appears to have been left behind by now, and what may very well have been a draft version of the memorandum did not actually reflect the progress that had been made since in developing the engine. It cannot be seriously believed that there was ever any intention by Bulleid to deliberately deceive his own employers.

There is a definite reference to feed-water heating, an idea that was not in the end carried forward to the prototype. This particular aspect was not in itself unduly complicated and might have given the added advantage that less water would have to be carried, and less water equals less overall weight. Perhaps the feed-water heating facility was in the end not included as a greater benefit could be achieved with TIA water treatment (a French invention for the chemical processing of water to neutralise its scaling and corrosive properties), which would be more beneficial to an engine working in the South of England, where much of the water is hard. Unfortunately TIA water treatment is not compatible with feed water that contains any globules of oil, which would have inevitably been the case with condensed water having already passed through the cylinders in the form of steam. An oil separator would then be needed, again technically feasible, but another added complication. For once Bulleid wisely decided to play safe and conventional cold water injectors and water treatment were provided.

Meanwhile, behind the scenes the Superintendent of Operations (in 1937 the post-holder was F. Bushrod OBE, but it is not certain if he was still in the chair at the time in question) was concerned over approval being given for 25 new machines with so many 'unorthodox and untried ideas'. The Superintendent is quoted as suggesting that trials be carried out with just a single prototype. Such conservatism – or perhaps fear – might similarly have affected other senior members of staff, but evidently not all. A number of individuals were clearly taken by the charm and charisma of the CME, who it is known was well able to cajole individuals towards his way of thinking.

Ready to face its waiting public, No 36001 is virtually finished. A numberplate – one of two, as there was an identical one at the opposite end – has now been fitted, but three items remain: the dust cover for the oscillating gear at No 2 end, connection of the steam-heat pipe from the bogie to the body (the pipe is lying across the buffers), and a cover for the transfer gearbox above the centre cab steps. The photograph was taken in Brighton Works some time between 21 and 25 June 1949.
National Railway Museum

Even so, the result was a compromise proposal, which would be put to the next Board meeting for sanction. This was for just five engines of the new type, and with no mention of any conventional tank engine replacement.

The following day, 5 September 1946, the (in)famous confirmation arrived:

'From the General Manager; to the Chief Mechanical Engineer.

With reference to Minute 79 of the meeting of the Progress Committee held yesterday; the Traffic Manager informs me that he has had a further discussion with you upon this matter and he now recommends we proceed with the building of five engines to Diagram 7326. I shall be glad if you will proceed accordingly.'

This, then, was it. 'Leader' had the go-ahead. However, Diagram W7326 was only a stage along the way, and a lot more would happen before a final working diagram was completed. Despite this, Order No 3382 was issued to Brighton Drawing Office on 11 September confirming the task: 'Build five tank engines to Diagram W7326.'

Richards and his colleagues were, however, clearly not pinning all their faith in the new design, for just a few weeks later, at the beginning of October 1946, he submitted his official requirements for motive power, which were placed before the Rolling Stock (Repairs & Renewals) Progress Committee at Waterloo:

'In reply to your letter of the 5th September and referring to minute No 79 of the Progress Committee Meeting held on the 4th September. The case justifying the construction of 25 new passenger tank engines is given below. At the present time and, indeed, for the past 45 years the most powerful passenger tank engines on the Western Section have been those of the M7 class, 104 of which are still in existence. These engines were built between the years 1897-1911 and although the last 49 embody slight improvements, the whole class was based on a design prepared in 1897 and now, therefore, nearly 50 years old. They were originally built for L&SWR suburban traffic and were, in due course, rendered redundant by electrification. They are now being used as general utility locomotives, 25 working empty trains between Clapham Junction, or other stock berthing points, and Waterloo, and the balance on local and branch line services on the Western Section. They are completely out of date and inefficient by modern standards, and their continued existence prevents any improvement on the services they operate. In the report to yourself dated 1.12.1944, upon our locomotive position in 1950, prepared by the Deputy General Manager and other Chief Officers, the whole of these 104 engines were condemned, and this recommendation was confirmed in the corresponding report upon the 1955 locomotive position submitted on 3.9.1946. The report dealing with the Engine Building Programme during the years 1947-1955 recommends the building of 60 new tank engines, diesel or steam, in addition to the 25 tanks already proposed, and I now recommend that the latter be constructed. It is understood that the five engines to be built will be a guide as to the building of the subsequent 20.'

Perhaps Richards still held on to a vain hope that another more simple and straightforward design might materialise. But again it is interesting that nowhere does anyone appear to consider any of the existing larger stock of tank engines worthy of further builds.

G. L. Nicholson, within the Traffic Manager's Department at the time, recounted the following in correspondence to the author in 1984, while also, perhaps modestly, commenting that his own part in the 'Leader' story was only 'marginal'. But it was Nicholson who managed to persuade the General Manager of the day, 'much to Bulleid's displeasure', that the original building order should be reduced from 25 to five. In the same letter to the author, Nicholson continued, '...which – as events turned out – was still four too many...'

Nicholson also gave his own views on Bulleid:

'OVB was a man of extraordinarily complex character and gifts. His normal demeanour seemed quiet and almost unassuming. This concealed a quite enormous determination to have his own way. He was extremely astute, and would normally pursue his ends with a combination of charm and guile, backed up by argument, sometimes well reasoned, often assertive, and an almost overwhelming power of persuasion and conviction that he was right. Like many another, he could become pretty unpleasant if he thought he was being thwarted. He was a difficult man to argue with. In bad times, such as failure on his – or his Dept's part – to deliver in accordance with previously declared promises, he would quite unscrupulously conceal the true position, even if this entailed further misleading undertakings he knew he could not fulfil.

A dominant characteristic was his total devotion to the unorthodox, quite frequently merely for its own sake. It was heresy or near heresy for any member of his design staff to present him with anything that "looks like an ordinary engine". As a general rule he disliked conforming to normal practice: ie his own brainchildren would not only *be* different: they must *look* different, even when they were not much different. (The Q1s, for example. Or what useful purpose was served by his numbering system?) This constant pursuit of the unorthodox sometimes warped his judgment with almost ludicrous results, like those awful buffet cars on the Victoria-Portsmouth main line electric mu's; or still more awful, "Tavern" cars on the main-line expresses out of Waterloo.

The "Leader" saga well illustrates a rather more serious aspect of this characteristic. The OVB objective throughout was, I feel sure, to produce a revolutionary, powerful and all-purpose steam loco, counter to emergent electric/diesel main-line traction, and thereby to crown his reputation. (A perfectly laudable objective for a devoted steam man, though in the context of the times, neither the concept nor its execution says much for his judgment.)

He saw his opportunity when his management decided it wanted to replace the M7s. No one but Bulleid would have dreamt of trying to transform the humble tasks these old locos were engaged on into such a specification as that for the "Leader". When – sensibly and prudently, but very likely guilefully as well – he asked for the Traffic Manager's "exact requirements", what happened?'

Nicholson then went on to relate the accepted sequence of events leading to up to the well-known memorandum:

'I fear such a mundane interpretation would have had little effect on OVB, who proceeded to mesmerise his management into thinking they needed a loco of the "Leader"'s potential capabilities for such work. Assuming there was a case for the "Leader", it certainly wasn't for the purpose set out in the TM's note of 3.8.45. Something like that was, I fear, the genesis of the "Leader" fiasco.

OVB, with his really remarkable innovatory talents, his vision and his energy, was a splendid chap to have around when and as long as he was kept on a very tight rein, as he was under Nigel Gresley.

But there was no such rein on the Southern – nor later, in Ireland. The tragedy was that his persuasive powers were such that for the only time in its history the Southern found themselves provided with large numbers of modern express locomotives. Neither the MNs nor the WCs could be regarded as successful. When they were in good nick, they were splendid to drive, masters of their job, comfortable to ride on, bags of steam. But they were atrociously expensive in coal and water consumption, and oil – oil all over the system! Depot maintenance staff, whether mechanical or shed, disliked them for their inaccessibility, unreliability and so on. Their casualty rate was high, and so were their operating costs. Eventually they were all rebuilt – at considerable cost – but then became, so far as I know, useful citizens indeed.'

At the next Board meeting of 3 October 1946, there is a record of a curious comment relating to the new design:

'Mr Bulleid also said that only one of the new Passenger Tanks would be completed in June 1947, and that the remaining four would follow as soon as possible thereafter. The Traffic Manager intimated that from an operating point of view it would be better if the five engines were constructed for coal burning in order to ensure greater mobility, particularly in regard to depot allocation, and the Chairman requested the Chief Mechanical Engineer to proceed accordingly.'

So once again the suggestion of oil-firing occurs and is rejected – almost for the last time. Bulleid's comments on both crew members being able to undertake their tasks seated would also now no longer apply. That said, on the Southern Railway and elsewhere this was a period when locomotives were being converted to oil, and it is the opinion of the present author that Bulleid was perhaps somewhat ambivalent regarding the whole fuel issue and was waiting to see how matters would develop.

As already mentioned, Diagram W7326, on which the 'Leader' build was supposed to progress, was but a stage in what would finally be produced. Yet there is no record of Bulleid having returned to either the Committee or the Board to seek approval for any variation in the design.

The basic concept had now been approved, and work progressed on the development of the design.

It was only a matter of time before a further drawing featured the inclusion of a driving cab at each end, at first with corridor connections added. Later would come the internal interconnecting corridor between the cabs of 'Leader' itself, which produced the crucial result of the boiler having to be offset. One is tempted to assume that innovations such as these were the product of Bulleid himself, but it is possible that such ideas could well have come from others among his staff. To lay every detail at the door of the designer would perhaps be unfair – or over-generous. Neither, though, should he be excused for not identifying when an idea presented to him was indeed a step too far. This brings us full circle to the discussion of corridor tenders in Chapter 1, and the question as to how the offset boiler was to be counterbalanced. This will be mentioned again later.

But regarding the corridor connections, the question must surely be asked as to why they were even considered necessary. For what purpose would a crew need to have access to the rest of the train, and what would warrant changing crews while in motion and *en route*? This was not the LNER or LMS – there were no long non-stop runs on the Southern. Indeed, there were also no water troughs that would have permitted such running. Possibly the explanation was to facilitate multiple working, with several engines under the control of a single driver, but as it seems that the engine was now to be coal-fired, a fireman would be needed on each machine. But still the ideas flowed, and it was but a short step to the incorporation of a connecting corridor between the cabs.

As already recounted, the early plans were certainly towards oil-firing, and what comes through subsequently is that the design, in so far as firing was concerned, was never really seriously altered to cater for coal. Indeed, in several of the projected designs at this stage the actual cab sizes are also obviously limited. The final stage was no external corridor connections and instead a connecting corridor between the driving cabs and firing compartment (the phrase 'central firing compartment' will be used hereafter, but only for ease of description, as the compartment was actually nearer one end than the other).

With the design team working at a feverish pace, rumours were of course rife. Whether there was a deliberate policy towards secrecy has not been established, but perhaps that was the normal procedure when a totally new design was being prepared. Some stories did leak out, however, not least of which was the potential isolation of the crew members. As I recounted in my previous works on this subject, steam men had a clearly limited viewpoint when it came to recalling the solitude 'enjoyed' by an electric motorman. (Indeed, there were on the Southern at this time some 'dual-links', whereby a driver might work alternately steam and electric traction.)

At that time much of society was isolated from technological innovation and had a correspondingly limited outlook. So while progress and development was clearly taking place, it was largely unknown to the masses. There was simply no knowledge of many of the technological achievements that had taken place with steam traction elsewhere. Contemporary work in France by the legendary André Chapelon will be spoken of later, but in America there were already designs that could perhaps have had an influence on Bulleid, for example a number of types where the driver and 'stoker' were separated. Often referred to as 'Camelbacks', the reason for placing a driving cab centrally alongside the boiler was so that the maximum space was available for the necessary very wide firebox used when burning anthracite or other fuels of low calorific value (these fireboxes usually also had two doors, one to each side). There was no mention of problems with the crew being separated, although each man still had reasonable visibility compared with that available to the fireman of 'Leader'; there was also provision for application of the brakes from either compartment. However, the two driving and firing areas were not really intended to be accessed while in motion. Most of these engines had been built around the turn of the 20th century, although some were still in service until the 1940s.

Also in America, but far larger, was the Southern Pacific line's 4-8-8-2 'Cab-Forward' design. These were of necessity oil-fired, with the boiler turned around so that crews would not have smoke and fumes to endure when working through tunnels.

Finally, there had already been an American design where the boiler was clearly offset from the centre line but without any difficulty over weight or weight distribution. Indeed, it is suggested that between 2,000 and 3,000 steam engines of the 'Shay' type, with an offset boiler, were successfully worked in America; these balanced the offset boiler by having vertical cylinders and a solitary geared drive on one side only. However, 'Shays' were used almost entirely for slow-speed haulage on lightly laid track, invariably involving timber haulage. But the offset boiler did work – it just had to be counterbalanced!

With work proceeding on the conversion of Atlantic No 2039 *Hartland Point* for sleeve-valve operation, and also on the 'Leader' design, Bulleid gave a broad hint at what was to come at the centenary meeting of the Institution of Mechanical Engineers:

'A new type of heavy, mixed traffic tank engine is under construction and these engines embody further developments of the innovations introduced in the tender engines, all with the object of developing a steam engine as easy to maintain and operate as possible. As the locomotive is carried on two six-wheeled bogies, the whole weight is available for adhesion and braking and the engine can run over 97 per cent of the company's lines.'

A further, perhaps more public, hint at what was to come came just a few months later in his presidential address to the Institution. This was in turn picked up by the journal *Modern Transport*, which really made public the whole concept for the first time:

'In the early days of railways the locomotives were purchased from outside builders and the railway company was content to operate them and allow them to be maintained by the builder... In order that the repairs could be done economically the necessary machine tools and other equipment were provided gradually and it was soon appreciated that this equipment was equally suited in manufacturing new locomotives...

It will inevitably be suggested that the accepted methods of design or construction cannot be expected to give substantially better results. That is to say, the results were as good as could be expected with the designs, materials, finish, and methods of operation which were used. Consequently if we are to reach the higher level of achievement in continuity of service, which is now required, a new conception of the steam locomotive is also needed. Such thoughts caused us to question the accepted ideas and forced us to investigate the locomotive as

regards, (1) design, (2) use and (3) servicing. The very age of the steam locomotive has acted against its further development, for its bad features have come to be accepted as inherent and inevitable. It is these bad features which enable other forms of transport to compete with it, and consequently such features must be eliminated if the steam locomotive is to survive. Our investigations soon satisfied us there that was room for improvement under all three heads...

What sort of locomotive may we expect to see if it is to meet the majority of our future requirements? ... The locomotive should be built (1) to be run over the majority of the company lines; (2) to be capable of working all classes of train up to 90mph; (3) to have its whole weight available for braking and the highest percentage thereof for adhesion; (4) to be equally suited for running in both directions without turning, with unobstructed look-out; (5) to be ready for service at short notice; (6) to be almost continually available; (7) to be suited for complete 'common use'; (8) to run not less than 100,000 miles between general overhauls with little or no attention at the running sheds; (9) to cause minimum wear and tear to the track; and (10) to use substantially less fuel and water per drawbar horsepower developed...

The culmination of Bulleid's dream – and Riddles's nightmare: No 36001 is seen alongside the coaling stage at Eastleigh on 16 August 1950 while involved in the trials referred to in detail in the next chapter. It had naturally been assumed that the class would be successful – the type of failures and difficulties associated with the birth of 'Leader' on the Southern were unknown to local railway officials and it must therefore have also been hard to comprehend how such a situation had been allowed to occur, or indeed was occurring. If success had been forthcoming, a memorandum of 15 September 1949 from the Repair & Renewals Committee stated that the 'Leader' class would work Oxted line services. A cautious caveat added that other routes would be considered following 'some experience of the performance … particularly after the delivery of the new Class 4s' – referring to the LMS-design Class 4 2-6-4T engines then being assembled at Brighton but destined for work on the Southern Region.

A subsequent memorandum of 20 December 1949 from T. E. Chrimes, the Motive Power Superintendent at Waterloo, confirmed that the 'Leader' class would be based at Brighton to work between Brighton and London (Victoria or London Bridge) via Oxted. This would no doubt include what was always known as the dreaded 6.10pm departure from Victoria, which had for years been the subject of complaints from its regular passengers.

Terry Cole from Steyning adds an interesting comment regarding the working of the Uckfield route at that time. 'It is worth remembering that there was an acute motive power crisis on the Central Section in 1949, particularly on the London-Tunbridge Wells West via Oxted, London-Brighton via Oxted, and Uckfield or East Grinstead services. The "I3s" and other 4-4-2Ts were life-expired and the Standard 4 tanks were still under development at Brighton. The result was that the "Q" class freight 0-6-0s were drafted in to Tunbridge Wells West to work the London expresses. The "Qs" were the largest engine which could turn on the TWW turntable. You can see the attraction of a heavy and powerful class of engine – 'Leader' – to work these services, and one which did not need turning.' J. H. Aston

A new type of Southern engine has been designed, and the construction of five has been authorised. The engine will incorporate the following features and it is hoped will satisfy the design criteria given above. The locomotive is carried on two six-wheeled bogies, the general design of which follows that of the bogies I designed for use under the company's electric locomotives... The engine develops a torque the uniformity of which is comparable with that of a nose-suspended electric traction motor, but has a higher speed range and the unsprung weight is less. The capacity of the boiler has been made greater relative to the cylinder horsepower than in the case of any previous Southern locomotive. The cabs at the ends will give an improved look-out. The engines are intended for working fast passenger trains of 480 tons weight over the difficult Southern Railway main line, and goods and mineral trains of up to 1,200 tons; that is to say, something above the heaviest trains that would be required on the system. They carry sufficient fuel for 200 miles...'

It seemed as if the Southern Railway could now leave its days as a private company and enter public ownership as the one company that had pushed steam locomotive design further than any other. Perhaps even privately this was the bequest that certain officials might also have wished for. At the time the success of the new design was being taken for granted, and it mattered not that there was still being issued a stream of both ideas and ideals that should – and, perhaps more importantly, would – be incorporated.

One of these was the interchangeable power bogie, a laudable concept and one that was perfectly feasible from an engineering perspective. From a cost perspective, however, a far greater fleet than the initial five engines would be needed both to justify maintaining sufficient spares and, more importantly perhaps, incorporating the innovations in the design. This concept – the interchange of bogies – was in the end never undertaken with No 36001, but, as mentioned in the following chapters, it might well have made a difference if it had!

So work progressed, but slowly – completion of the first set of main frames did not take place until May 1948, already a full year behind Bulleid's original prophesy. The stream – at times more a torrent or even a flood – of new ideas meant that construction was invariably slower than intended, although even the designer himself must have realised that the initial optimism of his timescales would be unlikely to succeed.

The concept of a fleet of engines based on the 'Leader' design, which would have justified on cost grounds the spare bogies etc, came nearest to fruition as a result of a Southern Railway Board minute of November 1947, whereby a further 31 of the class were authorised for construction. It would appear that neither Richards nor any of his more sceptical colleagues raised much objection. Perhaps the fight had gone – after all, nationalisation loomed. Thus no fewer than 36 'Leaders' were apparently to be built straight off the drawing-board.

According to G. Freeman Allan, the effect of ordering the additional engines was to give an almost 'hands off' signal to the newly nationalised system. But it would backfire. This was simply too much for what was then still a totally untried design. Accordingly, one of the first decisions of the newly formed Railway Executive was to rescind the building approval for the additional engines. Bulleid might still have an ally at headquarters in the form of Missenden, but perhaps even he could now see the need for a degree of caution. Possibly if the order had been for a lesser number – six, for example – if might have been approved. In the event, between November 1947, when the 31 were approved, and the cancellation in the early part of 1948 (the actual date is not known), no material was ordered and consequently no work started.

1948 was a testing time. The huge new organisation would take some time to settle, and very wisely the man in charge of Mechanical Engineering at the Railway Executive, Robin Riddles, decided to allow the four new 'regions' autonomy – while the dust settled. That is not to say that he did not keep a watching brief on progress at Brighton, with regular reports being expected. One of these concerned the spiralling costs; quoted in July 1948 as being £87,000 for the five engines, this was increased by 15%, to £100,000, just two months later. It would eventually rise still further, which at the time represented double the cost of producing a steam engine of comparable size and power to an existing conventional design. Small wonder then that the project was also unofficially referred to as 'Bleeder', a somewhat cruel reference to its escalating cost. Indeed, one unnamed official, when asked if there was concern over the finance of the project, is reported to have replied, 'Worried is not the word...'

Overall it still appears to have been a close-run thing in presenting the new British Railways with a project already sufficiently advanced that it was worthy of continuing. Had construction work not actually started and had the design existed only on paper, it is probable that No 36001 would never have materialised. Therein perhaps also lie some of the reasons for failure, which are discussed in far greater detail in a subsequent chapter – the whole thing was a rush job.

Bulleid's unique numbering system was to have been applied to the new locomotive, and because of the six-wheeled bogies it would have been CC101-5. H. A. V. Bulleid has suggested that his father sketched name ideas for the engines on an old envelope, including

MISSENDEN
Sir Eustace
General Manager Southern Railway Co

and

CHURCHILL
Winston PC OM
Prime Minister of Britain 1939-45

implying that this was before the subsequent naming of No 21C151 as *Winston Churchill* in 1946 and BR No 34090 *Sir Eustace Missenden Southern Railway* in 1949. The Brighton record book of nameplate drawings (full of detail for all the Light Pacifics built at the Sussex works) has no information on 'Leader' plates ever having been drawn or cast, and certainly they were never fitted.

Additionally, as S. C. Townroe recounted, two other names were likely, *Montgomery, Field Marshal* and *Walker, Sir Herbert*, both no doubt similarly detailed as per the first two. (According to Robin Tufnell, some of the names suggested in the works for the engine, including *Fred Carno*, were somewhat less polite.[2])

So it was to be under British Railways and not the independent Southern Railway that 'Leader' No 36001 was eventually completed. The finished design was very different, both mechanically and aesthetically, from Diagram W7326, but at least the corridor connection was missing! But in its place the host of technical innovations almost invited difficulty. Never before had a steam engine of such avowed complexity, novelty and with so many untried features succeeded. Indeed, many of the design features had never been tried before, and those that had, had not worked particularly well.

However, Bulleid and his team appear to have still been charged with optimism even if the messages from *Hartland Point* were disappointing. So much depended on the success of the project – so much, and with so little time in which to achieve it.

[1] Sir Eustace Missenden relinquished the role of General Manager in October 1947 and instead took a post on the new Railway Executive. He was succeeded at Waterloo by John (later Sir John) Elliot, and it is believed that he and Bulleid again enjoyed an excellent working relationship. Bulleid also now had the advantage of a useful ally on the newly formed Executive. In his autobiography, Sir John Elliot makes no mention of the 'Leader' project.

[2] Fred Carno – sometimes spelled 'Karno' – was a music-hall impresario, his 'circus' being a travelling comic opera troupe. The period in which he was a performer pre-dated Charlie Chaplin's movie career, but at the time of the 'Leader' project the expression 'Fred Carno's Circus' was still in regular use as indicative of a poor-quality product.

CHAPTER THREE

The Bold Facts

No 2039

Generations of railway enthusiasts visiting railway workshops – and even preserved railways today – have gleefully recorded the numbers of the machines they have seen, either complete or otherwise. Indeed, I recall reading with some wry amusement controversy relating to 'when a cop is a cop' – if the number of the engine is visible but there are perhaps no frames or wheels, does it still count? Or if the cab is in a heap on its own, does that count? It's a question of personal preference, but today, where preserved engines swap identities for little more than clever marketing, difficulties can arise – even more so when the stampings of other long-scrapped machines are found on common parts such as rods, wheels and axles. How much of a preserved engine is indeed original and how much is a 'new' replacement?

Why bring this up? Well, work on 'Leader' was approved to commence on 5 September 1946, although it was actually almost a year later in July 1947 that physical construction started. Therefore anyone visiting Brighton Works after the latter date and for the almost two years that it took to complete the engine could well claim to have 'spotted' it in its varying stages of completion.

Why Brighton was chosen is of interest, as it was then the only one of the three Southern Railway workshops (the others being Ashford and Eastleigh) that was considered to have spare capacity, allied to which it was also the location of the head office of the Chief Mechanical Engineer's department. Even so, most of the components were manufactured or machined at Eastleigh – the boiler, wheels, sleeves, etc. On 19 February 1949 an RCTS visit to

No 2039 *Hartland Point*, in many respects the forerunner of No 36001, is recorded in steam on her very first outing at Brighton on 5 November 1947. Unfortunately even under a magnifying glass it is not possible to distinguish the chalk writing on the cabside, while exactly what the man under the cab and the associated hose relate to is not certain (unless of course No 2039 was even then displaying a thirst for water, as at this stage no rings had been fitted). B. J. Miller

Work on the modifications to No 2039 is reported to have taken place between July and November 1947, although clearly a considerable amount of time would have been spent with little progress being made while the drawing office attempted to resolve the various engineering difficulties. The engine is seen here on an unspecified date, with the new right-hand cylinder in position and its associated sleeve standing vertically alongside – probably for the benefit of the photographer. On the ground it is possible to make out parts of the oscillating gear that will later be attached to the front; a piston is also visible.
National Railway Museum/J. G. Click

Eastleigh reported that components for the 'Leader' class, wheels, boilers 'and other parts, were on view'. In effect Brighton acted as an assembly plant in addition to being involved in the fabrication of the numerous items made from sheet. Whether Ashford, or indeed any other outside builder, was charged with the provision of any components is not recorded.

While 'Leader' and her sisters were in the initial stages of construction, elsewhere on the Southern Railway other experimentation was taking place regarding ideas that Bulleid anticipated would be incorporated in the main design. Timescale-wise this was perhaps strange, as the

more usual procedure would be to conduct, then analyse the results and data from, any experimentation prior to inclusion. With the 'Leader' project this was not done. As already mentioned, the new Labour Government had been in power since late July 1945, with the avowed intent of future nationalisation of a number of former privately owned industries including the railways. Although the House of Commons did not actually approve railway nationalisation until December 1946, there can be no doubt that this policy had been promoted as part of the original election manifesto and consequently there would have been both awareness and discussion of the topic in the boardroom of the Southern before this time. Consequently Bulleid would have known that his timescale was limited.

Experimentation thus first took place involving 'U1' 2-6-0 No 1896 following its overhaul at Ashford in mid-1946. The experiment was not immediately visible to the naked eye, however, as it involved the provision of an opening duct at the base of the smokebox, which was operated mechanically from the cab. Its purpose was to provide an opportunity to dispose of smokebox ashes, char and cinders at intervals during the journey, thus avoiding the otherwise necessary task of cleaning the smokebox at the journey's end. (This was similar to F. W. Webb's experiments on the LNWR in 1870.)

In theory this was a valiant scheme. The duct was only intended to be open on occasions and was thus unlikely to impair steaming in what should otherwise be a sealed environment. In practice, however, it is not believed that any truly useful data was obtained, simply because No 1896 was fresh from overhaul and therefore unlikely to reveal ideal results. A similar remotely controlled duct was later fitted to No 36001 for a time, but drivers soon became aware that its operation would result in particles of ash settling around the edge of the opening, preventing an airtight seal being formed. (It is rumoured that a supply of dung was carried, which, when surreptitiously applied to the edges, produced the desired effect. No comment was made concerning the additional aroma that may have resulted...) It is believed that No 1896 ran in this condition for only a short time, and no formal trial results have been discovered.

The matter of ash cleaning on 'Leader' was perhaps the first of numerous aspects of the design that were clearly given little thought when the decision was eventually made to settle for coal-firing. The enclosed environment of the smokebox and cab made ash disposal difficult, to say the least. The duct as fitted would have been of little practical use, save for depositing grit on to the moving parts – again perhaps contributory to later bogie problems.

A second far more serious form of experimentation commenced in July 1947 when former LBSCR 'H1' class 4-4-2 No 2039 *Hartland Point* was withdrawn from capital service to be fitted with sleeve valves, which were then being proposed for the 'Leader' design. Here again the question is why? With this experiment in mind, it would

Views of *Hartland Point* in the process of conversion inside Brighton Works are rare. This particular photograph was taken just a week prior to the first steam trials, but seemingly slightly later than the preceding illustration as the sleeve has now been fitted into place.

Mike Thorp collection

seem that a final decision had already been made that 'Leader' would be so equipped. If so, why bother with the experiments if the decision was already a 'fait accompli'?

Brighton stripped No 2039 of its original outside cylinders and front bogie, and in their place new cylinders were installed, fabricated from a steel shell with exhaust annuli at either end and single central admission annuli. Within the cylinder was a cast-iron liner made of fine-grade 'Mechanite' – also referred to as 'Meehanite'. Within this liner, and sealed with no fewer than 30 rings, was another Mechanite-grade sleeve valve, around the circumference of which were machined openings to correspond with the admission and exhaust openings of the liner. Finally, within the sleeve came the piston, although as would be expected the original bore was thus considerably reduced: the original 26-inch stroke was unaltered, but the 19-inch diameter became only 14 inches. Tractive effort measured at the standard 85% of boiler pressure was thus reduced from 20,070lb to 11,892lb, which in theory meant that the boiler would always have plenty in reserve, although the pulling power of the engine would be considerably reduced.

It has been suggested that both these and the later similar sleeves for 'Leader' were machined on an old lathe at Eastleigh, which had originated from the former LSWR works at Nine Elms, being the only one on the Southern that could accommodate the size of the item to be machined. Operated by just one man, it took up almost the length of one wall within the Eastleigh machine shop. As the sleeves for *Hartland Point* and 'Leader' were similar in length, it is reasonable to assume that all were produced in the same way.

The bogie alteration was necessary as the original item would foul what were both larger and wider replacement cylinders; it was thus replaced with the wheels from a 'D3' tank, which were of 3-foot diameter compared to the original 3ft 6in. (According to *The Railway Observer* the wheels used originated from 'D3' No 2366. This particular engine was not officially withdrawn until February 1949, but it could of course have been standing around out of use for some time. Another possibility is that the bogie came from No 2363, which was withdrawn in December 1947. There is also some doubt as to whether just the wheelsets were changed, or if an actual 'D3' front bogie was fitted.)

In addition to the cylinder changes, a multiple-jet blastpipe was fitted, and a new chimney. The location of the Westinghouse air-pump was also altered to the right-hand side of the framing from its original position on the left.

Operation of the valves was cleverly thought out, for in addition to a fore-and-aft motion a degree of axial rotation was imparted to the sleeves. The actual percentage figure has not been accurately determined, but from photographs it would appear to have been something in the order of 25° either side of the horizontal. As such, the valves in operation when viewed from the front imparted a 'figure of eight' motion while at the same time sliding back and forth.

This fore-and-aft motion was achieved by extending the ordinary valve spindles attached to the Stephenson link motion allied to rocking levers ahead of the frames, and protruding to either side. This was in some ways visually similar to the method used for controlling the valves of the outside cylinders on Great Western four-cylinder types. The axial rotation worked via a rotating shaft beneath the smokebox, which was itself driven through a 'Morse' inverted tooth chain off the leading coupled axle. Two new mechanical lubricators were also driven by this rotating shaft.

The axial rotation was provided in an attempt to equalise both wear and temperature, both of which could

otherwise cause fracture. Another possible cause of fracture would be lack of lubrication, so numerous oil feeds were fitted, all pump-driven from two Wakefield mechanical lubricators mounted in a far from ideal place at the base of the smokebox. No 2039 was not fitted with an opening ash duct.

Work on No 2039 progressed through the summer and autumn of 1947, with the engine finally ready for a steam test within the workshops on 5 November. At this stage no rings had been fitted, so understandably the results were clouded in more than one sense. A further external trial was arranged for 3 December, with Bulleid present; also invited was his brother-in-law, H. G. Ivatt, who held the CME's position on the LMS. No 2039 ran up and down the Brighton Works yard, but was still devoid of sealing rings, so the front was still shrouded in escaping steam.

Two weeks then elapsed, during which the 60 sealing rings were fitted, and No 2039 was steamed again on 15 December ready for its first run, albeit light engine. This was made as far as Lewes in company with 'E5' No 2404, the operating authorities seemingly determined to ensure there would be no breakdowns and consequent disruption of traffic. Without the benefit of any formal

The same right-hand-side cylinder assembly is now complete. The veritable plethora of oil pipes and feeds is apparent, yet even so there were numerous failures due to seizure. Did any of these crucial pipes ever become blocked? That is something not mentioned in any contemporary report. Although undated, the view must be after November 1949 as it will be noted that part of the side framing of the running plate has been removed ahead of the cylinders, no doubt to facilitate maintenance access. It would never be replaced.

National Railway Museum/J. G. Click

Seen from the opposite side, it is possible to view the two Wakefield mechanical lubricators placed beneath the smokebox – hardly an ideal location – and the sleeve extension onto which has been bolted the mechanism to operate the reciprocal motion.
National Railway Museum/J. G. Click

report, it is difficult to be exact about the results, although it is known that a number of rings broke on this first run and were replaced at Brighton Works.

Bulleid's aim in using sleeve valves was to increase the efficiency of the steam usage by reducing losses caused by condensation. The sleeve valve allowed virtually the whole cylinder to be permanently enveloped in a steam jacket, which became in effect a circular steam chest. This 'steam chest' afforded a volume some 3.25 times the cylinder capacity at maximum cut-off, 75%. With the addition of the large steam inlet and exhaust annuli,

Below: **Recorded on the turntable at Brighton, No 2039 displays the addition of the ugly wide stovepipe chimney that was fitted at the time of conversion. This might indicate that modifications were also carried out to the blastpipe, although this cannot be confirmed.**
National Railway Museum/J. G. Click

a free flow for the steam was ensured, with consequential free running.

However, any advantage gained was offset by the increases in mechanical complexity and identified difficulties due to friction losses. It would take the various test runs to establish if a steam-tight seal could indeed be maintained, especially across the exhaust ports and front radial outlet slots for the extension drive lugs.

No 2039 on test

The seasonal traffic peak of Christmas 1947 no doubt precluded any serious attempt at test running with No 2039 until the start of 1948, so it was not until the first day of public ownership, 1 January, that No 2039 worked former SECR three-coach set No 597 between Brighton and Eastbourne. (It is believed that this same three-coach set was used on a number of occasions behind No 2039.) This was an empty stock working, the guard instructed to ensure that passengers were not permitted to join the train at the various station stops that were made in order to provide information as to the acceleration characteristics of the engine in its modified form.

No 2039 is being prepared for duty at Brighton in February 1948, possibly around the time that it was being utilised on the duty that involved running light to Lancing, then taking carriage underframes to Eastleigh. It is not known if the return from Hampshire to Sussex was light or with another working. H. M. Madgwick

At this stage all was well, and no doubt buoyed by the success there followed what was an almost daily test, again north-east from Brighton, to Groombridge via Lewes, a distance of some 30 miles. Although not stated as such, it is reasonable to assume that the train was able to use the nearby triangle to turn, and return the same way. Again it is unfortunate that no formal records of these trials have survived, although the runs would undoubtedly have been monitored by members of the Brighton test section. What is known is that the modifications appeared to bear out the hope for a free-running engine, with 70-80mph reached with ease.

Some time in the same month there were also some light engine trials to Three Bridges in company with a 'K' class Mogul, which was evidently propelled by No 2039 in both directions. The presence of the extra engine was again no doubt a means of insurance against breakdown on what was the main London line.

Enough confidence had by now presumably been gained to find No 2039 a more cost-effective role, so from February 1948 she was put to work on trains of carriage underframes between Lancing and Eastleigh. Whether these were one-way trips with the engine returning light from Hampshire is not certain.

Unfortunately, however, by now all was not well, for despite the limited mileage actually covered, No 2039 had developed a capacity for prolific consumption of water, and no doubt coal, so the fireman's work would have been similarly increased. Rumour has it that No 2039 would

Right: **This is the only known view of No 2039 at Eastleigh itself, with the railway cottages of Campbell Road in the background. Possibly the engine has not long arrived, although unfortunately the identity of the driver alongside is not recorded.** S. C. Townroe

leave Brighton for Lancing and Eastleigh with a full tender tank, but would have to stop for water at least twice en route. Usually these stops were at Chichester and Fareham, and this on a run totalling no more than some 65 miles. This equated to something in the order of between 53 and 87 gallons per mile, up to 3.5 times what would usually have been expected. To evaporate this amount of water the equivalent coal consumption was also high, and likely to have been in the order of 60lb per mile. Not unexpectedly, therefore, the engine was observed back in the works by the end of the same month, February 1948.

Repairs – or modifications – were undoubtedly carried out, and between March and June there were a number of runs from Brighton to either Lewes or, it is stated, Cowden, just north of Groombridge. There was at least one run to Hastings, as evidenced by the accompanying timings sheet for Saturday 29 May 1948 (which relates just to the anticipated timings to be achieved and does not mean that the trial either took place or was indeed completed).

It is not known if the other runs were all light engine or with empty stock in tow, although certain of the Cowden trips involved a single bogie utility van and two Royal Mail vans, Nos s4951/2. The latter two vehicles are reported as specially allocated to this working.

What is certain is that in June a three-coach set was taken from Brighton to Tunbridge Wells West at least once, after which the same load was worked on several occasions

Leaving Brighton for Groombridge – the lack of any headcode will be noted. This was a regular run for the engine, and often the same three-coach set was used. This particular test route was selected due to the limited traffic volume after Lewes, and would also be the one often later used with 'Leader'. National Railway Museum/P. Ransome-Wallis

between Brighton and Hastings – possibly to the latter location at similar timings to those mentioned above. As at the start of 1948, the results were again encouraging, so the load was increased to between four and five bogie vehicles once more to Tunbridge Wells West, a working that continued twice daily until some time in July.

The rest of July and August 1948 are something of a mystery, but it is known that in September 1948 No 2039 was seen at the head of a train of bogie utility vans, although the destination and whether it was empty stock is not certain.

Details for the autumn of 1948 are likewise uncertain, but No 2039 is known to have been in Brighton Works again for much of this time. Possibly little actual progress in the way of maintenance or repairs/modifications was actually made, and the length of time out of service could well be because any previous urgency had already 'evaporated', and Brighton was running at almost full capacity with its Light Pacific building programme, as well as the construction of No 36001 and the other normal repair projects.

12—BRIGHTON AND HASTINGS.

	a.m. arr.	a.m. dep.	p.m. arr.	p.m. dep.			a.m. arr.	a.m. dep.	p.m. arr.	p.m. dep.
Brighton	...	9 20	...	1 55		Hastings	...	11 10	...	4 35
Kemp Town Jc. ...		9 23		1 58	Test Trips with Engine	Bopeep Jc. ...		11 14		4 40
Lewes	9 37	9 40	2 11	2 13	S.2039 hauling 5 bogies	St. Leónards W.M.	11 16	11 18	4 41	4 43
Southerham Jc. ...		9 42		2 15	C.M.E. A/c.	Stonecross Jc. ...		11 40		5 0
Polegate	9 58V	10 6	2 33V	2 40		Polegate	11 44	11 47	5 4	5 5
Stonecross Jc. ...		10 10		2 44		Berwick	11 54	11 57	...	
Bexhill Ctl. ...		10 26	3 0	3 6		Southerham Jc. ...		12 9		5 20
St. Leonards W.M. ...		10 30		3 10		Lewes	12 11	12 12	5 22	5 25
Bopeep Jc. ...		10 32		3 12		Kemp Town Jc. ...		12 25		5 38
Hastings	10 36	...	3 16	...		Brighton	12 28		5 41	...

Timings for No 2039, Saturday 29 May 1948. *T. Cole collection*

December 1948 also did not seem to bother the operating department as much as the previous year in so far as using No 2039 was concerned, for at the start of the month there were a series of light engine runs as far as Hastings, often twice each day and usually at weekends. Then on 19 December came the chance to excel, for the engine was set the task of hauling an Officers' Special between Ashford and Brighton (how the engine came to be at Ashford is not reported). All was well until the train left St Leonards, near Hastings, when there was a sudden fracture of the right-hand valve rod. Who was on the train and the purpose of the special is not reported, but it cannot have done the credibility of No 2039 any good, as the motion had to be completely taken down in the nearby shed yard, followed by a tow back to Brighton.

For almost three months nothing is known, although it may be reasonable to assume that No 2039 simply languished at Brighton. However, during this time it was also obviously repaired, for on 14 March 1949 it is reported to have been in charge of a revenue-earning passenger service, the three coaches of the Hastings-Birkenhead through service, which No 2039 was booked to work between Brighton and Redhill. In view of her previous unpredictable performance and the fact this was a main-line working, it was perhaps surprising that no pilot was provided; presumably someone behind the scenes had exerted pressure to ensure that a sleeve-valve engine could be entrusted to work in a reliable fashion. It does not take a genius to imagine who that authority probably was, although the faith was rewarded, for both the outward and return workings were accomplished without difficulty. This would be the only time that No 2039 would ever work a fare-paying passenger service. (The Birkenhead through trains had only been reinstated a few months earlier on 27 September 1948 after a lapse of some nine years. SR/GWR stock was used on alternate days, with No 2039's task classified as Brighton Duty No 530. At Redhill the Hastings portion was attached to one from Margate and Dover and the service then continued towards Reading and its ultimate destination.)

Two days later the engine worked an empty three-coach set north from Brighton to Redhill again, and, as on

14 March, without a pilot. All was well until Earlswood, when adverse signals were encountered – due, it is believed, to the train running early, evidencing the free-running characteristics of No 2039 once again. Unfortunately, however, when a 'clear' indication was received No 2039 stubbornly refused to move in either direction. Later examination revealed that the engine had stopped with the ports in a totally 'blind' position, which meant that no steam could enter the cylinders regardless of the setting of the reversing gear. Whether this was a fault in design, manufacture, assembly or valve setting was never revealed (perhaps never even investigated and established!).

Delays to other traffic were mounting, so 'E' class 4-4-0 No 31587 was hastily summoned to drag No 2039 and her train the final short distance to Redhill, other services being delayed by almost 25 minutes. The return to Brighton later in the day was made with the same pilot engine – clearly this time no chances were being taken.

Some form of alteration was no doubt carried out, as on 1 April – the date would be destined to have a somewhat wry irony later – No 2039 again ventured out, this time on

Above right: **Climbing out of Brighton bound for Lewes, No 2039 is hauling three different vehicles. During the period when the engine was on trial, and prior to leaving for Ireland, Bulleid at first lived at Steyning, a short distance from Brighton. In 1949 he moved, albeit temporarily, to a flat in Brighton owned by Miss Billinton, a sister to the former CME of the LBSCR. Despite having offices at Waterloo and on occasions of course travelling to Eastleigh or Ashford, he was ideally placed at Brighton, where, during Southern Railway days, the principal drawing offices of the CME's department were located. Following nationalisation Bulleid's area of mechanical responsibility effectively shrank and consequently he could spend considerably more time only at Brighton and, more specifically, on the 'Leader' project.** W. N. J. Jackson

Right: **Possibly with the same rake of coaches seen in the earlier view at Brighton, No 2039 is recorded here at Uckfield. Judging from the steam escaping from the cylinder drain cocks it may be that the engine is preparing to depart, or, at the risk of sounding cruel, attempting to depart. Indeed, when running, No 2039's front end was often enveloped in steam. The length of the cylinders allied to the extended lugs at the front gave the impression that the cylinders were longer than they were, although as the crankpin position had not been altered on the coupled wheels, the stroke was in fact the same as before.** National Railway Museum/P. Ransome-Wallis

Above: **At Brighton on 14 May 1948, No 2039 is apparently awaiting duty, which at this time was mainly trial runs to either Lewes or Cowden. The other three surviving members of the 'H1' class were also still to be seen on occasional main-line workings, including the Victoria to Newhaven boat train – two other members of the class had been withdrawn in 1944. Together with No 2039, the class would become extinct in 1951, although the last of the other type of LBSCR Atlantic, the 'H2' class, would survive until 1958.** Arthur Taylor

Right: *Hartland Point* **is in store at Brighton with nowhere to go on 24 July 1948. It is believed that the engine spent much of July and August in the same position, although whether this was due to any defect is not clear, as there would not appear to be any parts missing. Possibly even at this time there were some who were wary as to the future potential for 'Leader', bearing in mind the similarity of valve design and continuing failures with No 2039.** T. C. Cole

a three-coach special from Brighton to Ashford and routed via the coast line and Hastings. Bulleid and another member of his senior staff were on the footplate as observers and were thus able to view at first hand the difficulties experienced by the driver in restarting after a signal stop near Ore. The record reveals that some 7^{1}/$_{2}$ minutes were spent in attempting this restart.

The final confirmed run in which No 2039 participated (although no date is given) took place a short time later when the engine was again rostered to head what was deemed a 'works train' between Lancing and Eastleigh, thought to have consisted of four passenger vehicles.

After this came a period of open store at Brighton until the engine entered the works on 14 June 1949 with the

Fresh from overhaul and now identified as BR No 32039, the engine still has nowhere to go. She entered Brighton Works on 14 June 1949, surprisingly perhaps, for overhaul, after which she would have been expected to undertake running-in then a return to normal service. But No (3)2039 in her sleeve-valve condition was well known and with a far from enviable reputation. Consequently, after overhaul (was she ever given any running-in trials?) she languished in basically the same spot for something like 18 months. F. Foote/Mike King collection

somewhat strange intention of restoring it to its original form; however, as referred to earlier, the class was already considered life-expired, so instead No 2039 remained untouched inside the works pending a decision regarding her future.

Somewhat surprisingly, that decision was for overhaul but with the sleeve valves retained, so No 2039 was given what would in effect be a major refurbishment, which even included a replacement boiler sent especially from Eastleigh. She emerged by 2 September 1949 as BR No 32039 painted in unlined black, but perhaps significantly without any ownership insignia or wording. Presumably some test running would have been involved following the overhaul, but this is not reported.

Following overhaul – and presumably a satisfactory period of trial (and running-in?) – the engine was allocated to Brighton shed and intended for normal work. How this could seriously have been anticipated must be open to question, as unless some major modifications had been made she would surely have behaved in exactly the same way as before. Indeed, her reputation was known

Slightly later No 32039 has had her chimney sheeted over, a sure sign that she is stored. It has been suggested that at some stage the front buffer beam was strengthened, but this cannot be confirmed from photographs. RCTS

and, possibly due to instructions from the shed management, she was always ignored and may never have been used as intended.

The rest of 1949, all of 1950, and the start of 1951 were spent in the same way, the engine obviously deteriorating in store without being used. In February 1951 official notice was received to move No 32039 to Eastleigh for assessment, but inspection at Brighton revealed that she was unsuitable to make the journey under her own power (whether this was a boiler defect is not reported), and she was instead towed to Hampshire by 'C2X' No 32438.

Not surprisingly, inspection at Eastleigh revealed the same as had been found at Brighton, and that a further overhaul would be required in order to restore the engine to traffic. This time it was not forthcoming, and No 32039 quietly disappeared from the scene, being noted on the scrap lines at the works on 24 February 1951. She was finally dismantled at Eastleigh in March 1951, although at least one of the nameplates survived.

Construction of 'Leader'

'A new type of heavy, mixed traffic tank engine is under construction and these engines embody further developments of the innovations introduced in the tender engines, all with the object of developing a steam engine as

Inside Brighton Works on 25 June 1951, a member of staff is possibly warning off the cameraman. This did happen at Eastleigh, at least one photographer having the film removed from his camera by a senior works official after having recorded No 36001. Don Broughton collection

easy to maintain and operate as possible. As the locomotive is carried on two six-wheeled bogies, the whole weight is available for adhesion and braking and the engine can run over 97 per cent of the company's system.'

So O. V. S. Bulleid himself had stated at his lecture to the centenary meeting of the Institution of Mechanical

Engineers in June 1947. As we have seen, prior to that time little if anything had been made public, and slightly less than a year later (March 1948) a visitor to Brighton Works who reported on his findings to *The Railway Observer* was only able to record: 'It is reported that Brighton Works is soon to build five high-pressure locomotives to an unconventional design, to be known as the "Leader" class. They will be continuous-framed, carried on two six-wheeled bogies, with a cab and a set of cylinders, fitted with sleeve valves at each end. After the first five engines have been tested, a further thirty-one will be constructed. A set of cylinders and valve gear of the pattern to be used were, until recently, on test at Brighton.'

At this stage the reader may be excused a wry smile, but – as referred to in the Introduction – to apply hindsight to the knowledge then available is to immediately view the project in the wrong context. It is clear that there was secrecy surrounding it at the time. While the staff on the shop floor at Brighton were obviously 'in the know', those

at Eastleigh probably just saw the requirements for boilers, sleeves, axles, etc, as simply another works project. Moving ahead somewhat, there is a well-known view at Brighton where a member of the works staff can be seen waving the photographer away, while at Eastleigh some time later an individual had his camera seized and the film confiscated by the Works Manager. At the start the SR no doubt wished to maintain a degree of secrecy, while later, with the engine clearly not performing as intended, there was no wish to publicise matters any more than was absolutely necessary.

'Leader' at Brighton

Assembly of 'Leader' and her sisters really began around the very end of 1946 or the start of 1947. Certainly the first orders for material were placed with suppliers in December 1946 (as referred to earlier, Board approval had been obtained in September 1946), and it may be stated with reasonable certainty that actual construction would have commenced soon after. (The various design details and the politics and considerable discussion that took place

Filed away in the drawing store at Brighton is this tantalising glimpse of what the intended works plate for the 'Leader' class would have been like. Measuring 8 inches by just over 3$\frac{1}{2}$ inches, there is unfortunately no indication of whereabouts on the engine the item would have been fitted – assuming of course that it was *not* fitted…

behind the scenes are referred to in the preceding chapter.) What is not known is what material was actually ordered at this stage, and it may well be that it was just orders for steel supplies as a number of crucial design features had still to be both agreed and worked out. The drawing office at Brighton was of course working at full stretch on the proposal, in particular the sleeve valves, although it would appear that this particular aspect was finally completed in the spring of 1947. Possibly the complexities involved, which had no doubt been discovered in the planning stage, had led to the decision to use *Hartland Point* as a mobile test-bed – certainly the timing of work on that engine, July 1947, would tie in. However, it should also be mentioned that *Hartland Point* – or perhaps more accurately 'a modification to an existing engine for assessing the suitability of sleeve valves etc' – does not appear to feature in any SR Board minute of the period. This in itself is of interest as the cost of the modification would surely have exceeded the amount of finance that the CME – or probably any departmental head – could authorise without Board approval. There is absolutely no suggestion of course that anything underhand was involved; more likely, the September 1946 approval to proceed was a blanket approval to cover all work, with the

CME authorised to spend his allotted budget on the new design as he felt best.

Practically, though, there was little to view at Brighton until May 1948, when the first set of main frames was completed. Part of the difficulty lay in the almost continual changes that were taking place both in the drawing office and in the workshop itself. Much of the work was carried out almost on an 'ad hoc' basis, either because the drawings had been so modified as to be incomprehensible or a drawing was simply not available. It therefore did not bode well even at this early stage.

The situation at Eastleigh is also not clear, although as the components manufactured here, principally the boiler,

The culmination of a dream, but one that would eventually turn into a nightmare: the repainted No 36001, with holes drilled for the numberplate, although this has yet to be fitted. The date is not confirmed, but could be either 21 or 22 June 1949, with the engine emerging into the daylight for the first time after the works door incident described in the text! It appears that O. V. S. Bulleid was present – understandably so – and he is seen on the right of the photograph walking towards the No 2 (bunker) end of the engine.
National Railway Museum/J. G. Click

cylinder castings and wheelsets, were less susceptible to last-minute change it is reasonable to accept that work in Hampshire was proceeding at perhaps a calmer pace. According to Bradley, the Works Manager at Eastleigh, had '...very wisely avoided involvement with the Leaders...', but this is obviously not correct bearing in mind the components that were constructed there. As these items were completed they were transhipped to Brighton, one boiler at least being noted outside the Sussex works on 6 May 1948, although dates and details of other transfers are not reported. It is likely that such movements were undertaken as items were completed rather than all the parts for one particular engine or all of the same item. Indeed, as recounted earlier, it is the present author's view that despite authority having been given for an initial build of five engines, not all the main components were completed for the fifth engine, while the SR's authorisation for a further 31 of the type given by the Board in November 1947 was a gesture only, with no material ordered and certainly no actual construction commenced.

Following the various 'entertaining' incidents within Brighton Works itself – as described in the photographic captions – No 36001, as it had finally been identified, finally saw the light of day on the morning of Tuesday 21 June 1949. This was slightly later than intended, since when the engine had first been towed toward the doors of the works it had hit the surrounds and 'modifications' were necessary to allow it to escape! (What these modifications were – presumably simply the removal of a few pieces of frame around the door rather than modifications to the external parts of the engine – were not specified.) Of course 'Leader' was destined to make several more visits to the works in the course of the next few months, so it may be that she always entered and left via the same route. (She was the longest individual vehicle ever to use Brighton Works, locomotives on their own having a much shorter wheelbase; carriage stock, which would have been of a comparable length, was not handled at the locomotive works.)

No 36001 remained on view outside the works overnight, visible to trains passing on the main line, the plan being to run the first trial the next day from Brighton station, no doubt in a similar way to the earlier tests with No 2039, which would replicate normal station-to-station working. All started well, and on the Wednesday morning No 36001

backed down to Brighton station, whether for inspection or trial is not certain. Immediately luck ran out, as any potential running was quickly cancelled due to a failure of the engine to reverse, resulting in 'Leader' having to be towed back to the works for attention.

The fault was traced to a broken operating rod for the middle sleeve on the No 1 (smokebox end) bogie, while the oscillating gear associated with the sleeve to the same cylinder was bent. These items were repaired or replaced, the necessary components probably being taken from stored stock in hand and originally destined for another engine of the type. (Interestingly, this failure to the No 1 bogie was only the first of several that would involve the same component. No 1 bogie was the one allegedly reversed while on test at Brighton, then given steam to run in the opposite direction...!)

The failure to reverse was destined to become a not uncommon problem later for other reasons; the steam cylinder mounted centrally underneath the main frames and intended to reverse the direction of both bogies simultaneously was notoriously unreliable. Whether this was design failure, a manufacturing fault or something else was never established. (Similar criticism of design/manufacture was levelled at a number of other ancillary but nonetheless essential components.) Shortly afterwards recourse was often made to an 'economy size' crowbar, which would be used to 'assist' the steam cylinder to reverse as intended.

Three days were spent in the works, and it was not until 25 June 1949 that the first run was finally made. This was 'light' to Oxted via Lewes and Groombridge in company with an 'E4' tank. No mechanical problems were encountered, the record showing that the steep 1 in 60 gradient out of Lewes was accomplished with ease, although to be fair it should have been, as No 36001 was running light engine.

Left: **Alongside the main line at Brighton on 21 June 1949, No 36001 is in full view of passing trains. It cannot be emphasised enough the early impression that the engine must have made on both the travelling public and the considerable number of railway staff. Nothing like it had ever been seen before, and while there might have been some caution in so far as the more technical members of staff were concerned, simply due to the extreme number of novel features incorporated, there was no reason to believe that it would not work – and work well. After all, Bulleid designed engines to succeed.** H. M. Madgwick

Below left and below: **On 22 June 1949 the engine has successfully run the short distance to Brighton station from the works, possibly for inspection, although by whom is not reported. Unfortunately 'Leader' failed to reverse and had to be unceremoniously hauled back for inspection, modification and repair. It is believed that this is what is recorded here, the group of men alongside, without exception, viewing the new machine.** Don Broughton collection

Back outside the shed again, it is now the fitters who are paying attention. Men lean into the works of No 2 bogie, although it was not at that end that the trouble lay. Possibly they are checking to confirm whether valve problems have also occurred at this end. Don Broughton collection

Finally left alone – without an assisting engine, anyway – No 36001 waits for what will be a works visit and necessary repairs.
Don Broughton collection

At Groombridge a stop was made for water, and it was quickly discovered that the water column would not swing out and over the high profile of the engine to where the filler cap was located on top of the roof. This was no fault of the design, but purely a simple error on the part of the trial planning that no one had evidently considered. As water was urgently required, recourse was made to a small hose connected to a tap in the porter's office. Clearly the rest of the run could not be completed, as the same problems would have occurred at Oxted. There was therefore no choice but to abandon the working for the day and return to Brighton. A quick 'Heath Robinson' compromise of a copper chute and extension leather bag was carried on all later tests, in effect extending the reach of the Central Section water columns. (Another solution would have been to have water filler locations 'amidships' as on some of the first-generation main-line diesel locomotives that still needed to take on water for the steam-heating boilers.)

Possibly due to the time that would be necessary to reach a solution to the water problem, the next test run, on the very next day, was more ambitious, and involved a trip along the coast line through Chichester to Eastleigh, although still in company with an 'insurance engine',

this time 'K' class 2-6-0 No 32343. The purpose of this particular trip may indeed have been politically motivated, as upon arrival she worked to the running shed first and possibly the fire was dropped – certainly she was serviced. She was then shunted while in light steam into the nearby works by a somewhat grimy 'D15', No (30)464, the contrast between 'Leader' – still at this time in relative clean 'shop grey' – and the somewhat sad-looking Drummond engine accentuated by the contrasting liveries (as well as the fact that almost 40 years separated the designs).

Below and bottom: **Following the first trial and its associated 'water column' incident described in the text, the next outing took place on 26 June and involved No 36001 – by now with numberplates attached – working via Chichester to Eastleigh, once more in company with another engine, although No 36001 was doing all the work. At Eastleigh the fire was dropped at the shed, and No 36001 was shunted from the running shed into the yard in front of the works – No 464 was delegated for this task. Already an understandable amount of soot and grime has started to mar the top of the engine.** George Wheeler

Left: **Believed to have been taken on 25 June 1949, this photograph shows the engine ready to embark on its first main-line run, albeit 'light'. After the experience of three days earlier, and no doubt aware of the already experienced eccentricities of No 2039, the operating authorities were taking no chances, and before No 36001 was allowed out another engine was summoned – an 'E4' tank – which was coupled to 'Leader' for the trial.** Don Broughton collection

This remarkable photograph by Harry Attwell – a member of the Brighton test staff – shows 'Leader' taking water at Oxted by means of the improvised extension leather bag and copper chute. Even so, taking water with the adaptor took almost an hour. The problem was simply that the arms of the existing water columns on the Central Section of the Southern Region were not high enough to reach the roof-top filler of 'Leader', the height comparison with the Maunsell tender alongside all too obvious. (Were similar difficulties encountered with the Light Pacifics working in the Brighton area?) For the intended operational service of the 'Leader' class it was said that only five water columns would need to be modified to enable the type to run between London, Oxted and Brighton, the cost of this modification set at £200. It is not clear whether these modifications were in fact carried out. H. W. Attwell

No 36001 would remain at Eastleigh for three days, the whole time, it is believed, being spent outside the front of the works close by the office block. One immediate task was to add the then current BR 'cycling lion' emblem centrally to both sides of the casing, and the number 36001 was applied on the sides beneath the emblem. The cast numberplates had also been added by now, probably before she had left Brighton, as they were certainly not present on 21 June. At this stage the engine was still in plain grey with no lining out. More importantly, during this time several official – and some unofficial – photographs were taken while she was inspected by a number of senior officials, including Robin Riddles and Roland Bond from the Railway Executive as well as members of the Association of Locomotive Engineers. No doubt for the benefit of the 'great and the good' she was

also moved up and down the yard, which was achieved without incident.

Up to now the astute reader will no doubt have noticed that the name of Bulleid has rarely been mentioned relative to the first runs of 'Leader', and it can only be conjecture as to the whereabouts of the designer at this time. Certainly he would have been appraised on a regular basis as to progress, and this would continue for some time. Interestingly a contemporary note gives the impression that Bulleid had, in the last few months at least, become somewhat impatient with the (lack of) progress in completing the first engine. When No 36001 had first emerged from Brighton – two years late (June 1947 must always have been a hopelessly optimistic target) – Bulleid is said to have impatiently decided that Eastleigh should fit the multiple valve rings as Brighton had complained of difficulty with the task. It seems that Brighton did in fact manage to do the job in the end, as there is no written or photographic record of the engine enveloped in steam for the first trips to Groombridge or on the way to or at Eastleigh; if this task had been undertaken at Eastleigh Works it would doubtless have been necessary to do so within the works itself.

No attempt was made to weigh the engine at Eastleigh at this stage, and now might be an appropriate time to mention a conversation at Brighton between G. L. Nicholson and Works Manager L. J. Granshaw. When Nicholson asked, 'How are you going to balance the offset boiler?' the reply from Granshaw was, 'That is a good question – we are still trying to find the answer.' The

Outside the front of the works the engine was spruced up ready for inspection and official photographs. It appears that this included a body clean and a complete repaint, again in grey, while the bogies were at least cleaned and finishing touches added in the form of the then current BR emblem and locomotive number transfers on the centre of each side. Finally the rims of the wheels were picked out in what appears to be white paint. It was at this stage that the only known two colour views of the engine were taken, both by Stephen Townroe. (He recorded the engine from this spot in both colour and black and white, obviously using two different cameras. His well-known colour view of the engine has the painters in slightly different pose.) S. C. Townroe

weight-table at Eastleigh would have revealed that no answer had by then – or indeed ever would be – satisfactorily found! (Townroe later commented to the author that he was present when 'Leader' was eventually weighed and witnessed the needles going beyond the marked measurements, the only time he ever saw this happen.)

Bulleid's faith in the merits of Eastleigh was insufficient to ensure that the engine remained on the South Western Division, and instead she was made ready for a return to Brighton on 29 June 1949, this time alone. Whether Bulleid was really in charge of the decision-making process at this time is open to doubt; it is more likely that the Chief Mechanical Engineer of the Railway Executive, Robin Riddles, was content to allow Bulleid to supervise the trial running while at the same time ensuring that any potential disruption to traffic was kept to a minimum. Certain of the routes around Brighton were deemed to be of 'secondary' status while at the same time able to take an

engine of the size of 'Leader'. By comparison, there were potentially fewer available lines radiating from Eastleigh, although the thought of No 36001 venturing to Andover via Romsey, or Bournemouth via Ringwood, is interesting.

No 36001 therefore left Eastleigh, travelling via Botley to Fareham and the coast line; as she had completed her previous two trips without mechanical incident, she was this time unescorted. Unfortunately this confidence was misplaced, for although the engine did reach Brighton alone, a considerable amount of knocking was heard *en route*, clearly emanating from No 1 bogie. The engine also sounded decidedly 'off-beat'.

Examination at Brighton revealed that the same operating rod to the middle cylinder of No 1 bogie had again fractured, while at the same time the associated sleeve of the same cylinder was broken in four places. That to the left on the same bogie was also displaying evidence of seizure. The dilemma now was whether it was the sleeves that were contributing to the operating rod failure or vice versa. Bulleid was of the opinion that the sleeves were simply too tight, with insufficient room for expansion, and consequently all three sleeves fitted to No 1 bogie were reduced in diameter by 18 thou (0.0018in) – this modification was, however, only made to the No 1 bogie. (As intimated, it is possible that this work involved the components being sent to and dealt with at Eastleigh, which may go some way to explaining why it was not until 7 July that the engine was ready for its next trial.)

Two runs were then made from Brighton the short distance to Falmer and also to Groombridge – the records

Others were also on hand to record the scene, although whether this was by chance or whispered knowledge is not certain. Seen for the first time, this series of three views was recorded by an unknown photographer, perhaps surprisingly at a time when an awful lot of 'brass' was around.

Above: **It was also at this time that a young Eastleigh apprentice by the name of David Burnett happened to venture out to admire the engine from ground level. A tall man in a well-cut suit approached him and asked if he would like to look inside. Not unnaturally David said yes, and spent a few minutes finding his way around and through the corridor. When he emerged, the same man was waiting for him and asked his opinion. David responded that he was impressed and hoped that they would see more of the type. He then made to move off, but as he did he noticed the Assistant Works Manager rush up and address the stranger as 'Sir'. It was of course none other than Bulleid himself. After having quickly dealt with the Works Manager, he turned around to the assembled group of VIPs nearby and exclaimed, 'This young man has seen it first, now you can all have a look if you like.' For one young Eastleigh apprentice, this not unnaturally left an indelible impression.** David Burnett collection

Above left: **A small-scale but non-working model of the 'Leader' boiler prepared at Eastleigh and shown to the VIPs at the time of the June 1949 visit. It showed the use of the dry-back firebox and siphons, but its subsequent fate is not recorded.** David Burnett collection

Left: **A close-up of the steam-driven oil feed pump on the side of the main frames.** David Burnett collection

Below: **This is one of the official views of the engine from that period – the others were of the plain side and one end. No 36001 is seen, slightly unusually, with all three access doors closed – this would rarely happen again until after September 1950. Notice also the grab handle for use in accessing the firing compartment, the steps to which could not be located immediately beneath the door.** National Railway Museum

Left: **Cleaned and on parade: the engine could certainly draw interested parties, whether in the form of senior officials or the workers themselves. Of interest in this particular view, compared with that of the same end of the locomotive taken at Eastleigh just beforehand, is that the cab roof ventilator is open and the steam-heat pipe at the front has now been refitted – No 36001 had arrived at Eastleigh without it, possibly having had it removed in connection with the previous failure at Brighton. It is believed that the man in the cloth cap in the centre of the right-hand group is Alf Woods, the Eastleigh Works test driver.** National Railway Museum/J. G. Click

Bottom: **This final Eastleigh view is another unofficial record. The date is 28 June 1949 and the 52 men in the group are members of the Association of Locomotive Engineers together with some from the Railway Executive; it is believed that Messrs Bulleid, Riddles and Bond are among them. For this occasion the engine was in light steam and moved gently up and down the works yard. The more official photographer is seen in the right foreground. Possibly the local Hants & Dorset buses in the background had been used to bring members of the party from the station to the works.**

Below: **Leaving Eastleigh 'light' for Brighton on 20 June 1949. The photograph was taken from inside the works fence; the coaches in the background are not coupled to the engine but stabled in the nearby sidings.** David Burnett collection

are not clear if the engine travelled to Groombridge via Falmer or if there was one trip to each location, or even two runs to each location! Whatever, a repeat was made the next day.

Nothing was done over the weekend, and the next trial over the same route was booked for Monday 11 July, but for some reason it was cancelled at short notice. This may not necessarily have been due to a fault with the engine – it could well have been a simple traffic or operating difficulty. In the event, the run was made – without incident – on the 12th.

Nothing was scheduled for 13 July, but on the 14th a light engine trial was made to Crowborough, with Bulleid and Granshaw, the Brighton Works Manager, on board. Mimicking what would later be described as the occasional 'impish' behaviour of the designer himself, 'Leader' performed faultlessly while its designer was on the footplate, but a repeat of the same run in the afternoon witnessed another failure to the No 1 bogie at Barcombe Mills, this time with all three valve rods fractured. It was stated that there was also some consequential damage to other (unspecified) components, perhaps implying that the failure was both sudden and dramatic and possibly even at some speed. (Trial working would have involved working at cut-offs not normally associated with normal working – 45% or more – for long periods. This was a necessary measure, but would place additional strain on the valve and cylinder components.) A tow back to Brighton ensued, the cumulative score at this point being three failures out of nine runs, with just 360 miles covered. It was hardly an auspicious start, and was destined to get worse.

It was nine days before the necessary repairs were completed, during which time the opportunity was taken to paint the outline of panels along both sides, in red and black. Probably at the same time, and certainly by 17 August, the BR insignia and number were removed from the centre of the engine and replaced by numerals

Having experienced no trouble on the run to Eastleigh, confidence was high for a solo return to Brighton and the start of test-running proper. Unfortunately the journey was not without incident; although the run was completed, all was clearly not right and after arrival at Brighton No 36001 was in the workshops again. It is believed that this particular view was taken on the occasion of her arrival back at Brighton, as it is also the only known view showing the engine at Brighton in the original livery style that had been applied at Eastleigh. *National Railway Museum/J. G. Click*

only on both sides and at each end. No 36001 had now carried her number in six separate locations, twice on each side and on a cast plate on either end. No BR emblem was applied, and none would ever again be carried – perhaps in a slightly naïve belief that it would avoid potential embarrassment.

The necessary repairs having been undertaken, No 36001 next ventured forth on 23 July, again bound for Crowborough. No problems were encountered on the two trips that were made, and next day there was a new destination, Seaford, also intended to be visited twice. However, as had occurred before, on the first run there were no reported difficulties but approaching the destination for a second time the valve gear of No 1 bogie again developed trouble (this time it was just the right-hand valve rod and associated sleeve), and another slow return to Brighton was necessary.

It was later revealed that at the time of the Seaford failure No 36001 had indeed been running at a higher speed than would otherwise have been expected and in full forward gear – 75% cut-off. As this was a light engine trial, this was presumably on the direct orders of the testing staff on board and would not normally have been a regular procedure in traffic, although of course in operational service such behaviour would occasionally be required dependent upon the load and gradient. Even so there must have been a number of puzzled expressions, for 100 miles had been completed over the previous three runs without incident, and a failure to the right-hand valve rod and sleeve alone was both a new and worrying development.

Additionally it appears that while official reports had so far only detailed the failures associated with the reversing and No 1 bogie, there were in fact other problems. One of these involved the dry (brick) lining of the firebox, which from an early stage had displayed a tendency to collapse into the grate. Additionally, rumour

Top right: **Light engine trials from Brighton: while receiving attention in the works after the return from Eastleigh, the opportunity was taken to alter the livery – why has never been fully established, although the removal of the BR insignia could be taken to imply a degree of slight embarrassment even at this early stage. Unfortunately the paint used to effect the change appears to be lighter than that used at Eastleigh.** Don Broughton collection

Right: **No 36001 is seen at Seaford some time in July or August 1949. The year that 'Leader' was born, 1949, also saw the introduction of two other projects originating from Bulleid's mind: the Tavern cars and the double-deck electric train sets. It could never be said that here was a man constrained by conventional thinking! Perhaps more poignantly, Bulleid was awarded a CBE in the New Year Honours list.**

has it that L. J. Granshaw, while supervising a steam test of No 1 bogie at Brighton during construction, when the bogie was supported off the ground to allow the wheels to rotate, instructed the engine to be reversed while still in forward motion. The mechanism could not cope with this, and there was a general failure involving numerous bent components; these were supposedly straightened locally, with Bulleid never advised of the incident. This may go some way to explain the initial failures to the No 1 bogie, although by this stage no doubt all of the affected components would have been replaced anyway consequent upon the failures of 29 June and 23 July.

Repairs following the Seaford failure are now known to have involved not just the valve rod and sleeve but also the relining of both sides and part of the back of the firebox, again the necessary components probably 'borrowed' from those earmarked for another engine in the series. Meanwhile, work on the second engine, No 36002, was progressing slowly, all effort being concentrated on the first of the batch. Later an all-out effort to submit Nos 36002/3 as complete machines would lead to a delay of about five months in completing other outstanding build orders at Brighton, including 'West Country' Pacifics Nos 34091-4, which in turn led to similar delays in all the other build dates for the Light Pacifics right up to what would be No 34109.

It was to be almost three weeks before No 36001 ventured out again, on what was destined to be the commencement of a six-day series of runs, all light engine, commencing on 12 August. The destinations were to be Crowborough, Seaford and Lewes. The first two locations are in opposite directions geographically, so it is not clear if the intention was to run Brighton-Crowborough-Brighton-Seaford-Brighton, or some other alternative. What is known is that Crowborough was actually visited on no fewer than seven occasions during the six days. More importantly, these were the most successful trials to date, with just one failure at Seaford on 15 August due to an unspecified securing pin working loose and falling out of the valve gear. Running repairs were successfully completed and the engine was able to resume its run without incident. As with No 2039 earlier, it was stated that 'Leader' was both free-steaming and free-running, 70mph being attained without difficulty.

While it would now appear that 'Leader' was at last starting to show promise, a fresh problem with the firebox lining was starting to cause concern. Already this had begun to show signs of detaching itself from the small securing clips intended to hold it in position, with the result that the firebricks fell into the grate. This problem was noted in the official record of the run, together with the comment 'control of the regulator and reverser erratic', which referred to problems in maintaining the desired pressure within the steam chest, while the reverser was difficult to 'notch up'. Difficulty with the reversing gear has been spoken of before, but that concerning the regulator was another new obstacle; indeed, it almost

seemed as if when one problem was controlled a new one developed. However, there is some consistency in the difficulties being experienced, as the ongoing problem with the sleeves would have affected accurate steam distribution to the steam chests. Bear in mind that there were six of these – one around each cylinder – so if, for example, the No 1 bogie sleeves were causing problems, steam distribution generally could well have been affected. The consequences of necessary running adjustments to the valve gear should also be considered.

However, with some success at least being achieved, 'Leader' was once more tasked with a load trial consisting of ten bogie vehicles weighing 248 tons, which it was scheduled to haul unassisted between Brighton and Eastleigh on 18 August. It is believed that this trial was planned for several reasons, to continue the load trials after what had been some reasonable light-engine success, and also to enable the engine to at last be weighed at Eastleigh Works. (Why this had not been done before in June 1949 is not clear – perhaps it was nothing more than the Eastleigh weight-table not being available.)

It is also believed that Granshaw was on board the Eastleigh run, although Bulleid certainly was not, being on holiday in Perthshire with fellow members of the Association of Railway Locomotive Engineers (who were using the final funds of the Association following Riddles's decision to terminate its existence; this in itself was somewhat controversial, although further discussion is beyond the remit of this book). Nonetheless, a steady stream of telegrams made their way from the South Coast to Scotland, two of which are quoted (possibly in part only) by Day-Lewis: 'Successful trial trip of 100 miles on Saturday, taking engine to Eastleigh tomorrow' and 'Successful Brighton to Eastleigh on Sunday, arrived on time, no trouble during trip, reverser much improved'. These telegrams appear to refer to the Crowborough and Eastleigh runs, although it should be said that they do not correspond with the actual days for 1949 (or 1950) and should therefore be regarded with some suspicion (in all cases the dates and records of trials are taken from the official reports held at the National Railway Museum).

Further evidence that the telegrams' content may be open to doubt is that the Eastleigh run was not in fact without incident, as part of the firebox lining collapsed *en route*; this run was thus officially classified as a failure.

Repairs were carried out to the lining at Eastleigh, and the ash duct in the smokebox was now also welded shut – 'natural remedies would no longer be required!' This of course meant that future smokebox cleaning would involve the traditional method of a man and a shovel, made all the more difficult due to the enclosed space involved. More serious were the results discovered when the engine was weighed – in Townroe's presence – for instead of the anticipated 110 tons spread over six axles, with a maximum of 18.33 tons per axle, the actual result was more like 130.5 tons, or 21.75 tons per axle. Even more serious was the differential between the two sides, that where the boiler was located causing the pointers to travel off the scale beyond their maximum range of 25 tons. (It has not been possible to ascertain the weight on the opposite side.)

While this was undoubtedly a shock to those present, it could not have been unexpected, as evidenced by the comments made earlier at Brighton. What is perhaps more surprising is that no note of this weight differential had arisen before. Had there been no experience of the engine 'lurching' at any time? It was certainly noted on at least one later run from Eastleigh. (Conversely, subsequent improvements to the oil supply to the pedestal guides – referred to later – were reported as having had a marked effect on the quality of the ride, any previous harshness giving way to a smoothness more akin to that of a passenger carriage.)

With hindsight it appears surprising that the weight issue was not considered a major problem at the time, although it would of course reach the attention of the Chief Civil Engineer before too long. Obviously Bulleid would also have been informed, although unfortunately there is no record of the telegram relating to this issue, for even if the second of those quoted by Day-Lewis above is taken at face value it could just be said to refer to the trip to Eastleigh and not the outcome of the works visit.

Probably due to the weight issue, No 36001 was rostered to work back to Brighton on 20 August as a light engine. However, even this was unsuccessful, as at least one further sleeve valve failure occurred again on No 1 bogie and the engine was failed at Barnham – possibly being

towed back to Brighton later. The same return trip also saw a further collapse of the firebox lining.

When No 36001 eventually reached Brighton (it is not confirmed if this was on the 20th, although it probably was as the authorities would not wish to have the engine parked as an obvious failure) it was another works visit for repairs. The firebox lining was attended to, and the maximum cut-off was reduced from 75% to 65%, although this had the side-effect of poor starting performance. According to official records the opportunity was also taken to fit a spark arrestor, but it may be questioned as to whether this was the actual device provided or if a form of mesh intended to impart some degree of smokebox cleaning was actually fitted.

On 20 August 1949 'Leader' was returning light from Eastleigh to Brighton after having being weighed, and failed at Barnham with sleeve-valve problems. It is seen awaiting either a tow or a cautious continuation under its own power. Brighton later added two small vertical uprights welded to the front framing to measure the degree of movement of the reciprocal motion of the sleeves relative to known parameters. It was hoped that in this way it would be possible to identify changes in the degree of lateral movement. Unfortunately it was not successful and the 'markers' were later removed.
W. N. J. Jackson

Trials recommenced on 30 August and continued for four days with light-engine working to Crowborough. Once again the almost 'puckish' behaviour of the engine was demonstrated, with an almost faultless performance for the first three days, and only a single firebrick dislodged on the last day of working, 2 September; however, this was enough to classify the run as a failure in the official records.

What was to follow was without doubt the most ambitious test to date. No 36001 was set to take a train of empty stock through from Brighton to Victoria via Oxted and return, which was scheduled to occur on Monday 5 September 1949. The train weight was also marginally the heaviest yet, at 260 tons, and was made up of eight bogies. Fortuitously a full account of the trip from E. Walton, a Head Office Inspector, sent to the 'Chief Trains Clerk', has survived, and makes interesting reading:

'Test Trip with "Leader" Class Engine No 36001 with 8 coaches, Brighton to Victoria via Uckfield and Oxted and return Monday 5th September 1949.

'The result of the above Test trip was most unsatisfactory. The train left Brighton 9.50am, Right Time, stopped at Buxted, short of steam. Stopped again at Edenbridge Town short of steam and train was shunted to yard for 10.18am Brighton to Victoria to pass. In view of the bad running I decided not to risk a run in the London Area and arranged for the trip to terminate at Oxted and return to Brighton. Left Edenbridge Town with full head of steam but stopped on Hurst Green Junction Up Inner Home signal, again short of steam. After a stop to "Blow Up" it just managed to crawl into Oxted. Here our troubles really started. The engine was short of water. It was run to a water column but to my amazement was unable to take water owing to the fact that the only water inlet is on the top of the engine casing and the only suitable columns are those with a high "Swan Necked" jib or a hanging leather hose. Decided to berth stock at Oxted and run engine light to Brighton. Oxted could not hold the stock so decided to take stock to East Grinstead to berth, calling at Lingfield to take some water from tap on down platform with Cattle Dock hosepipe. Took sufficient water at Lingfield to get to East Grinstead and left. Stopped at Dormans short of steam. Eventually arrived at East Grinstead

and berthed stock. Again unable to take water at Crane. Connected Fire Hose to Hydrant and took enough water to get to Brighton. Would not trust engine on Main line so travelled via Sheffield Park. Arrived at Sheffield Park and shunted for traffic. Again unable to get water from Water Column so shunted to Up siding, borrowed garden hose from timber yard and connected to tap in Pump House. Got enough water to take engine to Lewes. Phoned Brighton to send assisting engine to Lewes to tow engine home. Arrived at Lewes, found Water Crane at Lewes had a "Swan Neck" jib and by bending leather hose was able to get enough water to take engine to Brighton. Stopped assisting engine at Falmer and travelled under own power to Brighton, arriving 6.25pm after leaving Oxted 1.17pm. Engine berthed in Workshops at Brighton and as far as I am concerned have no desire to see it again.

'In the event of further Trial Trips of this engine under traffic conditions, I suggest that the load should be restricted to 3 coaches and suitable arrangements made for a water supply to be available on the route chosen.'

The particulars of the test trip are given in the accompanying table. Additional to the above report is a comment from the late H. W. Attwell to the author that on the climb to Dormans, just north of East Grinstead, following the decision to terminate the trial, 'Leader' had almost stalled on the 1 in 210 gradient approaching the station. It is not believed that Bulleid was on board to witness the sad spectacle.

The route taken as described in the report is also very interesting, providing confirmation that the journey north

Engine No 36001. Driver Capelin, Guard Giles.
[The Fireman's name is not reported.] Load – 8 coaches. 260 tons.

	Booked	Actual	
Brighton	9.50am	9.50 am	
Lewes	10.7	10.11½	4½ mins signals, Kemp Town Jct
Culver Junction	10.12	10.17½	1 minute loss by engine
Uckfield	10.19	10.27	2½ minutes loss by engine
Crowborough	10.33	11.6	25 minutes loss by engine; short of steam
Reigate Mill Jct	10.38	11.10	1 minute regained by engine
Eridge	10.40	11.12	
Ashurst Jct	10.44	11.14½	1½ minutes regained by engine
Edenbridge Town	10.58	11.30-11.54	25½ minutes loss by engine short of steam
Hurst Green Jct	11.7	12.5-12.20	17 minutes loss by engine short of steam
Oxted	11.10	12.26pm	3 minutes loss by engine short of steam
Oxted		1.17	
Lingfield		1.30-1.58	Engine taking water
Dormans		2.9-2.22	Engine short of steam
East Grinstead		2.31	
East Grinstead		3.31	Engine taking water
Sheffield Park		4.12-5.24	Shunted for traffic
Lewes		5.48-6.7	Engine taking water
Brighton		6.25	

was via Lewes and the return via Sheffield Park and the 'Bluebell' line. The operating authorities were intent on keeping 'Leader' away from the main lines as much as possible to avoid any risk of delays to ordinary traffic consequent upon a breakdown. No 2039 had unfortunately already paved the way in this respect – Bulleid's 'experiments' did not have a particularly good reputation!

Obvious questions should be asked. Had the engine started with its water tank full? Had not the problem with the water supply already been identified and the adaptor made up? Presumably – and surely for no other reason than forgetfulness – the said adaptor was not carried on board.

Back at Brighton the engineers considered that the spark arrestor fitting may have contributed to the poor steaming, so it was simply removed and a second London trial arranged for three days later, Thursday 8 September. The load behind the drawbar is believed to have been similar, while it is likely that the same route was taken again. Unfortunately the result was almost identical, although this time the train managed to reach Oxted, just 7 miles north of Dormans and still only 33 miles from Brighton. Victoria was a further 20 miles away.

Again a report and timings are available from Inspector Walton:

'Test Trip with "Leader" Class Engine No 36001 with 8 coaches, Brighton to Victoria via Uckfield and Oxted and return Thursday 8th September 1949.

'The result of the above Test Trip, the second, was again unsatisfactory.

The train came to a stand at Buxted, Engine short of steam. After passing Crowborough, it was running well but got signal delays from Birchden Junction onwards, having lost its path over Ashchurch Jct due to the delay at Buxted. The train was shunted at Edenbridge Town for 10.18am Brighton to Victoria to pass and then proceeded to Oxted where the trip was terminated with the intention to return to Brighton. The engine had to take water at

Above: **On the same day No 36001 awaits the opportunity to move south towards Brighton. The first proposed trial to Victoria was scheduled for 5 September 1949, which was coincidentally the third anniversary of the date when approval for construction had been given. It would not be a very happy birthday. The incident with the water supply difficulties on this run is mentioned with considerable force in the report. Bearing in mind that 'Leader' had already been out on trial since June, all in the Brighton area, it seems very strange that this had not been noticed before. It will be noted from the text that the second abortive London run on 8 September did have the 'adaptor' carried; perhaps on 5 September someone simply forgot it!**
National Railway Museum/J. G. Click

Left: **This view is possibly also from 5 September 1949, showing the engine and crew 'resting' after the shortage-of-steam incident. Amongst those on the platform at Dormans are Doug Smith and W. H. 'Joe' Hutchinson of Brighton, both of whom had been involved in the project from the very start. Whether it was of any significance regarding the London trip failures, in charge of No 36001 for both runs was Driver Capelin. For the successful test runs of 16 and 19 September Driver Long was in charge; Bill Long was the engine's regular driver for the majority of the Brighton trials. It should not of course have made a difference – a steam engine incapable of being used except by a select few is of little use. But did Capelin know the difference between the necessary driving technique for 'Leader' and a conventional engine? Even if not, surely there would have been someone on board to tell him.** H. W. Attwell

Oxted for the return trip to Brighton and whilst this was being done it was found that the Fire Box Brick Lining was damaged and the Engine became a partial failure and could not take the stock back to Brighton. Oxted could not berth the stock and it was taken to Edenbridge Town by the "Leader" class engine and berthed there. Arrangements were made to take the stock from Edenbridge Town to Eastbourne where it was required for the weekend working. An adaptor was carried on the engine to enable water to be taken from an ordinary Water Crane but even so it took almost an hour to top up the engine water tank.'

Particulars are again provided in the accompanying table.

It may be worth spending a moment at this stage to consider the implications of the failed London runs. Although there is no factual evidence to support what follows, it is likely that both Bulleid and what were still a number of very loyal and supportive Brighton staff were only too acutely aware of the need to prove the viability of the engine in service, with BR headquarters at Marylebone being ever more inquisitive as to both progress and cost. Accordingly the London trials were no doubt arranged as a showpiece, to confirm the engine as both a viable and useful asset, but sadly the results from both days would only have the opposite effect.

Why was steam pressure not regained and the run continued? Another alternative would perhaps have been to double-head the train. However, the latter may be quickly dismissed as more counter-productive, while in the case of the former it should be recalled that most of the senior SR staff were only too acutely aware that the reputation and therefore the future of No 36001 already hung in the balance, and a failure on a busy commuter route somewhere in the London area would have probably sealed the end for the engine there and then. In reality there was no choice – No 36001 returned to Brighton light engine, and if anything the future was even more uncertain than three months earlier. (According to Robert Tuffnell in his work *Prototype Locomotives*, the intention of reaching Victoria with No 36001 'was sharply vetoed by order from Marylebone'. This comment raises many questions, the most obvious being simply 'Why?', and likewise what was the point of starting off in the first place? Unfortunately nothing further has been unearthed to elaborate on this comment.

A 'Leader' would eventually reach London – two members of the class in fact, Nos 36002 and 36003 – but neither would be in steam, being quietly hauled to store at New Cross Gate pending a decision as to their future.

It is interesting to note that at this stage there appear to have been no more difficulties with the sleeve valves, although the reader should be dissuaded from believing that the problem had been totally overcome. Investigation was now centred on the continued poor steaming and the instability of the firebox lining. While it could be said that the two problems were interconnected, this was not for the moment thought to have been the case.

Indeed, so far as the poor steaming was concerned, Bulleid was of the opinion that the difficulties were traceable to the front-end design, and accordingly the size of the chokes was reduced within the multiple-jet blastpipe, although this resulted in a new problem of fire-throwing. At the same time it was stated that a

Engine No 36001. Driver Capelin, Guard Twigley. [Again no Fireman is named.] Load – 8 coaches. 260 tons.

	Booked	Actual	
Brighton	9.50am	9.51am	1 min Sigs
Lewes	10.7	10.8	
Culver Junction	10.12	10.13	
Buxted	10.26	10.39	
Crowborough	10.33	10.55	21 mins Loss by Eng, short of steam
Eridge	10.40	10.59$^1/_2$	2$^1/_2$ mins Regained by Engine
Birchden Jc	10.42	11.0-11.7	Sigs
Ashurst Jc	10.44	11.10	
Edenbridge Tn	10.58	11.26-11.51	Shunted for Traffic
Hurst Green Jc	11.07	12.2	
Oxted	11.10	12.4pm	Terminated
Oxted		2.5	
Hurst Green Jct		2.8	
Edenbridge Tn		2.14	Stock berthed
Lt Engine			
Edenbridge Tn		2.49pm	
Ashurst Jct		3.19	
Birchden Jct		3.20	
Eridge		3.22	
Redgate Mill Jct		3.24	
Crowborough		3.28	
Uckfield		3.40	
Isfield		3.46-4.00	Shunted for Traffic
Culver Jct		4.6	
Lewes		4.13-4.25	Waiting Traffic
Brighton		4.44	

'more resilient' type of firebrick lining was installed, but whether this was the cast-iron bricks known to have been fitted later is not certain.

It must be said that the steaming modifications were very much a hit-and-miss affair. The engineers from the test section, W. H. 'Joe' Hutchinson, Harry Attwell and their colleagues, did their very best on the trials, but were often restricted by a lack of available scientific test equipment. Brighton – indeed, the Southern Railway and later Region – had nothing like the sophisticated measuring and monitoring equipment that was available to the other three 'Big Four' companies, although 'Leader' would 'benefit' from dynamometer car trials later.

The modifications occupied a week of works time, and 'Leader' next ventured out on 16 September, twice bound for Crowborough and with a different load on each occasion. Still the valve gear appeared settled, while the firebox repairs held firm, although steaming remained erratic.

Further modifications to the blastpipe orifices meant another three days without work, but when the locomotive ventured out next on 19 September there were further similar problems. There followed another modification to the blastpipe and the engine was set to work on further two trips with varying trailing loads the next day, 20 September. Clearly these modifications were relatively simple, as proven by the limited time spent at Brighton between successive test runs for the work to be conducted.

Another attempt was made overnight at Brighton to reach a successful mechanical compromise, and the engine was made ready for another load trial on Tuesday 20 September, once again destined for Crowborough.

This time the destination would not be reached, for in the Uckfield area a distinctive 'crack' announced the failure of one of the sleeve valves again, affecting the middle cylinder on No 1 bogie (again) at a point where the forward extensions were attached to the oscillating gear. Dismantling of the associated parts by the travelling fitter who accompanied every trial allowed the engine to return to Brighton, although it is not known if on this occasion it was just light engine.

At least one fitter accompanied the engine on each trial – often it appears that there were two – together with the other observers from either the test section or design office. 'Leader' had one advantage in this area: with three cabs there was usually plenty of room. One record that 'Leader' did achieve was the carrying of no fewer than 18 observers on the engine at the same time! The redoubtable French engineer and friend of Bulleid, André Chapelon, was just one of many distinguished visitors who were invited to travel on 'Leader'. Chapelon, who was perhaps the greatest steam designer the world has ever seen, also visited Brighton during the construction phase and was

At Uckfield on 20 September 1949 No 36001 has failed after the run referred to in the tables. Of the four men in the group, the one on the extreme right is believed to be Driver Bill Long. It was after this final failure to the sleeve-valve mechanism that the decision was taken at Brighton to remove the oscillating gear from the No 1 bogie. Possibly the successive sleeve-valve failures were exacerbated by the combination of differing metals making up the cylinder, sleeve, rings and pistons, all of which would expand at slightly different rates when heated.
H. W. Attwell

reported to be particularly interested in the sleeve valves and the boiler with its siphons. According to Bulleid's son, 'H. A. V.', in his own book, 'He [Chapelon] ... could see their potential.' Unfortunately history would decree that time was not on Chapelon's side either.

The travelling fitters took with them no special tools, and necessary repairs were undertaken with a standard kit, although supplemented by hammers of various sizes, a crowbar or two, and probably a few expletives from time to time.

This was proof, if it were needed, that the sleeve-valve mechanism was still not 100% reliable and in consequence the bold step was taken to remove the oscillating gear completely from No 1 bogie, while at the same time the Mechanite 'valve guides' were replaced by an identical component made of steel. The reference to the 'valve-guides' being replaced in this way is taken from one of the official reports on the engine, and is the first time that such a component was referred to. Could it have meant the cylinder liners? Surely time would have been needed to manufacture such components, yet No 36001 was out of service for just two days before she was steamed again, complete with modifications. It would appear that the oscillating gear associated with No 2 bogie was left intact, proof again of earlier comments that the sleeve failures seemingly only affected the one end. Another comment from the same time referred to necessary patching of some of the lower firebricks consequent upon them being badly worn – but how exactly do you 'patch' a firebrick...?

The details and report for the run on 20 September were as follows:

'Trial trip of "Leader" Class Engine,
Tuesday 20th September, 1949.

'The arrangements shown in LCD [London Central Division] Notice No 952 for the above were quite satisfactory. The train was formed as under:

'Engine 36001 – Driver Long
10 vehicles – 271 tons – Guard Morris, Brighton.

'Running was as under:

	Booked	Actual	
Brighton	9.50	9.50	
Kemp Town Junction	9.53	9.54	Signals
Falmer	9.58	9.59	
Lewes	10.7	10.8	
Culver Junction	10.12	10.14	
Uckfield	10.19	10.21	
Crowborough		10.33	

'Owing to trouble developing in the valve gear of the engine the train terminated at Uckfield where it was shunted without causing delay to other traffic.

An engine was requested to haul the stock back to Brighton, this left at 11.58am.

The "Leader" engine after receiving attention of fitters left under its own power for Brighton at 1.20pm, running at reduced speed as under:

	Arrive pm	Depart/ Pass pm	
Uckfield	1.20		
Culver Junction	1.34		
Lewes Home Signal	1.41	2.5	
Lewes	2.7		
Falmer	2.18		
Kemp Town Junction	2.25		
Brighton	2.28	2.34	To Loco Works

'It is possible the 1.12pm Ore to Brighton was delayed by this engine.

Redhill Control were kept advised of the position at Uckfield.'

A different Inspector was involved this time, A. E. Gayland.

Leaving aside the question of how to patch firebricks, let us instead turn to Bulleid's own part in the continuing saga. Retained by the Railway Executive to oversee the trials and, hopefully, the commissioning into service of 'Leader', his control over the whole project appears to have been lessening, although this may well have been at his own insistence. It is the opinion of the present author that outside forces were involved, with at least one engineer, Ron Jarvis, placed in a senior position by the Railway Executive, in effective control of the project and reporting directly back to Riddles. (Bulleid had been originally due to retire from BR – he received a presentation set of

The occasion of Bulleid's official retirement from the Southern Region of British Railways: shortly afterwards he would agree to continue in a consultancy capacity to oversee the continuing trials of No 36001. Also in the group are Sir Eustace Missenden (left) and Sir John Elliott (centre).
British Railways

cutlery at Waterloo on 23 September – with effect from the end of that month, and had indeed already been appointed consulting engineer to the Irish national railway system with effect from 26 April 1949, 'to take effect as soon as Mr Bulleid can become available'. But as September 1949 passed, an olive branch in the form of an extension to his tenure with British Railways was formalised, allowing Bulleid to remain in theoretical control of the 'Leader' project until the end of 1949, despite the comments made earlier in this paragraph.

Notwithstanding any allegation of political interference, No 36001 was made ready to test the various modifications in the form of a series of light engine runs between Brighton and Crowborough between 23 and 25 September. A total of five runs were made, amounting to some 235 miles, all of which were successful in so far as the sleeves were concerned, although again the firebricks were reported as needing 'slight attention' following the final run. For this latter reason the official report on the engine deemed the tests of 25 September a 'failure'.

The staff possibly now took the opportunity of a belated day off, as the next series of trials commenced on Tuesday

27 September and involved a relatively light load of just five bogie vehicles to Lewes, Crowborough, and as far afield as Oxted. Over four days a total of 447 miles were covered, with no mechanical difficulties encountered but steaming still erratic.

Despite these steaming problems the same trials were scheduled to be recommenced on 3 October and, as might be expected, the same difficulties occurred. Additionally, and for the first time, both drive chains feeding the oil circulation pumps became detached, and while these were relatively easy to replace, when the same defect threatened on the second day the governor valve to the pumps was immediately suspect. With lubrication such a crucial issue, this sequence of tests was again terminated. Once again the firebricks were found to be in poor condition after the last run.

It is at this stage in the official records that the first mention is made of the provision of cast-iron firebricks, although, as stated earlier, it may well have been that they had been in use earlier.

Testing resumed on 9 October, the destination now Groombridge and the load a paltry 150 tons. Four men were on board: Brighton driver Bill Long and fireman Ted Forder, both of whom had been involved in most of the trials up to now, a works fitter, and test engineer Harry Attwell. At Crowborough the engine once more failed, this time in spectacular fashion with the cast-iron firebricks having melted into the fire on one side of the firebox, and the other side threatening to do the same. The resultant heat for the fireman in the firing compartment was considerable, although approaching the point of failure there had ironically still been difficulties with poor steaming.

There were no circumstances under which the test could continue, and after allowing a suitable 'cooling off period' (probably for all concerned), No 36001 was once again returned light engine to Brighton.

At this stage it might be appropriate to consider the actual steaming qualities of the engine. The boiler of 'Leader' was without doubt a superbly designed steam-producing vessel; Bulleid was a master of boiler design and this was probably his best ever. Even allowing for the

Left: **Fireman Ted Forder from Brighton poses in the cab. Despite being young in years, Ted was the regular man associated with many of the trials of the engine, although a list of the runs when he was on board is not available; this would be useful in relation to the controversy surrounding the reports of some of the September 1949 runs, as mentioned in the text. The impression is gained that Ted was proud to be tasked with the trials of 'Leader' and took exception to being misquoted over the alleged heat of the engine.** Ted Forder collection

Right: **This is the scene at Crowborough on 9 October 1949 and No 36001 has again failed, but this time with the firebrick incident. Bill Long, the Trials Driver, is on the left, with fireman Ted Forder in the centre. 'Leader' was destined to spend almost two weeks out of service following this incident. It will be noted that the oscillating gear is still present at the No 2 end.** H. W. Attwell

lack of a water jacket around the sides and rear of the firebox – normally one of the hottest parts and in consequence where most steam is generated – the provision of the thermic siphons allied to excellent water circulation more than compensated for this omission. Let there be no doubt – the locomotive's firebox and boiler could certainly generate steam. The trouble was that it was not being used efficiently. The heat produced on that fateful day can only be imagined, as a temperature in the order of 2,700°F would be needed to melt cast iron!

However, such a temperature was an exception, and an unacceptable exception. In practice, the central firing compartment of 'Leader' was often cooler than the cab of a normal steam engine, although condensation and consequent humidity was a problem that was never resolved. It is often quoted that the temperature of the firing cab could reach 120°. Wrong – it was actually measured at 122°. However, on the same day a reading in the cab of a 'Merchant Navy' Pacific produced 140°, proof if it were needed that by being deliberately economical with the truth incorrect information will result. This was just one of the many aspects used by 'authority' and supposedly informed journalism to condemn the project out of hand. Yes, 'Leader' was hot, but others were hotter. (According to Antony Bulleid, by March 1950 'the firebox was stokeable by an asbestos-clad fireman'. This somewhat sweeping comment has not been borne out anywhere else, and was never mentioned to the author by any of the crews who worked the engine at the time.)

As an alternative to the cast iron, conventional, albeit thicker, firebricks were used. These were some 3½in thick and were attached using larger, and thus supposedly stronger, securing hooks. Another problem was that the firebricks were multi-functional; their main role was of course to retain the heat of the fire, but a secondary task was to protect the plain sheet sides of the firebox from what would otherwise be severe heat distortion. When the bricks fell or became dislodged the side wall was thus distorted by the radiant heat of the fire, which in turn altered the position of the securing hooks. It was a no-win situation – the more the heat, the greater the distortion,

and the greater the distortion the more chance of the firebricks falling, with the consequent generation of even more heat. This in turn led to a rapid temperature rise in the subsidiary water tank (the 'mantle-tank') around part of the exterior of the firebox. This was not intended to be a steam-producing area, merely an additional water storage unit, which, it appears, was a somewhat late addition to the design; its purpose was hardly to increase the water capacity as a few gallons here would make little difference (the exact capacity is not known). Instead it was suggested as being necessary to afford some form of 'insulation' between the potentially hot firebox sides and the man working in the compartment. Unfortunately, as it was thus part of the feed-water supply, the water generally became hotter than desirable for efficient working of the injectors, which then would themselves not work!

Almost 14 days had now been spent out of service and it was not until Saturday 22 October that the engine was ready for another trial run. Testing would now often continue over a weekend, for several reasons: most obviously, there was a degree of urgency over the whole project. Bulleid himself was likely to be around for only a further two months, so it was very much a race against time to produce a workable engine. Additionally, line occupancy, as well as stock and staff availability, was sometimes best achieved at weekends. The various wages-grade men involved were no doubt also glad of the overtime generated by the project. But there were also other

incidental benefits from working with 'Leader'. Bulleid himself is recalled as being particularly generous, with a cash tip of £1 regularly given to the crew each time he travelled on the engine. (It has been stated that Bulleid even had to seek permission from Marylebone Road if he wanted to travel upon it, but as he was notionally still in charge of the project this is perhaps unlikely.) Another official also involved was likewise recalled for his generosity, and would share bars of chocolate with the driver and fireman at a time when such confectionery was still on ration.

With all eyes therefore on the modifications made, No 36001 successfully took another featherweight train of just 150 tons from Brighton to, it was said, 'Oxted and Crowborough'. (Again, did this mean two separate tests or were the destinations simply written in reverse order?) All was well on the 22nd, and also on the 23rd, the intention being to repeat the same tests over the same route the next day. But on 24 September, when the plan had been to cover a similar schedule as the previous two days, what is believed to have been the first major failure to affect No 2 bogie occurred with the fracture of the middle sleeve. This happened near Lewes, although the direction of travel at the time was not stated.

Investigation at Brighton revealed that the cause was probably fatigue affecting the extensions of the sleeve valves, and as a result, the oscillating gear was removed from this bogies as well. With the oscillating gear now no

longer a feature of either bogie, testing recommenced on 29 October, the engine visiting what was then new ground, its destination being Tunbridge Wells via Crowborough. For the two days in this series the runs were understandably 'light engine' and to the same destination. Subsequently, however, and continuing through until 13 December, varying loads of between 153 and 255 tons were taken daily. The trials were often split, with different trailing loads in the morning and afternoon. (This was again purely for operational convenience and would sometimes simply depend upon what stock was available at the time. As with No 2039, the trials would also invariably commence from Brighton station, which would then enable a realistic comparison to be made with actual operating times.)

Without doubt this period of running, representing a total of 27 days' working, was the most consistent success of 'Leader' at any time. True, there still some difficulties with the steaming as well as the firebox lining, while occasional mechanical defects in the form of broken valve rods and circlips still occurred.

Bulleid was on board on a number of occasions, one memorable run with him being recalled by the crew; as the engine was about to start the $4^3/_4$-mile climb from Buxted to Crowborough, its designer said, 'Come on, let's get to the top as quickly as possible ... then if anything is going to fail at least we will find out what and why.' The crew of course diligently obliged, even if the unexpected demand for steam meant that the fireman was ill-prepared for the effort and the engine surmounted the summit with just 120psi on the gauge. Even so, the distance had been accomplished in the astonishing time of just $4^1/_2$ minutes, less than half of the normal timetable allowance of 10 minutes. Ironically, nothing untoward occurred, but unfortunately the date of the run is not recorded. More unfortunately, a second trial over the same route on the same day, but this time without the presence of Bulleid, resulted in failure.

On another occasion Harry Attwell, of the test section, was riding alone in the rear cab when there was a

Above and right: **...and away! As with film footage, there is a lack of sound recordings of the engine and it would be most interesting to know what sound the engine made. Presumably, because of its six cylinders, the blast would have given the impression of rapid acceleration; did it behave audibly in a similar way to 'Mallet'-type designs, where each bogie did eventually tend to get 'in sync' with the other? Notice the height of the coal above the roof line, and the whole engine being considerably higher than the coaching stock.** National Railway Museum/J. G. Click

sudden 'crack-crack', which initially implied the immediate failure of two of the sleeve valves – however, it transpired that the noise was no more than the engine passing over two fog signals!

More serious was when freak circumstances created a partial vacuum in the engine when it entered Crowborough Tunnel, which could have had fatal consequences for the six draughtsmen being carried at the time.

However, despite the apparent success now being enjoyed there was considerable gloom at Brighton on 19 November 1949 when information was received that a directive had been issued by Riddles instructing that all work on the other engines in the series, Nos 36002-5, was to cease immediately. Bulleid's thoughts at this time were not recorded, but it must have been disheartening for many of the others, who had all worked so hard up to now. (This no doubt followed from the Riddles/Bond/Bulleid discussions just prior to this date, which were reported by Townroe to the author – see the final chapter.)

Even so, the trials of No 36001 were unaffected and it was planned to commence a new series of runs on

14 December, although these were cancelled by the operating authorities for the simple reason of a build-up of traffic due to the Christmas peak. Instead, 'Leader' again ran light to Eastleigh for weighing, and returned in similar fashion the same day. It is believed that the measurements taken included weighing one end only at a time, information that could then be used by Brighton in the modifications that were to come. The return journey was completed without incident, and back at Brighton the fire was dropped and she was once again stored either inside or certainly in the vicinity of the works, where she

No 36001 is ascending the bank near Lewes while on trial in the autumn of 1949. This was the view that appeared in *The Times* on Friday 4 November under the heading 'A new and unusual type of locomotive'. The caption was incorrect as it referred to the new design being constructed at Eastleigh. The same view was subsequently reproduced in another railway book and incorrectly captioned, suggesting that the fireman was taking a breather – it does perhaps look as if someone is leaning out of the centre cab. Under a glass, however, what appears to be a head is in fact the elbow of someone standing with his back to the window. Times Photographs

would remain until 26 January 1950. Bulleid, in the meantime, had of course departed for his new post in Ireland, although his BR consultancy, enabling him to advise further on the engine, was extended further until 31 March. However, much of his time was now spent in Dublin, and it is possible that after December 1949 he would only ever set eyes on his creation once more.

The weighing visit to Eastleigh would have revealed exactly the same findings as previously, and it is likely that there were now two instructions relating to the engine. The first was an attempt to balance the sides to a state nearer equilibrium, and the second was an instruction from the Chief Civil Engineer at Waterloo that he would not tolerate an even heavier engine on the routes out of Brighton. The option was to seek another location, and really the only place available was Eastleigh. Indeed, possibly around this time Bulleid is alleged to have exclaimed, seemingly in exasperation, 'Send it to Eastleigh – Townroe will get it working.' (Stephen Townroe was the Shed Master at Eastleigh, and someone whom Bulleid obviously held in the highest regard. However, Townroe, perhaps modestly, believes that the comment was, 'Send it to Eastleigh – Turbett will get it working,' referring instead to the Works Manager, who for a time also acted as deputy to Bulleid.) According to 'H. A. V.', in a chapter

penned by Mrs Bulleid, and probably relevant to this period, Bulleid 'was very worried and "put out" when the Civil Engineer of the Southern Railway was difficult about the weight of Oliver's engines – thought them too heavy and demanded drastic lowering of weight, which Oliver said was unnecessary, and almost impossible to achieve in keeping with his designs'.

The time out of use for 'Leader' was probably spent in attempting to redress the weight imbalance, and thus included two complete changes of springs. At some time more clearance was given to the axlebox pedestal guides, and the type of oil supply to the guides was also changed. While all this undoubtedly helped, the most effective method of balancing was simply the obvious: adding pig or scrap iron along the corridor side (some commentators have recounted that old brake blocks and firebars were used). The total amount used eventually weighed several tons and it has been suggested that it reached a height of 2 feet within the corridor. Additionally recourse was made to pieces of slab steel both underneath the floor and vertically against the casing. The weight of scrap thus added is not absolutely confirmed, although when finally accepted for test the axle weights were known to be in the order of $24^{1}/_{2}$ tons. The corridor obstructions meant that the driver and fireman were now basically marooned from each other, and unable to assist each other in an emergency.

Time was also spent on various other modifications, including further work on the valve gear, brakes, lubricators and, it was stated, the whistle; whatever was the defect or modification to this component is not recorded.

At some unspecified stage the firebrick lining was also increased to a staggering 9 inches thick. These larger bricks certainly cured the problem of the instability of the brick sides, but of course also effectively reduced the grate area from the original 43sq ft to just 25.5sq ft. Even so, 'Leader' would still generate steam in volume!

With the work completed, No 36001 was steamed again on 27 January 1950 for a light engine trial to Tunbridge Wells, and all was well. Further slight spring adjustments were then made at Brighton Works, together with

weighing in the workshops – Brighton had originally been unable to accurately weigh the whole engine, although with some figures now known it is believed that one end at a time was measured.

On 2 February the engine again visited Eastleigh for weighing and no doubt to verify the changes made. The run and its return on the same day were again completed without incident.

As regards the engine itself, the concern of the CCE was understandable. After all, 'Leader' now weighed in at something just under 150 tons, equivalent to almost 25 tons per axle – considerably greater than an original 'Merchant Navy', with a maximum axle weight of just 21 tons. (To be fair, any engineer will confirm that axle weights are in reality a notional figure, and even engines within the same class could display marked variations dependent upon spring adjustment and settings. Additionally, certain classes could be far more punishing to both trackwork and bridges from the 'hammer-blow' effect.)

Notwithstanding, the CCE decreed that 150 tons was to be the absolute maximum, and in order to remain within that figure there was now a restriction on the amount of coal and water that could be carried – only 3 tons of coal and 2,600 gallons of water were permitted, compared with the design capacity of 4 tons and 4,000 gallons. There were also allegations that No 36001 in both her original and subsequent heavier form had spread the track, but these were never proven, although by inference may well have contributed to her later demise.

At Brighton 'Leader' was still awaiting a decision from the hierarchy, and behind the scenes much discussion was indeed taking place. For his part, and despite being occupied at Inchicore, Bulleid still appears to have been trying to ensure that his creation could live, and attempted to arrange a meeting with Missenden and Riddles at which no doubt he would have used his persuasive skills to best effect, but for reasons that are not clear this did not take place. In all probability the other parties were far from keen on such a meeting, as it could have resulted in definite decisions having to made there and then. Even Missenden, Bulleid's former ally, privately might well have had an 'out of sight, out of mind' perspective.

Having failed to arrange a face-to-face discussion about the engine, Bulleid's next shot was a letter to both men, almost an admission of defeat:

'I am quite satisfied the engine can be made a useful and valuable locomotive and Mr Granshaw, the Locomotive Manager at Brighton, with the help he is receiving from Mr Jarvis, the Chief Draughtsman, can be relied upon to see that this is done.

I shall always appreciate deeply having been permitted to follow the development of the "Leader" engine so far, as it has given me much valuable information for future work.

I would like to add my acknowledgment of the help I have had from everyone concerned and especially the courtesy I have always had from Mr Riddles.

Above: **While in store at Brighton over the winter of 1949/50, decisions concerning No 36001 were being made elsewhere. The engine is coupled to a 'WD' 2-8-0, several of which were being overhauled at Brighton around this time.** Don Broughton collection

Left and below: **'Leader' is seen during here during her last days at Brighton in the first few months of 1950, after which the engine was permanently transferred to Eastleigh. These two views also prove that the engine was cleaned at least once, while all the pipework has also been restored! Note the position of the windscreen wiper on the left-hand window, identifying this as the No 2 (bunker) end; 'Leader' was driven from the opposite (left-hand) side at the No 1 end, with the windscreen wiper correspondingly on the opposite side. The man in the black coat and beret is the redoubtable John Smith who ran the photographic company 'Lens of Sutton' for many years.** T. Cole and B. J. Miller

As I do not think my services are necessary any longer and as I feel I may well be an embarrassment, I shall be obliged if I can be released from the arrangement made last September. I shall be available for consultation if desired and if I can be of any help at any time I shall always be only too pleased to give it.'

Meanwhile, a somewhat more critical appraisal had been prepared by R. G. Jarvis and submitted to Riddles:

'I have been asked by Mr Warder to express my views on this experiment as the Regional Chief Technical Assistant responsible for design. No personal criticism is inferred in the remarks which follow, and the views expressed represent my views which may well be at variance with those of the designers of the locomotive, on the basis that if doctors can differ, so may engineers.'

Jarvis continued by repeating the aims Bulleid had first set himself, then to compare these with the actual results:

'(1) The weight will restrict route availability.
(2) The enclosure and lubrication of engines, axleboxes and springs is very unsatisfactory.
(3) The increased steam chest volume and port areas, and the reduced clearance volumes, may only have a minimal effect on thermal efficiency judging by recent tests at Rugby Test Plant.
(4) Replacement of firebox water-legs by firebricks is not successful.'

His view was that 'the disappointing progress made with the locomotive to date is to a much greater extent attributable to the detail design than to the broad conception'. He felt that there was an essential need for self-aligning axle bearings, that the fireman's confined space was very unsatisfactory and dangerous in the event of a blowback on entering a tunnel, and that the valve gear was unsatisfactory on three counts: the out-rigger drive to the valves, the bad effects as wear developed, and the fear of thermal distortion in the fabricated cylinders. He would also have preferred smaller wheels.

His conclusion was that, 'The design has certain attractive features, it has many problems to solve, and it has some fundamental defects. That the locomotive could be made to work I have no doubt, but a great deal of experimental work will be necessary. It all depends upon how much money can be permitted for the modifications which will entail virtually a complete re-arrangement.'

It would be reasonable to suppose that the 'Leader' would have been condemned there and then, but no. After some deliberation, Riddles finally decided to accede to Bulleid's original comment that the engine should be sent to Eastleigh. However, there it would be subject not just to testing, but full-scale dynamometer car trials.

Accordingly No 36001 steamed quietly away from Brighton on Thursday 13 April 1950 bound for Hampshire.

The feelings of the Brighton staff were not recorded, some no doubt sad, others probably glad to see it go. 'Leader' was like that – there were never any half measures, it was like it or loathe it. Time would tell which way the men at Eastleigh would respond.

(In my original work on the saga of No 36001 I stated that the modifications and alterations necessary to correct the weight differential were carried out at Eastleigh in April and May 1950. This may have been incorrect, a more accurate description being that Brighton and Eastleigh shared the task. Certainly this involved the fixing of transverse struts along the corridor to a depth of 2 feet, which was then filled with the various items of steel ballast already mentioned. The individual responsibility of the works is somewhat academic, as the results are well known.)

Testing from Eastleigh

With Bulleid now no longer involved, Riddles was the man in directional control, while Granshaw assumed overall charge. R. G. Jarvis was tasked with issues relating to the dynamometer car trials.

As with the rumours over the weight of No 36001, so rumours regarding her working had preceded her arrival at Eastleigh. No sooner had the engine arrived in Hampshire than the ASLEF representative approached the shed management to say that ASLEF staff would not work the engine for fear of danger to the fireman in the event of the engine turning over onto its corridor side,

A new home at Eastleigh amongst the piles of ash of the running shed: theoretically the slab sides would have enabled the engine to pass through a carriage washing plant, but this was never done.
Don Broughton collection

preventing any escape from the central compartment. In many respects this was a totally logical comment to make, the firing compartment having just the single door, and any alternative exit along the side corridor now difficult if not impossible due to the presence of the additional weight.

The matter was left in the hands of Stephen Townroe, who was a devotee of Maunsell rather than Bulleid, an affinity based upon the logic of an operating man; whereas a Bulleid Pacific was excellent on some days, but the design made it erratic and difficult to maintain in its original form (this was some time before the rebuilding of so many of the Bulleid breed intended to produce a more reliable machine). This situation compared with the simpler Maunsell designs, the 'King Arthur' type in particular, which were both predictable and simpler to maintain. (The 'Lord Nelsons' were perhaps a little more difficult, but with coaxing, Townroe and his Inspectors

Below: **Shortly after arrival at Eastleigh, No 36001 undertakes an early trial to Fratton. It had of course been hoped that the dynamometer car tests would start as soon as possible, and the purpose of these runs was to enable the engine crews and fitters to become as familiar with the machine as possible. Preparation and disposal duties for these runs were often delegated to any available crew, so a number of young Eastleigh firemen were able to gain an impression of the engine.** Collection of Mrs Talbot

Below right: **This is the only known view of the engine at Fratton, although the date stated on the rear of the photograph, 29 September 1950, must be open to doubt. The height of the engine relative to the coaches will again be noted, although the driving cabs of 'Leader' were not over-generous with regard to headroom (it had always been intended that the driver would undertake his duties seated).** D. R. Yarney

were often able to educate both driver and fireman accordingly. Townroe's preference is made plain in his masterful work 'Arthurs', 'Nelsons' and 'Schools' at Work.[1]) As an aside, Bulleid's original choice for a locomotive on which to experiment with sleeve valves was indeed a 'King Arthur', but this was vetoed by the SR traffic department as being potentially too useful a machine to lose. Did Townroe have a hand in that as well?

But a man like Stephen Townroe did not rise to the heights of Shed Master – and later District Motive Power Superintendent – without both knowledge and guile, and an effective compromise was reached when it was agreed with ASLEF that its members would only work the engine on the basis of trials alone and that a major redesign would be necessary before it would be accepted into general service. Society had indeed changed over the years – one can only imagine the reaction of someone like Dugald Drummond to the circumstances that prevailed in 1950! (It is suggested that Alf Smith, the regular driver of 'Leader' on its trials from Eastleigh, was not an ASLEF member, but an NUR man!)

It was not until 5 June 1950 that No 36001 was finally ready for its first trial from its new operating home, although it was now limited in not only the amount of coal and water that could be carried, but also its speed, a 50mph maximum being confirmed by the CCE. This speed limit had allegedly been in place for the latter part of testing from Brighton, although compliance was sometimes doubtful.

Steam was raised and 'Leader' was made ready for what was to be the first of the pre-dynamometer car tests, the actual recorded runs using the former LNER vehicle due to commence soon afterwards. As I mentioned in my

previous book, the same dynamometer car was used that had been attached to *Mallard* in 1938 when the world speed record for steam was broken. But with 'Leader' it was not speed that was to be measured, but something more basic – a justification for survival.

On the morning of 6 June 'Leader' was attached to a train of ten vehicles weighing 332 tons, the heaviest load the engine had yet been set to haul, and, with No 2 end (the bunker end) leading, left Eastleigh for the 21-mile trip to Fratton, on the outskirts of Portsmouth. At this time it was being handled by the works trial crew, although a number of other observers were on board. One of these was fitter Reg Rowde, who recalled the engine giving a considerable lurch just south of Botley and coming within what appeared to be a hair's-breadth of hitting a signal post. 'We all held our breath...,' he later commented. To be fair, the fault was with the track and formation, the area in question in the vicinity of Botley consisting of much unstable subsoil and the cause of much subsidence, and consequent remedial work, over the years.

The return working later the same day was accomplished without incident; even when No 36001 was brought to a stand near Eastleigh South signalbox, she pulled away again without hesitation or slip. Similar successful runs were made on the next two days.

The engine then entered the works again for what was stated to be attention to the main steam pipes and also the grate. What was involved with the former is not known, although the latter resulted in the removal of the rocking grate and its substitution with a drop grate. On the subject of the grate, a necessary modification to compensate for the decrease in grate area was a reduction in the size of

the blastpipe nozzles, which in turn resulted in excessive fire-throwing. Rather than fitting a spark arrestor as before, this was now addressed by adding a brick arch, something that had certainly not been present before, but while this cured the fire-throwing it had a tendency to cause the fire to creep backwards, with flames licking around the firehole door. In turn this led to a more difficult situation for the fireman, and meant that on occasions he would wrap hessian sacking around his legs. Judicious use of the blower, which was controlled from within the firing compartment, helped to suck the fire the other way, but the trouble was that from his hidden position the fireman often had little knowledge of his actual location on the line, the only alternative being to have the blower operating for the majority of the time.

Heat was also a problem within the cab at the No 1 end of the engine, where the smokebox protruded into the driver's working environment, despite the presence of 'Magnesia' or similar lagging covering the whole of the smokebox, with the smokebox door handles protruding through it. Accordingly for crew comfort during the trials a timber partition was installed to separate the driving compartment from the smokebox, although its presence made life still more difficult so far as smokebox cleaning was concerned, the very aspect that Bulleid had originally 'designed out' with his ash disposal chute. (The task of smokebox cleaning was often given to the younger fireman at Eastleigh, who would thus become involved in various aspects of the preparation and disposal of the engine.)

It was anticipated that the actual dynamometer car trials would occupy the first two weeks of July 1950, and as a preliminary test a further run was arranged for Monday

12 June over what was to be the dynamometer car test route for all the runs: Eastleigh-Woking-Guildford. This was also seen as an opportunity to assess the recent modifications to the grate and steampipes.

However, the problem with running trials from Eastleigh was one of line capacity. Eastleigh to Portsmouth (Fratton) or perhaps even in the opposite direction towards Romsey would have been reasonable, but elsewhere from Eastleigh on the Bournemouth to Waterloo line, north or south, the situation was very different indeed. Line capacity was at a premium, which meant that the only pathway the operating authorities could provide was to leave Eastleigh immediately after the 5.05pm Bournemouth West to Waterloo train had departed, which, on 12 June, was hauled by No 30850 *Lord Nelson*. (This was invariably a standard 'Lord Nelson' class turn, and the very service that would later come to grief at Shawford some two years later, on 29 July 1952, when the driver of the engine forgot that he had been routed along the up local line instead of the more normal up through route. The result was an undignified falling over at the bottom of the embankment, made worse by the fact that Stephen Townroe lived very close by and was quickly on the scene.)

No 36001 had a record load of 337 tons at the drawbar upon leaving Eastleigh, again comprising ten bogie vehicles. In charge were driver Alf Smith and fireman Sam Talbot, who, it is thought, were also involved with all the subsequent main-line runs with the engine. Despite the load, No 36001 pulled away without hesitation, and was reported to be going as well as No 30850 by the time Shawford was passed 4 miles later. Indeed, there was some comment from those on board that they would encounter a signal check as they were undoubtedly catching up! But just a mile later steam pressure was seen to be falling, first to 240psi then fairly quickly to 190psi, at which point it stabilised. With the thought of a further 14 miles of climbing before the summit was reached – the

Ten vehicles are the load between Allbrook (Eastleigh) and Shawford, which means that it must be the evening of 12 June 1950. The train is heading north on the up through line bound for Woking, with an incorrect headcode. The engine is going well, with no visible excess steam escaping apart from a normal amount from the oil pumps on each bogie. As with the earlier tests from Brighton, the stock used was simply whatever was available to suit the weight required by the testing crews.
Henry Meyer

reason for this route being chosen for the intended trials was thus apparent – the decision was reluctantly taken to come to a halt at Micheldever for a 'blow-up' (the stop may have been in the Wallers Ash loops just before Micheldever). Here boiler pressure was restored and a successful restart made.

Most of the later trials also called at Basingstoke on the way to Woking, although this is not mentioned on this occasion. Instead, at Woking the engine ran round, no doubt took water and was inspected, being generally made ready for the return working. (The formal intention was to terminate the trial at Woking, then propel the dynamometer car to Guildford where both car and loco would turn on the turntable. A similar propelling movement would then take place back to Woking. In this way the crew could work with the cooler No 2 end leading.)

However, it appears that the trial had now lost its return path, so it was not until some hours had elapsed that Control could allow the engine back out onto the main line. Eastleigh was reached again at 2.30am. For the return run it was the smokebox (No 1) end leading, the engine not having been turned en route. (The return runs were always under the command of the Woking Control Office, and the engine's generally unreliable performance meant that it may well have been the cause of a number of delays to other services over the course of the subsequent tests.)

Investigation at Eastleigh quickly revealed the reason for the sudden dropping off in steam pressure – a buckled flange plate was allowing the smokebox to draw air. It was but a straightforward matter to effect a suitable repair.

A further test over the same route, although this time with a slightly reduced load of 320 tons, was arranged for 15 June, probably to a similar schedule. With the previous defect now rectified, it would have been expected that the engine would have behaved in a predictable manner, and indeed it did – not as intended, but running short of steam en route! The cause on this occasion was not reported.

As far as Smith and Talbot were concerned their opinion of the engine confirmed not just the heat that had to be endured, but also that the firing compartment was at times akin to a 'Chinese laundry'. This was exacerbated by steam leakage from the injectors, which were located under the compartment. With steam apparently also leaking from a number of fittings and flanges in the same area, the result was an almost steady stream of condensation.

After a weekend of rest, trials had been due to recommence on Monday 19 June, but instead this was cancelled to allow No 36001 to enter the works. Here the valve events would be checked, the blastpipe cap changed and a start made towards some of the fittings that would be necessary for the dynamometer car tests. It was reported as well that the welding of the boiler was examined, although this is the first time that there had been mention of such verification since construction, and by implication it was a sinister development.

Checking the valve events of a machine fitted with sleeve valves was not a straightforward task, and Eastleigh had no jigs available for the task. (Did Brighton?) Accordingly it was necessary to move the engine slightly forward or back with a pinch-bar, which remarkably could be accomplished with ease by just one man, such was the advantage of the use of roller-bearings.

'Leader' was released from the works towards the end of June and ready for what was probably intended to be the final trial before a full assessment with the dynamometer car, which had been scheduled to commence on the 29th. Eight coaches were in tow and, with steam raised, the engine set off north for Woking.

However, something was very wrong almost from the moment the train pulled out of the yards at Eastleigh, as there was a distinct knocking noise from No 1 bogie, more pronounced as steam was applied and increasing in intensity as the engine accelerated. Nothing like this had ever been heard before and there were no doubt a number of puzzled faces on board.

It had long been the practice, both at Eastleigh and previously at Brighton, to remove sections of the floor of the end cabs to observe the movement (or otherwise!) of the oscillating gear attached to the sleeves, but on this occasion there was no immediate sign of distress from any of the components that could be seen. Perhaps on the basis of 'perhaps if we ignore it, it will go away' or even 'if it is important, it will get worse', the trial trip continued northwards. Unfortunately the latter scenario proved correct, for 9 miles after the start, when passing Winchester Junction, the knock changed to what was described as a deep hammering sound, which also corresponded to each revolution of the wheels. Under the circumstances, and undoubtedly for fear of what had, or indeed might next develop, the engine was immediately eased and the trial halted at Micheldever, which was the next available location where the stock could be suitably deposited.

No doubt the engine was then examined as thoroughly as possible. In the light of what would transpire it would be fascinating to learn what was found – or even not found – but no details have come to light. It was clear that there was no way the trial could continue, and the engine was worked light back to Eastleigh at a slow speed. Once again there is no report on this return run, but it would no doubt have been accompanied by similar metallic sounds.

Safe in the running shed the fire was dropped and the engine towed to the nearby works for examination. Regardless of the day's events, this visit was a planned one as it was still necessary to complete some further connections necessary for the dynamometer car trials.

The investigation into the noises at first centred on a possible fracture to the right-hand sleeve and cylinder of No 1 bogie, but this was found to be intact and opinion was that the fault lay in the vicinity of the right-hand axlebox. However, examination of this meant that the bogie would need to be rolled out, and despite Eastleigh being able to lift the body, the works seemingly excused itself from undertaking the task immediately on the basis that it would have no means of supporting the body once the

Left: **The aftermath of the broken crank axle, seen in Eastleigh Works on 3 July 1950.** John Bell

Below: **X-ray examination of the second crank axle, of No 2 bogie, revealed that this was also likely to fail in the near future. The defective area is highlighted in the workshop by white paint.** John Bell

bogie was removed. This was perhaps a slightly inconsequential statement, as with a will surely conventional sleepers could have been used – after all, engine frames under repair were often supported in this way. However, for whatever reason it was decided to send for the two wooden supporting trestles that existed at Brighton, and which had been used during the construction process (appearing in several of the construction phase photographs).

Brighton forwarded the necessary items – similar in appearance to a carpenter's saw-horse, although of course larger and more substantial – together with, it was stated, an assortment of spares. The latter were no doubt intended to cover every eventuality that might be encountered, and were no doubt purloined from the parts intended to complete Nos 36004/5.

On 3 July 1950, four days after 'Leader' had last been steamed, the all-important pair of trestles arrived. The body was then lifted and supported on the trestles after the bogie had been rolled out. After this No 1 bogie could itself be lifted. The result was a 'worst-case scenario': complete failure of the centre axle, which had fractured near where the axle was pressed into the driving wheel.

Not unnaturally an immediate check was made on the crank axle of the No 2 bogie, which, despite not displaying any audible signs of weakness, was immediately shown as likely to fail in the future, having the same fatigue cracks when examined using both mechanical and X-ray techniques. The only conclusion was that with a similar defect on both axles, this could only be a design fault,

although dark murmurings concerning defective manufacture that had contributed towards the failures would be made later. It was a devastating blow, which would surely spell the immediate end to the trials.

Surprisingly, however, Riddles ordered the engine to be repaired and the trials to continue. Accordingly replacement crank axles were fitted, together with any other necessary repairs. With hindsight it would have been better to replace both bogies with perhaps those from No 36002, which were of course complete, but this was not done.

Meanwhile, the expense of having a full complement of engineers standing by waiting to undertake trials with the dynamometer car had not gone unnoticed, and it was decided that they would be better employed gaining information that could be used as a 'benchmark' against which 'Leader' would subsequently be measured. In view of the size of 'Leader' and its notional power output – on paper at least – one might have expected something like a 'King Arthur' or even a Light Pacific to be used for this purpose, but instead the choice made was to use a 'U' class Mogul, No 31618.

Rumour has it that this particular engine was selected as it had long been regarded as shy for steam and, regardless of the test results against which 'Leader' would be measured, it might well afford an opportunity to assess the 2-6-0's poor reputation.

No 31618 was made ready with various attachments, and on 10 July the first dynamometer car trial was undertaken. It was quickly realised that the engine had been a bad choice, being in 'a poor condition' according to the test crew, while the left-hand trailing axlebox ran hot, so the test was terminated at Basingstoke. No 31618 returned light to Eastleigh for repair and no doubt emerged a far more reliable engine as it eventually survived in traffic until January 1964. In that the trial had been intended to utilise the test crew, the outcome so far was not very satisfactory, as everything was now back where it had been on 29 June.

Strangely, there is no record of any progress in the replacement crank axles for 'Leader' at Eastleigh, and the same applied until the second week of August. Was it simply due to pressure of work in other areas in the works, or was the lack of urgency the result of what was seemingly now already a foregone conclusion? Do not imagine that the delay was due to tests being made on all the 'Leader'-type axles that existed in order to find a pair that were suitable. That was not done, or the nearly complete No 36002 would not have remained intact and untouched (save for the dismantling of the valve gear for subsequent towing movements) from the moment work was suspended on 19 November 1949 until she was scrapped. This lack of progress is even more surprising when it is recalled that Marylebone Road would have been aware of the ongoing situation and the probable 'standing time' of the engineers associated with the dynamometer car. (Did these men perhaps even go back to Doncaster in the meanwhile?)

In the event somebody (who and when are not known, but that is not really important) decided that the next stage would be further 'benchmark' trials with another 'U', this time No 31630. Again it took time to prepare the engine and the first test was not until the end of July 1950. In all, three runs were made between Eastleigh and Woking, No 31630 performing faultlessly on each occasion with varying loads and burning 'South Kirby Hards No 1' weighed into 1cwt bags. The tests concluded on 2 August.

It will be recalled that, due to its weight, the Chief Civil Engineer had set a maximum speed of 50mph for 'Leader', which was consequently also the maximum speed set for No 31630, which averaged 45-50mph, the differential between average and maximum being therefore minimal.

No 36001, meanwhile, was eventually released from the works on Monday 14 August, and the next day a trial was made to Botley and return. The same run was repeated on the 15th. The distance covered was in the order of 5 miles each way daily, a total of 10 miles per round trip, yet according to a note in the official records 'Leader' used something in the order of 2,000 gallons of water in each direction.

Eastleigh, Saturday 19 August 1950, and No 36001 and the dynamometer car are made ready for the trials that will commence two days later. Pursey C. Short

This incredible figure needs both some elaboration and some discussion. First, remember that the CCE had prohibited the engine from carrying its full complement of water and coal due to weight. Water capacity was now restricted to 2,600 gallons instead of the design capacity of 4,000 gallons. So how much was 'Leader' carrying? Next, there were no water columns at Botley – or anywhere between Eastleigh and Botley – so there was no chance of replenishing supplies. Third, did not No 2039 use a similar amount running between Lancing and Eastleigh? And finally, if 'Leader' was indeed using that volume of water – and we may assume that it was not leaking from the tanks – how much coal and consequently effort by the fireman was involved? It is still remarkable that the boiler was able to evaporate that amount of water from a grate area now reduced to just 25.5sq ft.

Suspicion, then, must be centred upon the sleeve valves. Possibly the pistons and valves had been removed or disturbed during the replacement of the crank axles. The wastage of steam past these was what had affected No 2039, and was seemingly now affecting No 36001 as well. But how could the engine have entered the works on 29 June *without* any appreciable steam loss or excess water consumption – surely these would have been referred to in official records had that been the case – yet *emerge* in that condition? And what exactly was the amount of water

carried on board or used on the Botley trips. Somewhere someone was not being honest.

A third test was planned for 17 August, but this was cancelled as a connecting rod, this time from No 2 bogie, was striking the casing of the oil bath. Again, possibly the casing had been disturbed when the replacement crank axle had been fitted. Indeed, aside from the one failure of 24 September 1949, as detailed previously, this was the first reported failure of the No 2 bogie. (Other problems associated with the oil bath on unspecified dates included corrosion of the motion pins, caused, it was stated, by water finding its way into the oil bath and not being drained away. Also, as with the Pacifics, there was a tendency for the chains to stretch, and although a modification in the form of a 'skid' was prepared, this was never fitted. Broken circlips were another common problem, which allowed the motion pins to fall out. (This was not the fault of Bulleid or the design, being attributable to the outside manufacturer of the circlips, but it will not have helped the working of the oscillating gear.)

Repairs were quickly completed and a further light engine trial was arranged to Fratton on 18 August. As before, the works trials crew were in charge – not believed to have been Messrs Smith and Talbot this time – and surprisingly no mention was made of excess water consumption. Instead it was recorded that the engine was now ready for its long-awaited dynamometer car tests, which would commence on Monday 21 August.

'Leader' was made ready on No 1 road at Eastleigh running shed. The dynamometer car was attached, and the necessary cable connections made in order that various instrument readings could be taken. After this, and with its complement of observers, engineers and, of course, crew, the engine left the shed ready to collect its train of empty stock from the carriage sidings alongside the station.

The load behind the drawbar, including the dynamometer car, was $231\frac{1}{2}$ tons, which was to be increased as the tests progressed. The schedule would see the trials being made at the same time of day as before and continuing to Woking. Here engine and dynamometer car would detach and propel to Guildford, 6 miles away, for turning. In theory, of course, 'Leader', having a cab at each

The former North Eastern Railway/LNER dynamometer car.
Don Broughton collection

100

Above: **Viewed from its plain side, 'Leader' presents a bland appearance. The former grey panels are now streaked with dirt, hiding the black and red lining that had been applied. Notice the vents in the roof 'amidships', which correspond to the location of the firing compartment.** National Railway Museum/J. G. Click

Right: **To assess fuel consumption accurately, the amount of fuel at the start and end of each trip had to be measured. There was only one way to do this – human muscle-power. As with the earlier tests with No 31630, each bag contained 1cwt of 'South Kirby Hards No 1'.** National Railway Museum/J. G. Click

end, could have accomplished the task without this added complication, but Alf Smith said that he would only undertake the work if he could drive from the bunker end, and it was for that reason that the turning operation was undertaken.

In addition to the driver and fireman, a fitter was also booked to travel, his principal duty being to assist in the preparation of the engine. However, in this area there was little for the driver to do. Bulleid had incorporated in the 'Leader' design some of the advantages of the internal combustion engine, so little in the way of preparation was required. All the important components were designed to be either pressure or flood lubricated; indeed, it was stated that there were only two oiling points on the whole engine that the driver needed to attend to! (Unfortunately the present author has not been able to discover where these two lubrication points actually were, and with the passage of time it is unlikely that the information will become available. A possibility – confirmed in conversation with former Eastleigh fitter Eric Best – is that the two *may* have been identical, and in fact referred

Having satisfied the appetite of the engine, it was now time to quench its thirst. No 36001's tank is being replenished by fireman Sam Talbot (on top) outside the front of Eastleigh shed. The height and flexibility of the hose will be noted, compared with the earlier view at Oxted. Notice too what appears to be a canvas cover on top of the coal bunker; this was applied after fuelling and appears in several of the views of the engine while it was based at Eastleigh, although its purpose is still not clear. Alongside is 'King Arthur' No 30784.
National Railway Museum/J. G. Click

to points confirming the oil level within the holding tank that fed the Wakefield mechanical lubricators, three of which were mounted on each bogie.)

Monday 21 August is reported as having been a wonderful summer's evening, so perhaps the gods would at last look kindly on the project – perhaps even the official record of the run would reveal as much:

'The start from Eastleigh was slow, and the boiler pressure fell quickly from 270 to 210lb in six minutes, although the regulator was only partly open with 170lb in the steam inlet pipes. Exhaust pressures of 12 and 12$\frac{1}{2}$lb, and exhaust temperatures of 244° and 246° Fahrenheit were noted, also a high smokebox vacuum of 5$\frac{1}{2}$ inches was recorded.

Below left and below: **Ready to go!** National Railway Museum/J. G. Click

Two minutes later, although the steam chest pressure had fallen to 140lb psi, the exhaust temperatures continued to rise to 256° and 280° Fahrenheit and the smokebox vacuum to 7in. of water. The regulator was eased to give 100psi in the steam chest and allow the pressure to rise in the boiler. The drawbar arm in the dynamometer car indicated unusual vibrations, and as the exhaust temperatures continued to rise it was soon evident that all was not well with the engine working. Due to very hard work by the fireman the boiler pressure rose and was maintained at about 240psi for the remainder of the journey. Under these conditions the temperature in the fireman's cab was abnormal [but the figure was not recorded].'

The test continued as intended as far as Woking, with arrival as scheduled at 8.15pm. Engine and dynamometer car then propelled down to Guildford for turning, where Messrs Smith and Talbot were able to take a breather of sorts while the engine was examined prior to the return run. Unfortunately this examination revealed that the mechanical lubricators on No 2 bogie were faulty, and in order to reduce the risk of seizure while working under load on the return run, the test was abandoned and engine and dynamometer car returned light to Eastleigh the next day, leaving Guildford at 8.30pm. Eastleigh works refitted some new rings, while certain of the sleeves were also given lathe attention.

Above: **The shadows indicate that the time is clearly early evening, and 'Leader' is waiting for the off.** National Railway Museum/J. G. Click

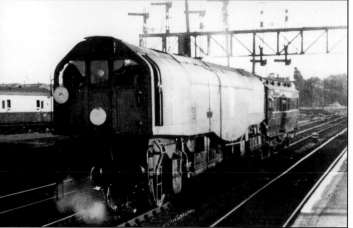

Left: **Having left the shed, it was necessary to run through Eastleigh station, then set back across the north end of what were then Platforms 3 and 4 to reach the carriage sidings.** N. L. Browne

Repairs having been effected, a further trial was arranged for Wednesday 23 August. The load this time was increased by one vehicle, making 264½ tons. Again the official commentary is somewhat revealing:

'Prior to starting the up journey from Eastleigh ... steam was blowing from the safety valves, but the boiler pressure fell to 185psi after 16 minutes. The exhaust pressures were again high and the exhaust temperatures gradually rose to

350° Fahrenheit, which is the limit of the working range of temperature for the indicator in the dynamometer car for this purpose. In order to reduce the coal and water consumption the engine was worked in 20% cut-off instead of 30% used on the previous test runs. Although this had the effect of reducing the smokebox vacuum, the engine continued to throw burning char from the chimney top. The actual running time was spoilt by a number of signal checks, seven in all, and four signal stops, which assisted in keeping up the boiler pressure. On the return journey from Woking steam was again blowing from the safety valves and a thicker fire was put on the grate before starting away. The regulator was adjusted to give a maximum steam chest pressure and the engine tried in 15% cut-off on the easier sections of route. This resulted in maintaining a higher boiler pressure and reduced the exhaust steam temperatures within the range of measurement, but there was no improvement in either coal or water consumption. The engine refused to start on one or two occasions and had to reverse before a drawbar pull of about 5 tons necessary to start the train could be exerted. All the figures and evidence collected at this stage were ample proof that a considerable amount of the steam produced was being wasted, either by leakage past the piston or sleeve valves of both engine units.'

This was damning evidence indeed, but some of the points raised need elaboration. What had been witnessed was no more than might have been expected after the precedents of 14 and 15 August when the excess water consumption on the Botley trial had been noted. Remember, too, that on those two earlier occasions the engine had been running light.

Assuming that 'Leader' was loaded only with the officially permitted figure of 2,600 gallons of water –

Coupled to its train, No 36001's route from the carriage sidings at Eastleigh appears to have been parallel with the running lines as far as Allbrook, running from there northwards via the Up No 2 Goods Line. Certainly that was the case on 20 August 1950. Les Elsey

and with a number of professional engineers riding with
the dynamometer car this must have been the case – on
the runs of 21 and 23 August it is almost certain, though
not confirmed, that a scheduled stop was made at
Basingstoke, where examination could be made and water
taken. Therefore 'Leader' appears to have managed – *with
a train this time* – to travel almost 26 miles from Eastleigh
to Basingstoke without running out of water. If this had
not been so, surely it would have been mentioned in the
official reports. The only available intermediate water stop
was at Winchester, but again this is not mentioned.

The conclusion therefore is that the runs of 14 and
15 August represented an inaccurate record, which formed
some of the evidence later presented in the official report,
and upon which Riddles would base his conclusions –
inaccurate evidence provided on which formal decisions
would be made.

That is not to say that 'Leader' was performing well,
however – far from it. The extremes in exhaust

temperature allied in particular to the exhaust pressure
within the smokebox clearly show that high-temperature
– and high-pressure – steam was being fed to the
cylinders from the boiler via the regulator and steam
chests and was exhausting straight into the smokebox
without performing any useful work. This would account
for the decreasing boiler pressure, unless the cut-off was
so severely reduced that the boiler, grate (and fireman)
could accommodate the demands for steam. 'Leader' was
wasting almost as much steam as it could produce. This
would also go some way to explaining the difficulties in
restarting the train, although this was also 'helped' by the
fitter shifting the reversing gear to the required position
with judicious use of the crowbar.

What was not widely known, and perhaps had been
deliberately kept from the dynamometer car engineers,
was that at Eastleigh this problem with steam leakage was
already common knowledge, and an unofficial method of
attempting to 'tighten everything up' when the engine was
cold had been arrived at. This method was simply to run
light up and down any convenient siding, the idea being
that steam passing through the sleeves and therefore into
the cylinders would expand the various components until

Above and below: **Apart from those actually involved, few people were on hand to record the exploits of No 36001 in the summer of 1950. One, though, was Henry Meyer, who despite visiting almost exactly the same location north of Allbrook, and unfortunately on unrecorded dates has managed to capture the engine on trials with what are two distinctly different rakes of vehicles in tow. Notice too the solitary headcode disc carrying the abbreviation for the word 'Special'.** Both Henry Meyer

they formed a better fit. That said, the same result would have been achieved after perhaps 10 miles of normal running, and if that had been the case the engine would have performed better as the runs had progressed, but this was simply not the case. Perhaps the running up and down did take place and did help a little, but not as much as those who instigated it would have wished. (In the opinion

of the present author only, this 'help' given to No 36001 was at the instigation of one Bulleid devotee – no name this time – who was determined to assist in the success of the project generally and especially in view of the fact that the designer was now no longer on the scene. While no doubt well intended, it did little to achieve the desired object.) Difficulties with the operation of the cylinder cocks were successfully dealt with.

The return run from Woking to Eastleigh was accomplished in the night hours, again with a probable stop at Basingstoke. The engine and dynamometer car were then turned and stabled once more for a further trial scheduled for later the same day. Once again the load was increased, this time to ten coaches, quoted as 290$\frac{1}{2}$ tons. According to the official record:

Above: Because of the evening timings, as well as its unannounced and totally unpredictable appearances, views of No 36001 north of Allbrook are few and far between. This is still the only known view, albeit of indifferent quality, showing the engine entering Winchester at about 7.00pm on 21 August 1950. This was also the very first of the dynamometer car runs with the engine. P. A. L. Millard

Right: The fact that No 36001 is at Guildford in daylight means that this photograph can only have been taken on 22 August. Again the cover over the bunker is visible, but it will be noted that it does not extend over the top of the water filler and TIA tank.
National Railway Museum/J. G. Click

'A fourth test run was made on 24.8.1949. When running between Eastleigh motive power depot to the reception sidings to pick up the trainload the cylinder cocks were open to get rid of the condensation. The cylinder of No 1 end can be seen from the dynamometer car and it was observed that an abnormal amount of water was issuing from the sleeve valves. The condensed steam was white and oily from the lubrication supply. When attached to the train, the boiler pressure was 275psi, and again a good thickness of fire was on the firegrate. The weight of the train for this test run was $290^1/_2$ tons, a light load for an engine of this size. Working in 30% cut-off with 140psi in the steam chest, the boiler pressure fell rapidly to 200lb. Good work by the fireman got the pressure back to 225lb but the pressure fell to 140lb approaching Winchester City, $7^1/_2$ miles from the starting point and a running time of 19 minutes. A stop had to be made to regain the boiler pressure, but as this so upset the booked path, the test run

A useful view for modellers of the top of the bunker area; note also that, unlike a carriage, 'Leader' was not of a uniform body width throughout, both ends tapering inwards. National Railway Museum/J. G. Click

was abandoned at Micheldever. On arrival back at Eastleigh depot a standing test very clearly showed that steam was blowing to waste and further tests with the engine in this condition were useless.'

Again this was a damning verdict, and one that could have spelled the end of the trials and, potentially, the engine. But analyse the comments further and more detail is revealed. The 19 minutes taken to travel between Eastleigh and Winchester represents an average speed of only just over 23^1/$_2$mph, which for 'an engine of this size' with a 'light load' is hardly a commendable achievement – even allowing for the figures representing start-to-stop times. What is not mentioned is the water usage, or should it be loss, for once again the supply had to be replenished at Micheldever using a half-inch hose connected to a standpipe on the station cattle dock. The whole episode was like something out of a Will Hay comedy, and reminiscent of the experience at Groombridge on 25 June the previous year.

It is clear, then, that 'Leader' was considered to have insufficient water on board at Micheldever for a return to Eastleigh, possibly insufficient even to reach Winchester on the return run. What we do not know is whether water was taken at Winchester on the way up, where the stop was made to rally the boiler. Assuming not, then No 36001 had evaporated something approaching 2,600 gallons of water in about 15^1/$_2$ miles, and still lost time in the process.

Perhaps even more amazing, though, is that this is the first mention of the emission of steam from the cylinder cocks in the way described. None of the photographs depicting 'Leader' on trial give any indication of steam leakage from the cylinders, although to be fair, the warm air at the time of year when the tests were run would make this more difficult to discern.

With the engineers concluding that further testing would be non-productive, the ball was again placed in the court of Riddles and his colleagues at Marylebone. This would be the third time that the future of 'Leader' was in the balance, the previous occasions arising from its weight and, more recently, the crank axle failure. Marylebone's response was swift and succinct – 'repair and continue'.

No 36001 is seen inside Eastleigh Works on the occasion of her last visit when all 144 rings were replaced. It would appear as if every vestige of the former oscillating gear has also been removed. T. J. Edgington

Accordingly, just three days after what could well have been the final run, 'Leader' re-entered the works and was basically given every attention it required. No 1 bogie had a completely new sleeve fitted to the left-hand cylinder and score marks smoothed over on the other sleeves. Additionally, all 24 rings were replaced on each piston and sleeve, amounting to 72 per bogie and no fewer than 144 for the complete engine; these items were stated to be of 'Wellworthy' manufacture. Other non-specified work was carried out on the No 2 bogie and elsewhere. (According to Townroe, Riddles and Bond paid a visit to Eastleigh some time in August 1950 and witnessed the engine running up and down the shed yard – this could well have been around this time.)

No 36001 finally re-emerged on 20 September and was steamed ready for a light engine trial to Fratton the next day. Alf Smith and Sam Talbot were on board as usual, and whether it was their words that were subsequently quoted in the official reports or those of an observer on

board is not certain, but the engine performed 'better than at any time in the past'. Most promising of all was that on return to Eastleigh close examination revealed that for the very first time there was absolutely nothing in need of attention.

However, No 36001 now had a lot of ground to make up. The interim report prepared by the testing staff while the engine had been in the works was hardly complimentary, although there was hardly any way in which the facts could be presented otherwise, even if on at least one occasion, as proven above, they veered somewhat from the truth. What Bulleid's views were in Ireland at this stage is not known, although in the light of what was to come later it is evident that he was being kept informed, though undoubtedly not through official BR channels.

Back at Eastleigh No 36001 was made ready for what would be the final series of formal dynamometer car trials over the same route, Eastleigh-Woking and return, due to commence on Monday 25 September 1950.

As before, the engine left Eastleigh at 6.45pm, immediately after the section was clear following the departure of the Bournemouth West-Waterloo service. The load was 241½ tons, which, although less than had been handled previously, was deliberately set almost as a 'running-in' load to allow the various components to bed in after the recent repairs.

For almost the first time, the official report gives a record of a true test in both directions:

'Eastleigh-Woking: The engine was worked mainly in 30% cut-off and partial regulator to give 110 to 120lb in the steam chest. As a result, the train speed rose gradually to 46mph on the rising gradients to Litchfield Signal Box... On the falling gradients from Basingstoke to Woking, the booked time was maintained, the maximum speed being 55$\frac{1}{2}$mph.'

'Woking-Eastleigh: The engine was worked in 25% cut-off with higher steam chest pressures. Signal checks spoiled the running to Brookwood, but with clear signals the steam chest pressure was put up to 200lb and this gave a drawbar pull of 3.38 tons, which accelerated the train from 20 to 41mph in 1$\frac{1}{2}$ miles. The regulator was eased at the 31$\frac{1}{2}$ milepost, the speed was 50.2mph. The maximum speed was 54mph at milepost 44.'

Back at Eastleigh the engine was again examined and, despite the previous evenings exertions, nothing untoward was found. Accordingly, the next day, 26 September, an extra vehicle was added, making the load 275 tons, comprising nine bogie vehicles. The same crew were in charge, Sam Talbot assisted to an extent by one of the many observers on board who would provide the weighed coal bags as required, although the cramped conditions for more than one man in the firing compartment made the work somewhat more onerous. Despite being totally familiar with the route, it was a new experience for the fireman to be unable to confirm where he was by sight, so it was not always easy to adjust the firing rate to compensate for changes in gradients.

With this heavier load, the engine departed once more:

'Eastleigh-Woking: Working mainly in 25% cut-off to Shawford Junction, the speed rose to 42mph and the exhaust pressure was up to 14lb with the result that a good amount of burning char was thrown from the chimney. The gear was changed to 20% cut-off, but the exhaust pressure rose again to 14lb when the speed was 53mph. When passing through Wallers Ash Tunnel at 53mph there was a shower of large pieces of burning char from the chimney top. Sectional running time was maintained to Basingstoke. During the downhill running to Woking, a maximum speed of 56mph was noted near Farnborough; this speed could have been exceeded if it had been desirable.

'Woking-Eastleigh: The engine put up a good performance by passing Brookwood at 42mph, a drawbar pull of 2.4 tons was maintained and the train speed rose to 50mph at milepost 31.'

Back at Eastleigh, apparently no defects were found and on Wednesday 27 September a heavier set of nine vehicles was provided, equal to 294$\frac{1}{2}$ tons.

'Eastleigh-Woking: The load was again increased to test the engine when working with higher steam chest pressures. There was some difficulty in obtaining suitable conditions owing to steam blows from the cylinder release valves when the pressure in the cylinders was above 210psi. At 21mph with a steam chest pressure of 195lb, the drawbar pull was 3.48 tons, drawbar horsepower 872 and the exhaust pressure 15lb. The boiler pressure gradually fell to 200lb. The regulator was eased to 130lb in the steam chest and the boiler pressure rose to 225lb in three minutes. At this point the speed was 51 mph...

'Woking-Eastleigh: A relatively good performance was made on the continuously rising gradient of 1 in 389 during which speed rose to 50mph in 12 minutes...'

Once more there is no record of any adverse comment upon the return to Eastleigh, but the record from the last run was already revealing areas of concern. The tendency for the cylinder release valves to blow at the relatively low pressure of 210psi meant that they were not operating correctly – they should have responded at the same rate as the boiler pressure, 280 psi. It is believed that the trouble was dealt with by simply blanking off this component because no one could be bothered to replace what were discovered to be a set of weak springs. The high exhaust pressures were another warning of boiler steam bypassing the sleeves.

The final detailed run with the dynamometer car was scheduled for Thursday 28 September, which was another fine dry evening (the weather had alternated between showery and dry over the four days of this final series of tests).

'Eastleigh-Woking: After passing onto the main line at Allbrook, the gear was set at 25% cut-off. The speed rose to 50mph in 12 minutes and the exhaust pressure rose to 12lb with a pressure of 195lb in the steam chest.

'Woking-Eastleigh: Special attention is drawn to the particulars of the engine performance from Woking when a speed of 50mph was attained in 12 minutes 44 seconds. There was no difficulty in maintaining adequate boiler pressure. During this period 9cwt of coal were put in the firebox...'

What is not stated in the official records, though, is that on this final run the engine was allowed to travel somewhat faster than before, the descent from Litchfield Summit to Eastleigh being taken at far more than the officially stipulated maximum speed. (Although no figures are given, according to driver Alf Smith this could well have been in the order of 70mph.)

Back at Eastleigh, engine and dynamometer car were first uncoupled, then 'Leader' had her fire disposed of. Either under her own power or perhaps shunted later, she eventually arrived on one of the sidings to the east of the running shed, cold and lifeless. Chains and padlocks were attached to the various cab doors – the authorities were determined that no one was to venture inside.

As far as most were concerned that seemed to be the end of 'Leader' and her sisters. Politically, the way ahead was seen to be the range of Standard steam designs as an interim measure, with later electrification or dieselisation according to technology and finance. Indeed, at this stage few engines to pre-nationalisation steam designs remained to be built, and it would surely take a small miracle to resurrect not only a non-standard design but one that had proved, to say the least and obvious to all, erratic in operation.

It must therefore have come as a considerable surprise when, just a few days after the completion of the last dynamometer car trial, with the dynamometer vehicle itself returned to its more usual haunts, arrangements were set in hand for a further series of tests. The dates involved are not totally certain, but suffice to say that it was some time during the first few days of October 1950. The first stage involved a thorough examination of the engine, which resulted in repairs to a number of flange joints, one of these affecting the blower, while various flexible steam pipes to the generators were also replaced. It is interesting to consider when exactly these repairs became necessary, for there had been no mention of any problems in the official report.

No 36001 was steamed again for a light engine trial between Eastleigh and Cosham on Saturday 14 October. Again the regular crew were on board, no doubt also with others. All went well and a full test was set for Tuesday 17 October; exactly what the purpose of this test was is not certain. Neither has it been possible to ascertain under what authorisation it was carried out. Popular belief has it that there were those among Bulleid's devotees who felt that the engine had still not had the chance to show its capabilities with the type of load the designer had intended; all the dynamometer car trials had been undertaken with only a limited weight, and the most that the engine had ever hauled was the 337 tons back on 12 June.

This time the load was 13 coaches, weighing 430 tons. Despite the fact that there would be no dynamometer car, the route and schedule were to be as before, with the engine turned at Guildford so as to be always working under load with No 2 end leading. Together with the usual crew, a fitter was on board, and also Bulleid and R. C. Bond of the Railway Executive. Undoubtedly this was the final time the designer would witness his creation.

Leaving Eastleigh, one observer described the start as 'effortless', although the engine did not behave totally as intended; at Basingstoke some 6 minutes were wasted while No 36001 stubbornly refused to move either forward or back in order to reach the water column.

An official summary of the run fortunately survives:

'The engine ran satisfactorily and whilst some time was lost on the easier sections, this could well have been avoided by slightly heavier working. The steam pressure and water level were fairly well maintained, but steaming was not entirely satisfactory during the heaviest conditions. The performance of the locomotive was such, however, as to indicate that a trial could be attempted with 480 tons.'

But why had this trial been undertaken in the first place? What information could now be achieved that could not have been gained from the dynamometer car? To run a test of this nature obviously took the will of at least one or probably several senior officials. But we cannot be certain what it was hoped would be achieved or, more interestingly, who was behind it.

Nevertheless 'Leader' was made ready for what would also be its very last outing, on Thursday 2 November 1950. No fewer than 15 coaches were attached, weighing 480 tons, the only concession being that due to the load an extra 5 minutes was allowed in the passing time for reaching Winchester Junction. It is known that on this occasion neither R. C. Bond nor anyone of his seniority was on board, although there were certainly some observers, as again a record of the run has survived.

Even with this colossal weight attached, No 36001 showed herself to be the master of the task set, with 50mph maintained almost throughout with a load greater than that given to a 'Merchant Navy' on the 'Bournemouth Belle' Pullman service – and this latter service did not have the disadvantage of a standing start from cold from Eastleigh directly onto a rising gradient. Indeed, every Bulleid driver I have ever spoken to confirmed that even with a larger 'Merchant Navy' Pacific 50mph was very acceptable throughout the climb north to Litchfield Summit.

En route at Micheldever it was even reported that No 36001's safety valves lifted, there was so much steam available. This was a truly remarkable performance, especially considering the load and the reduced size of the fire grate. No 36001 was even half a minute early at Worting Junction. This may have contributed to a signal stop, from which the 'Leader' pulled away without difficulty, but which resulted in a delayed arrival at Basingstoke.

There must have been jubilation on board, although this was soon tempered when examination of the engine revealed that the smokebox door had not been properly fastened when leaving Eastleigh and in consequence had 'sprung' at the bottom edge, allowing hot ash and char to drop onto the wooden flooring of the cab. This in turn was threatening to burn the floorboards, so the decision was reluctantly made to abandon the test and return to Eastleigh light engine.

Even so, No 36001 had one final trick up her sleeve – and the choice of word is deliberate! On running back to

Eastleigh, with little demand for steam, 'Leader' was allowed to fly. It has been suggested that she reached 90mph near Winchester, still riding as smoothly as a coach.

Back at her home depot the fire was dropped and the smokebox examined. All that was needed for a further trial was a replacement smokebox door, and four were of course available on Nos 36002-5. But it was not to be – whoever had authorised this final series of tests now similarly decreed there would be no more. Once again No 36001 found herself either among out-of-use engines or stabled alongside the shed, her access doors again chained shut. A decision was now awaited from Marylebone Road, and it would arrive just 18 days later.

On that date, 20 November 1950, Robin Riddles, as the member of the Railway Executive responsible for Mechanical Engineering, submitted his report on the 'Leader' project. The Executive had already been made aware of the goings-on at Eastleigh through an earlier report of 24 March 1950, but this would incorporate the final recommendations.

'Since my report dated 24.3.1950 was submitted, further trial runs have been made including two series of dynamometer car tests to determine the performance of this locomotive in comparison with a conventional locomotive of comparable power characteristics...

It was originally hoped that adjustment to the axlebox pedestals and slides would improve the weight distribution, but it is now evident that extensive redesign of the locomotive would be necessary in order to obtain a distribution which could be considered satisfactory for running in normal service.

It was therefore necessary in order that further trials might be run, to overcome the unsatisfactory weight distribution temporarily by the addition of $5\frac{1}{4}$ tons of ballast located on the locomotive in such a way as to produce a more uniform distribution of weight between the left and right sides...

Renewed running of the locomotive revealed a number of minor defects which culminated on 29th June after a total mileage of only 6,103, in the crank axle of No 1 bogie fracturing and breaking in two pieces. Examination of the crank axle of No 2 bogie revealed a number of small fatigue cracks and this axle would ultimately have failed in similar manner...

The locomotive had to be sent into the Works and new driving wheels and crank axles were fitted on both bogies. With the locomotive as at present built it is very probable that these replaced axles would also fail...

In view of the very high coal and water consumption, it was suspected that steam leakage was occurring and the pistons, sleeve valves and rings were renewed and

At Eastleigh on 21 October 1950, No 36001 lies forlorn and seemingly dumped. However, she was to have one last outing when she would take her heaviest load ever. The hole cut in No 1 end was to facilitate the necessary connections with the dynamometer car. H. C. Casserley

examined. Evidence of leakage was apparent and a number of new sleeve rings were fitted and all rings on pistons and valves were renewed... Such a marked deterioration in performance for a locomotive after only approximately 6,000 miles is exceptional and the trials have indicated that, with the present design, this rapid deterioration could only be corrected by frequently stopping the locomotive for examination and repairs to the valves and pistons ... compared with that of modern main line locomotives of more conventional design where the valves and pistons are normally only examined at intervals of 20-36,000 miles...

In the course of the trials attention was given to the operating conditions as far as the engine crews are concerned... Men have complained of the high temperature in the fireman's cab ... the fireman's position becomes intolerable if attempts are made to run the engine chimney first, owing to the very hot air which emerges from the corridor when running in this direction. With the present arrangement one of the aims of the locomotive is thus defeated and it would be necessary for turning to take place at the end of each journey.

There are only two alternatives which now present themselves in respect of the future of this class of locomotive. They are:

(a) To make a number of major modifications to the present design with a view to overcoming the difficulties which have been experienced and the difficulties which have been revealed;

(b) To scrap the locomotive so far completed and the other four in varying stages of construction.

The former course would involve the following in respect of the matters referred to above:

(1) The high coal and water consumption is due, to a large extent, to steam leakage past the sleeve valves, pistons and rings. It is also due to the high rate of combustion made necessary by the reduction in grate area, resulting from the thicker firebrick walls which experience shows to be essential.

   To correct these deficiencies would, in my opinion, involve a major redesign of the cylinders, eliminating the sleeve valves and replacing them with piston valves.

(2) To reduce the total weight of the locomotive by 20 tons, thus bringing it into conformity with the original diagram ... would be virtually impossible...

(3) ...At present the boiler is offset from the longitudinal centre line of the locomotive. The weight distribution could be corrected only by placing the boiler on the centre line, which would involve major alterations to the design of the locomotive or by a complete redistribution of the water tanks which also would involve extensive modifications.

   In either case it is doubtful whether the present access which exists between the driver's cab and fireman could be retained. This would involve an automatic device in the driver's cab on a similar principle to a "dead-man's handle" on electric stock (which would be an undesirable though essential complication), or three men would always be required on the locomotive when on the main line.

(4) The present axlebox assembly would require to be completely redesigned to give sufficient freedom to ensure the safety of the locomotive as a vehicle on the track, and to provide the necessary flexibility to eliminate breakage of the crank axle.

   It is not possible to say at this stage whether such redesign might not involve the elimination of the chains connecting the coupled axles and their replacement by coupling rods.

(5) It is difficult at this stage to suggest anything that could be done to ensure tolerable conditions for the fireman...

(6) The defects which are known to exist in the welding of part of the boiler of this locomotive would require to be rectified. Part of the welding of the boiler in the completed locomotive was subjected to X-Ray examination... The completed boilers for the other four locomotives, however, were not subject to any kind of X-Ray examination and I should not be prepared to allow them to go out into service until this precaution has been duly carried out.

   Expenditure amounting to £178,865 has already been incurred. So far it has not been possible, nor will it be possible, to place the locomotive in revenue-earning service without further heavy expense. I have not estimated what this further expense might be because, even were it incurred and all the defects eliminated, the locomotive, as modified, would offer no advantages compared with one of the conventional well-tried design.

I am compelled therefore to RECOMMEND that the second alternative, namely, the completed Locomotive and the other four in various stages of construction, should be scrapped and that the authority for their construction as part of the 1948 Locomotive Building Programme should be cancelled.

(Sgd) R. A. Riddles'

In just 44 words then (the final paragraph), the first engine, No 36001, together with her incomplete sisters, was condemned. This time there would be no reprieve.

It was now just a matter of time before more than four years of work was consigned to scrap. All that would be left would be paper and photographic records, and, after what was to come later, BR would no doubt have wished that both of these had been similarly scrapped.

No 36001 is seen alongside the running shed at Eastleigh, where she languished from November 1950 until being scrapped the following April. Bulleid is reputed to have said that had the engine been intended for use on other railways, water pick-up gear and more coal would have been carried. Les Elsey

In the meantime the almost complete No 36002, together with the less complete 36003, had been towed away from Brighton for storage within the confines of the under-used shed at New Cross Gate, on the former Brighton lines in South London, and just 7 miles 3 chains from Victoria, which No 36001 had so vainly tried and failed to reach twice in September 1949. Two 'Leaders' did eventually reach London then – but unfortunately not in steam, and for totally the wrong reasons.

Why move them away from Brighton? Simply put, they were probably a bit of an embarrassment, while 'out of sight, out of mind' could well have applied. Also, it is very likely that the works were short of space, as most works always were, so the logical thing would be to move the two machines away as there was no likelihood of permission being given for their completion. Following a spell then in the metropolis, Nos 36002 and 36003 were again quietly moved away, this time to Bognor Regis shed, where again the same 'out of sight...' view no doubt applied. (Both engines were at Bognor by at least 1 July 1950.) It should also be borne in mind that the whole 'Leader' episode was a 'hot potato', with many former Southern Railway staff at all levels having a strong affinity and consequent sympathy with the man whom they perceived as having put the Southern at the forefront of steam engine development and technology. They did not all take kindly to the curtailment of the project – although much of this

murmured comment was based on hearsay rather than fact. Also, half a century ago the movement of engines to what were then outlying locations such as both New Cross Gate and Bognor Regis meant that tracing their locations was far more difficult than would be the case in today's communications revolution.

Despite the wealth of detail relating to the movements of No 36001 almost from its birth and certainly up to 2 November 1950, no such detail is available for Nos 36002/3. Did they move together? Were they moved under cover of darkness? Were they sheeted over for the movement? All these questions are now unlikely to be answered, even from contemporary observations by members of the likes of the RCTS and SLS.

Eventually, and without further fuss, Nos 36002 and 36003 were again towed back to Brighton, where they were summarily dispatched by the cutter's torch. Once more the date of this is not known, although No 36003 was recorded being shunted by the Works 'Terrier' at Brighton on 23 May 1951, possibly succumbing shortly afterwards. Likewise, the incomplete No 36004 – mainframe and boiler, together with the remaining parts intended for 36005 – was reduced to scrap.

No 36001 herself languished alongside the running shed at Eastleigh until 25 April 1951, when she was towed the short distance to the neighbouring works and quietly dismantled. (This was the month after the demise of

Left: **The wait was now almost over, and this time there would be no reprieve. No 36001 is in its last days before being dismantled, with the doors chained and padlocked. The engine's final mileage is open to some doubt, but something between 6,000 and 7,117 may be considered as realistic. Despite its now proven appetite for coal and water, the other commodity that was used to excess was oil; No 36001 used – or more accurately wasted – more oil for lubrication alone than a later diesel engine would use in fuel over a comparable distance.** A. E. West

Below left: **It was also the end for** *Hartland Point.* **At a time before souvenir-hunters would unreasonably steal anything they could, the engine still retains its name- and numberplates on the Eastleigh 'dump' on 27 February 1951.** A. E. West

Right: **John Click was a thorough Bulleid devotee. An engineer by profession, he was involved with a number of the 'Leader' trials as well as later being seconded by BR to Ireland where he worked on the 'Turfburner'. A man of strong convictions, it is to be regretted that his own story of his days with Bulleid was never written.**

Below: **The engine record card for No 36001.**

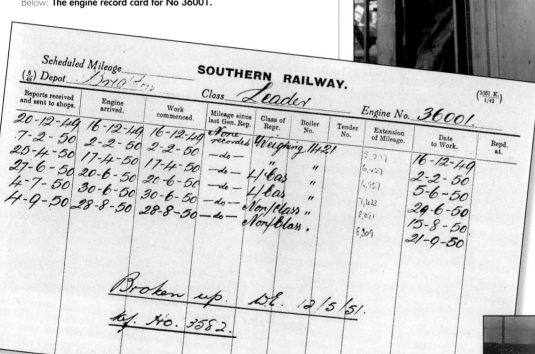

Below: **'Leader class engine in service'** was the slightly incorrect caption used by Bulleid when this view accompanied his article in the American journal *Mechanical Engineering.* **'Leader'** is actually preparing to depart from Brighton on trial – hardly 'in service'. National Railway Museum

Hartland Point, which, as recounted earlier, was also dispatched at Eastleigh Works.) The boiler of 'Leader' was lifted off the frame, and when separated from the engine there were clear signs of heat distortion to the dry sides. The actual cutting up occupied a number of weeks (it was the practice to work on any number of engines at the same time, while men would also be called away to assist in other areas when required). It was stated that certain parts, possibly the roller-bearings from the bogies, remained by the oil store until at least 1959/60.

At least one numberplate from both Nos 36001 and 36002 survived, together with the brass whistle from No 36001; the latter was for many years in the hands of the redoubtable Harry Frith from Eastleigh.

One puzzling aspect of the final days of the 'Leader' is the rumour – perhaps far more than rumour – that Bulleid, ensconced as he was by the spring of 1950 in his office at

Inchicore, contacted BR *with a view to the purchase of the whole class for shipment to Ireland.* This was confirmed to the present author in correspondence with the late Don Bradley, although unfortunately he passed away before further discussion on the subject could occur. There is no other information to either prove or disprove this quite amazing point of conjecture; the only other person who might have had knowledge of the subject was the late John Click, who was unwilling to discuss the matter.

What is known is that a small delegation from Inchicore visited Brighton some time after November 1949, more likely during the summer of 1950. The reason is probably easy to understand: Bulleid was already working towards what might loosely and a bit unfairly be described as 'Leader Mk 2' (the 'Turfburner'). Perhaps he was considering adapting or modifying the existing Brighton-built engines rather than starting from scratch. At least he would have had a complete class to start with, rather than just a single example, which was what of course occurred! Make no mistake about it – the Irish 'Turfburner' was a success as well. (The story of that locomotive is fully described in the book by Ernie Shepherd – details are in the Bibliography.) Whether Bulleid also wished to have the prototype, No 36001, is unclear, but probably not. The fact that the delegation went to Brighton is also interesting, although it was probably because there was something there to see as well as people who had sufficient knowledge and who were in sufficient authority.

In the event, no deal was struck. It would be unfair to say that this was because BR would not sell – it might have been that Dublin would not pay the price. Or it could have been that the engines were simply deemed unsuitable and required too much modification. Unfortunately, unless anything is discovered amongst contemporary BR or CIE papers, it is unlikely that any more light will ever be cast on the matter.

Bulleid had clearly not abandoned the theory of this type of double-bogie engine, with many of the same theoretical advantages of diesel and electric locomotives. Indeed, it was a theme he developed at a lecture to the American Society of Mechanical Engineers in New York in October 1949:

'The first of these new engines has run about 4,000 miles. Steam locomotive development has always been handicapped by the absence of proper testing facilities. We have to build the complete locomotive before we can try it and the trials can only be made out on the road. As is to be expected some troubles have arisen, such as broken ends to the sleeve valves and spalling [splintering] of the firebrick casing of the firebox, troubles which are being overcome. The engine has shown already the advantage of a double-bogie locomotive as regards freedom of running, ease in taking curves, and the great value of having the total weight available for traction and braking.'

The fact that he was pushing ahead at Inchicore should really be proof enough, but despite his age – he was already

68 in 1950 – Bulleid was clearly determined that the message of continued steam locomotive development would continue to be heralded to as wide an audience as possible.

This was further confirmed in an article by him that appeared in the American journal *Mechanical Engineering* in 1950 under the title 'Locomotive and Rolling Stock Developments in Great Britain'. In all probability the draft had been submitted some time in 1949, as the article was accompanied by a photograph of No 36001 on a train at Brighton station, clearly on a test run. The caption accompanying the view – presumably also prepared by Bulleid – was, however, somewhat misleading: 'Leader class engine in service'. (I think it is possible to forgive the man this indiscretion – at the time the article was prepared it was probably still expected that the class would indeed enter service. Nowhere has it been found that Bulleid acted other than in an honest and straightforward way.)

Even more interesting were two sections within the article describing both the 'Leader' design and the way in which Bulleid hoped to see steam traction taken forward:

'While in American eyes this is a small engine, its horsepower will be about 1,700 and consequently it will give as good results as a Diesel-Electric locomotive with a 2,000hp engine. How successful we have been in the new design remains to be seen, but the new features in the engine should give us better service, help to improve the performance of the steam locomotive and restore steam traction to favour.'

In view of what was already happening on the railways of America at this time, Bulleid's comments are slightly strange. His was already a 'voice in the wilderness', for steam across the Atlantic was even then being 'retired' (the American term for what we would call 'scrapped'). So at whom was Bulleid aiming his comments?

However, to emphasise his own personal belief in a future for steam, there followed clues as to what was still to come. In this it may be inferred that Bulleid already knew that under a nationalised regime and without his own guiding hand British Railways would never allow 'Leader' to work in traffic, although in his own mind he still intended to pursue his ideals further:

'While in the Leader class of engine the developments of the steam locomotive have been carried a stage further, there is still much work to be done. The use of blast to create draft should give way to fans so that we can control the production of steam accurately. The exhaust steam should not be allowed to escape to the atmosphere but should be returned to the boiler. Experimental work already done encourages the thought that these two problems can be solved, and I commend them to young engineers as worthy of investigation. I shall feel more than recompensed if I have shown that while the Stephenson locomotive may in some circumstances be dead or dying, this cannot be said of steam traction itself. If new designs be developed in the light of our present greater knowledge, and the servicing of the locomotive be brought up to date – in short, if only we can demolish the conservatism which is destroying the steam locomotive rather than give up any of its customary ways – then we can look forward to a revival of steam traction.'

(Elsewhere the article contained references to developments on the Southern Railway in particular, but while Bulleid's ideas and influence come to the fore once again, there was nothing else particularly radical.)

So, Bulleid clearly felt that steam could be developed, and what was to become the 'Turfburner' would be just another step along the way. Interestingly he states 'experimental work already done encourages thought that these two problems can be solved' – meaning the control of the blast by fans and exhaust steam being returned to the boiler. But where exactly had this been done? Certainly not during Bulleid's time on the Southern. The experiments with SR No A816 (1930-35) had been along similar lines, but were *before* Bulleid's time at Waterloo.

Elsewhere engineers were generally facing up to the fact that it was potentially easier to pursue a course of dieselisation and eventually electrification. There was also no doubt as to the political pressure in this area, and while a number of skilled steam engineers were still to come, in reality the days of the steam designer being consider pre-eminent were rapidly drawing to a close – with one exception, and not this time Bulleid.

At the risk of ignoring a number of contemporary skilled and competent engineers (who, given the opportunity, time and resources that had been available to their forebears, would no doubt have pushed steam further), there was probably only one other engineer contemporary with Bulleid who had the foresight and wisdom to make the case for steam in the modern world. That man was of course the legendary André Chapelon in France, who – in very cruel summary terms – used compounding and extremely free steam and exhaust passages to transform an already good steam engine into one that could only be described as phenomenal. What Chapelon did was to raise power output to figures almost unheard of within the French loading gauge – *5,000 horsepower at the cylinders*, an equivalent 4,000 drawbar horsepower at 50mph. What was even more remarkable were the coal consumption figures, never more than 2.64lb per hp/hr. The grate also showed itself able to develop 1,000hp per square metre. Truly this was a remarkable machine and, according to the Chapelon team, far from the limit that could in fact be achieved. On the drawing-board there were already plans for a 6,000hp steam engine. Another stunning fact is that all this was achieved back in 1946, with France still suffering the ramifications of war and occupation. While this book paints a picture of Bulleid as a man ahead of his time, he was very much behind the times when compared with the likes of Chapelon.

Unfortunately, in France politics would also play its part. The opportunity existed to both rebuilt and re-equip the French railway system after its battering during the years of conflict. In many cases this was the equivalent of a 'blank canvas', a fact that was not lost on the politicians of the day, and steam development was curtailed. Chapelon had shown it could be done, but it was not politically prudent, particularly in light of the fact that his steam engine and other projected designs would outperform any potential new electric locomotive then planned to be built. No, steam had to be seen as outmoded. Chapelon's other projected designs never got further than the drawing-board.

Regarding power output, it should be remembered that in the UK arguably the very best steam engines were Stanier's 'Duchess' Pacifics (and in saying so, I know I am entering the lion's den!). But even Stanier could not even approach the efficiency of Chapelon. The maximum output by a 'Duchess' was in the order of 3,000hp, still far short of what was taking place across the Channel.

Bulleid had long admired both the French nation and the abilities of its engineers. He was also fluent in the language, and had long maintained what was probably more than a professional contact with André Chapelon, the two men sharing a great admiration and friendship. It will be remembered that Chapelon travelled on the 'Leader' while the engine was on test from Brighton, and was reported to take a particular interest in the sleeve valves and firebox. Paradoxically it may be considered a little strange that Bulleid had not incorporated any of the French principles in the 'Leader' design.

Leaving aside the prospect of the further development of steam in both Ireland and France, with the 'Leader' project now cancelled and the engines physically no more, it could be reasonably expected that the experiment would be forgotten. But no – it was not long before murmurings concerning the whole project were being aired in certain of the more technical and professional railway periodicals.

It would only be a matter of time before the obvious blunt questions were being asked, as in the *Railway Gazette* of 25 May 1951, when an anonymous correspondent (but reported as writing from Woking) asked the perfectly fair question:

'I wonder if an appeal could be made through your columns for more information about this design? I know of no official information or photographs published about this interesting class [today it is of course well known that both existed in quantity], although it is now two years since the first one appeared from Brighton Works. As far as my information goes only one "Leader" class locomotive has ever been steamed and that has been lying out of use in the open at Eastleigh since early November. If this locomotive design is unfortunately unsuccessful there may be an attempt in official quarters to forget that it ever existed as has happened in the past with some experimental designs. It seems odd that the extensive trials with this locomotive should appear to have been abandoned just when they appeared to be meeting with a fair measure of success. The locomotive apparently made several quite successful runs to Woking about October last year.'

Who, I wonder, was this anonymous correspondent – although perhaps one shouldn't expect to find a serpent under very stone that is turned over! It could indeed just have been a genuinely interested outside party. British Railways did reply, but the response was curt:

'...for varying technical reasons the experiments with the prototype "Leader" class locomotive were not as satisfactory as had been hoped and to obviate the expense which would be involved in continuing them for a problematical return, it has been decided not to proceed further with this novel design.'

It was a fair and honest response, even if BR was now clearly on the defensive; words had to be chosen very carefully or they might possibly be turned against it. Unfortunately also the response is not credited to a particular individual.

There was still a marked degree of secrecy over the design, the costs, the trials and the reasons for curtailment. The formal report from the dynamometer car tests and the accompanying Riddles reports would not be made public for a further 30 years, during which time a number of incorrect and totally spurious allegations would be made and allowed to fester.

With hindsight the best option might have been to go on the offensive from the start. There were far fewer 'radical' journalists then compared with today, and 'trial by media' was fortunately still some way in the future. Indeed, certain of the 'Leader' ideas would be utilised in the future. The body-to-bogie mounting without a central pivot, with the body instead resting on 'Mintex' pads, was successfully copied for the SR-built diesel-electric designs Nos 10201-3. Some years later it was likewise copied for the first-generation main-line diesel-electric locomotives of what became Classes 40, 44, 45 and 46. Similarly the axlebox 'dashpot' springing was adapted for what was to become the BR Mk 6 bogie used under a number of electric multiple-unit vehicles including the '4REP' sets.

It was even thought that the 60 roller-bearings from the 'Leader' bogies might find use on the crank axles of the Bulleid 'Q1' design, which had a propensity to run hot, but in the end this was not pursued, due, it was stated, to the amount of modification required. This is perhaps strange, as at that time steam traction was still being projected well into the future and modernisation plans were still some years ahead; indeed, even after the latter had been formulated there would still be major expense on a considerable number of steam engines, notably the rebuilding of a number of Bulleid Pacifics.

But the whole 'Leader' project refused to lie down, even if according to official sources the subject was now closed.

It seems that neither Waterloo nor Marylebone was prepared to comment further, and maybe Eastleigh and Brighton had been told to do likewise. Yet slightly less than two years later the story against burst into the open in the form of the front page of the *Sunday Dispatch*. At this point it might be best to quote Bulleid's 1964 biographer, Sean Day-Lewis, who treats the episode in an honest and unbiased manner:

'The supreme irony came two years later ... when the Sunday Dispatch, a failing conservative newspaper, was suddenly tipped off about the story of the "Leader" class and decided that this was a magnificent stick with which to beat the concept of nationalisation – not because British Railways shelved the project, but because they did not do so earlier. It was the custom of such papers to find a story of this kind each week and blow it up to dominate the front page – no matter how old and stale the information. The "Leader" was certainly given the full treatment with a banner headline in thick letters, an inch deep:

"£500,000 WASTED ON THREE USELESS ENGINES RAILWAYS' BIGGEST FIASCO THEY TRIED TO HUSH IT UP!

Three huge railway engines, which cost altogether about £500,000 to build, now lie rusting and useless in sheds and sidings – silent and hidden evidence of the biggest fiasco produced by Britain's nationalised railways.

This situation comes to light as the result of *Sunday Dispatch* inquiries, prompted by the threatened increase in fares and allegations of mismanagement on the railways.

The engines, 67ft long monsters of the Leader class, with driving cabins at each end, were built in 1948 and 1949 to 'revolutionise' rail travel.

They were part of a £750,000 experiment undertaken by Mr O. V. Bulleid, chief mechanical engineer of British Railways, Southern Region.

I can reveal that the region's officials regard the experiment as one of their biggest failures.

It was a failure that had been hushed up.

From the start the plan to build Mr Bulleid's dream loco was kept secret.

But news leaked out late in 1948, when the designer gave the British Association some details of 'a revolutionary steam locomotive'.

The first of the Leaders, known to railwaymen as No 36001, was then being built at the Southern Region works in Brighton. It started its trials in 1949, and work began immediately on the other two.

From start to finish the 'revolutionary' gave trouble. Workers at the Eastleigh (Hants) sheds frequently saw No 36001 being towed back for repair by an 'old fashioned' engine.

The *Sunday Dispatch* for 18 January 1953 – inaccurate and sensationalist journalism at its worst.

Sunday Dispatch

152nd Year. No. 7,889. 2½d.

JANUARY 18, 1953.

Radio Page 6.

£500,000 Wasted On Three Useless Engines

RAILWAYS' BIGGEST FIASCO

They Tried To Hush It Up

By Sunday Dispatch Reporter

THREE huge railway engines, which cost altogether about £500,000 to build, now lie rusting and useless in sheds and sidings—silent and hidden evidence of the biggest fiasco produced by Britain's nationalised railways.

This situation comes to light as the result of *Sunday Dispatch* inquiries, prompted by the threatened increase in fares and allegations of mis-management on the railways.

The engines, 67ft.-long monsters of the Leader class, with driving cabins at each end, were built in 1948 and 1949 to "revolutionise" rail travel.

They were part of a £750,000 experiment undertaken by Mr. O. V. Bulleid, chief mechanical engineer of British Railways, Southern Region.

I can reveal that the region's officials regard the experiment as one of their biggest failures.

It was a failure that had been hushed up.

From the start the plan to build Mr. Bulleid's dream loco was kept secret.

But news leaked out late in 1948, when the designer gave the British Association some details of a revolutionary steam locomotive.

The first of the Leaders, known to railwaymen as No. 36001, was then being built at the Southern Region works in Brighton. It started its trials in 1949, and work began immediately on the other two.

One of the Leader class locomotives.

Towed Back

From start to finish the revolutionary "gave trouble. Workers at the Eastleigh (Hants) sheds frequently saw No. 36001 being towed back for repair by an old-fashioned engine.

Firemen who worked aboard her during the test period reported the Leader was the most uncomfortable loco on the track.

Ventilation in the centre portion, where they stoked in a corridor running between the two driving cabins, was very poor.

One worker told me:—"We knew the three Leaders as 'The White Elephants.' Some who had ridden in them used less polite descriptions."

"Frequently the 'Flying Tramcar,' as others called her, broke down.

Two In One

"She was a streamlined job with no smoke stacks visible. New everything about her was new in design. The Leader was one of the most expensive locos ever built.

'ARISTOCRACY DOOMED AND DAMNED'

Shinwell Outburst Over The Coronation Plans

A FORMER Socialist Minister of Defence and Secretary of State for War, Mr. Emanuel Shinwell, yesterday attacked Coronation arrangements.

He said, at Halesowen, Worcestershire, that he had the highest respect for the young Queen and wished her long life and a successful reign. But when he read that the standard-bearers at the Coronation were all from the aristocracy, and particularly from the military, he wondered at it all.

We were in a democratic age and wanted this age to usher in an era of peace.

What more appropriate than that the Queen should be accompanied by her friends and by those who represented the scientific world, the medical profession, the nurses, miners, farm-workers, steel-workers, the railwaymen.

They were the salt of the earth. He hoped those in authority would give a thought to the changes of the last 50 years and realise that aristocracy was "doomed and also damned."

FARES-RISE NOW MAY BE QUERIED AT WESTMINSTER

By GUY EDEN, Sunday Dispatch Political Correspondent

THE Transport Commission...

Police Ask To Free On Theft

A MAN who had sworn he was 250 miles away at the time of the crime for which he had been arrested was released from prison yesterday after action to get his bail reduced.

"Information has come to hand which, if it had arrived earlier, would have resulted in this man's release," a detective-sergeant told the West London...

ALARM OVER 'LOST' MAILBAG THAT WASN'T LOST AFTER ALL

By Sunday Dispatch Reporter

THE Mystery of the Missing Mailbag of Reading Station was solved late last night!

But only after detectives and G.P.O. officials had searched frantically for a clue—and only after someone at Reading Station had the good sense to count the mailbags which were left there.

Firemen who worked aboard her during the test period reported the Leader was the most uncomfortable loco on the track.

Ventilation in the centre portion, where they stoked in a corridor running between the two driving cabs, was very poor.

One worker told me: 'We all knew the three Leaders as "The White Elephants".' Some who had ridden in them used less polite descriptions.

'Frequently the "Flying Tramcar", as others called her, broke down.

'She was chain-driven – immense chains more than two feet wide were completely enclosed in an oil bath. They caused endless trouble.

'She was a streamlined job with no smoke stacks visible. Nearly everything about her was new in design. Leader was one of the most expensive locos ever built.

'She carried four tons of coal and 4,000 gallons of water. The familiar trailing tender was done away with. She was, in effect, two locos back-to-back encased in steel with one central firing point.'

Railway maintenance workers, annoyed at attacks being made on them, say the money lost on this experiment could have been better spent improving their working conditions.

Mr Bulleid, the designer of the Leaders, is now working in Eire.

FOOTNOTE: Nobody seems to have told British Railways' own magazine the story of locos 36001, 36002 and 36003. This month's issue gives pride of place to a review of the five years since nationalisation. Proudly the writer praises the unified building of locomotives, carriages and wagons. Large-scale production has, he says, 'considerably lowered the cost by millions of pounds'."

'Next day the *Daily Telegraph* followed up the story and got the amount of money spent on this experiment into rather better perspective:

"NOVEL ENGINE SCRAPPED
BRITISH RAILWAYS £150,000 TEST

A £150,000 experiment by British Railways to produce a revolutionary type of steam engine has been abandoned. The prototype, and two other partly finished engines of a new class of thirty to be called the Leader, have been broken up at the Southern Region Works, Brighton.

The engine was designed by Mr O. V. Bulleid, when he was Chief Mechanical Engineer of the Southern Railway. Later he became consultant chief mechanical engineer to the Irish Railways.

A British Railways spokesman said yesterday: 'The engine went on trial runs, but did not come up to expectation. Meanwhile a second was nearly completed and the framework of a third was built. All three have been scrapped.'

Firemen complained during the tests that they had to work under stifling conditions. But Mr Bulleid, now living in Eire, denied last night that the design was radically wrong.

'The locomotive was intended to meet the competition of electric engines, but built to use coal, the nation's fuel,' he said.

'It was almost an enclosed box, with a driving cabin at each end, going right across the engine. In the middle was space for the fireman with a corridor at the side joining the two ends. The boiler was completely welded and was the first of its kind produced in an English railway shop.

'It did not require turntables or go into the sheds before starting on a return journey. During the trial run out of Brighton station, the acceleration was superb.'

Mr Bulleid said he left the railways after nationalisation 'because I did not approve of it and when I was offered a post in Ireland I was pleased to accept.

'In my opinion, there was little wrong with the Leader. The tragedy was that it was built two years too late.' "

Presumably Bulleid had been contacted by the *Daily Telegraph* and asked to respond. His reply, if quoted correctly and not out of context, is perhaps slightly sad, giving the impression of a man divorced from reality.

So who then had tipped off the press? That is something we will again probably never know. It can be said with certainty, though, that it would not have been British Railways. According to Day-Lewis: '"Why should we wash our dirty linen in public?" is the official British Railways attitude, "The whole thing is still dynamite..."'

While the *Daily Telegraph* may have been basically correct in its report, no doubt provided with salient facts by a defensive British Railways, the *Sunday Dispatch* report displayed an example of investigative journalism at the opposite end of the spectrum. The damage was done, and while factually the matter may have been put straight, the readership of the *Dispatch* was hardly the same as that of the *Telegraph*. Thus was born the rumour, misconception, inaccurate reporting and outright criticism of almost everything Bulleid had ever had a hand in designing.

In his 1960 book *Unusual Locomotives*, Ernest F. Carter did his best to condemn the designer as a whole: '...in 1946/7, about 40 years after Sir Cecil Paget's grim experience with his unique locomotive, Bulleid's ill-fated six-cylindered "Leader" burst like a bombshell on the locomotive engineering world. He had defied traditional design and produced an engine which was as ugly as it was unconventional and as difficult to manipulate as it was inefficient. It was the first and last of its class and was broken up, its designer becoming Chief Mechanical Engineer of the Irish railways on the nationalisation of the British lines.'

Aside from a brief couple of sentences on the rebuilding of the Pacifics, that was it. The work and ideals of Bulleid condensed to less than a single page in a volume running to more than 200 pages.

Some years later, in 1987, G. Freeman Allen, in his

book *The Southern Since 1948*, begins what is, to be fair, a reasonable account of the project with the phrase: 'The genesis of this final definitely iconoclastic concept was the railway's immediate post-war requirement of more large-sized tank engines...' Unfortunately thereafter the facts are supplemented by the well-known criticisms of the design, although Freeman Allen does make one very interesting point at the end when referring to the controversy surrounding the *Sunday Dispatch* article of 1953: 'And so it went on, not forgetting, naturally, to give management/labour relations any disruptive stir the opportunity offered.' He quotes from the article, 'Railway maintenance workers, annoyed at attacks being made on them, say the money lost on this experiment could have been better spent improving their working conditions,' then adds, 'A likely story, when one reflects on the railway unions' anxiety two and three decades later to see the money invested in APT's painful development not cut off, far from it, but greatly increased.' In this last statement Freeman Allen may well be correct, but he was applying a 1980s perspective to a project of 30 years earlier.

Finally, in more recent times, Michael Rutherford, writing in the November 2005 issue of *Backtrack*, in an article on F. W. Hawksworth at Swindon, is of the opinion that, referring to an engineer who has 'spent all his working life in a drawing office environment or only one step removed from it ... Such a man is likely, when given the power, to either release all the pent-up frustrations of his early career by becoming wildly radical (as with the case with Oliver Bulleid) or to heed his works and operating subordinates who are inevitably conservative, wishing to keep things as they are and known and to change things either very slowly or imperceptibly.'

So was Bulleid indeed radical, or is that a slightly excessive description? Hawksworth could even be said to have been radical in the use of a 280psi boiler pressure on the 4-6-0 'County' class. Indeed, according to a discussion between the present author and the late A. C. (Tony) Sterndale, who was in the drawing office at Swindon at the time, Hawksworth is purported to have included the high boiler pressure simply because 'if it was good enough for Bulleid then it is good enough for us'. Perhaps it is all a matter of degree.

None of the three authors singled out has written anything incorrect, and any writer recording facts is perfectly entitled to his opinion; it is by assessing such opinion that a new perspective can sometimes be obtained. What is wrong is where an incorrect assessment and therefore opinion has been made that is then subsequently perpetuated (not, it should be said, by any of the three gentlemen mentioned above).

Interestingly, it does not appear that any of the other Sunday or daily newspapers picked up on the story back in 1953, while contemporary news reports, let alone movie footage of the engine while on trial, are conspicuous by their absence. Any news story will attract a finite amount of interest (in the days that followed the same newspapers were dominated by the inauguration of Eisenhower as US President, while at home the debate raged over the soon-to-be-executed police killer Derek Bentley). The story of 'Leader' quickly went cold, and perhaps just as well, for in Ireland, where British newspaper headlines seemed to have only limited effect, Bulleid might well have caused further uproar by unequivocally pronouncing, *à propos* 'Leader', that 'we will probably do something of the sort over here' (a distinct reference to the future 'Turfburner').

Returning to the *Daily Telegraph* report, and in particular the alleged quote by Bulleid that 'The locomotive was intended to meet the competition of electric engines, but built to use coal, the nation's fuel,' therein lies one of the continuing debates over 'Leader' – whether it was intended to burn oil rather than coal. Over the years many people have made reference to the fact that 'Leader' was intended to burn oil, but where is the evidence? Nowhere is it mentioned in official SR records, nor in Riddles's report. Indeed, the only known reference to suggest oil-firing is in some handwritten notes within the papers of the late John Click and now deposited at York. Here there is a distinct reference that oil was the fuel that Bulleid had intended, although unfortunately the note is undated, but it continues that the Traffic Department itself was opposed to the suggestion. The note probably dates from around 1948, before No 36001 had ever steamed but well into the design stage. The sheer awkwardness of firing the engine, with its offset firedoor, would seem to indicate that coal-firing was very much an afterthought.

Would oil-firing have made a difference? Certainly the disadvantages of oil were the smell, excess smoke if the burner and air flow were not correctly adjusted, potential leakage, and variations in temperature created within the firebox when the oil was reignited after the firebox had cooled down. While this latter aspect could never be totally avoided even in 'Leader', Bulleid had gone some way towards dealing with the problem with the dry-sided firebox. 'Leader' would in many ways have been an ideal test-bed for oil-firing; she was already running on trial in November 1949 when 'West Country' No 34036 was converted back from oil to coal-firing. It is perhaps a pity that oil was not pursued for No 36001; it might not have changed history, but it might have made it a bit more palatable.

In conclusion, therefore, with a fair proportion of the test runs reported as failures, there was little choice for Riddles and the Railway Executive but to condemn the 'Leader' project. As far as is known, only two writers have either had access to or cared to study the BR reports on the engine and trials – J. G. Chacksfield and the present writer – although prior to 1985 the official reports were not publicly accessible, excusing some past inaccuracies. It might be assumed that, with access to those reports, little else could be added. But something else has now appeared, which – albeit incomplete – casts new doubt on the

[Memorandum – 16 September 1949]

MEMORANDUM FOR:- Assistant to Superintendent of Operation.

Trial Trips of "Leader" Class Engine
Friday 16th September, 1949.

The arrangements made for the running of the above trips as shown in L.C.D. Special Notice No.944, were satisfactory. The train was formed of 5 passenger coaches and 4 vans, weight 249 tons.

Running was satisfactory, times as follows:-

	Booked	Actual	Booked	Actual
Brighton	9.50	9.56	2.22	2.26
Kemp Town Jct.	9/53	9/59	2/25	2/29
Palmer	10/2	10/2	2/37	2/40
Lewes	10/7	10/16	2/49	2/52
Culver Jct.	10/12	10/25	3.5	3.3
Uckfield	10/19	10.35		
Crowborough	10.33			

The late starts from Brighton were due to late arrival of engine.

X Stop at Lewes was to pick up the Chief Mechanical Engineer.

	Booked	Actual	Booked	Actual
Crowborough	11. 7	11.47	4/19	4/13
Uckfield	11/21	11/28	4/26	4/32
Culver Jct.	11/35	11/42	4/32	4/42
Lewes	11/44	11/58	4/46	4.49
Palmer	11/49	12. 0		
Kemp Town Jct.	11.52			
Brighton				

The 10 minutes late start with the 11. 7am trip was due to difficulty in uncoupling, the engine being unable to take water.

There was no need for the engine to take water. Brighton, throughout.

Engine 36001. Driver Long. Brighton, first trip.
Guard P. Gully, Brighton " second trip.
Guard Humphrey "

20½" Vacuum were maintained throughout.

A E G
H

T.W.
17th September, 1949.
MH

[Memorandum – 19 September 1949]

MEMORANDUM - ASST. TO SUPT. OF OPERATION.

Trial Trips of Leader Class Engine, Monday,
19th September, 1949.

The running of the trips from Brighton to Crowborough and back were very satisfactory.

Engine 36001, Driver Long, Brighton.

The 9.50am Brighton and return was formed of 5 passenger coaches and 2 vans, weight 180 tons, Guard Mills, Brighton.

The 2.22pm Brighton and return was formed of 5 passenger coaches and 4 vans, weight 217 tons.

Running was as under :-

	Booked Arr. Dep. a.m.	Actual Arr. Dep. a.m.	Booked Arr. Dep. p.m.	Actual Arr. Dep. p.m.
Brighton	9.50	9.50	2.22	2.21
Kemp Town Jc.	9.55	9.53 (sigs)		
Palmer	9 58	9 58	2 25	2 27
Lewes	10 7	10 5	2 30	2 35
Culver Jc.	10 12	10 11	2 44	2 40
Uckfield	10 19	10 16	2 51	2 48 (check)
Crowborough	10.33	10 22 (distant on) 5. 5	5. 5	3. 2
		10.32		
Crowborough	11. 7	11. 7		4. 4
Uckfield	11 21	11 18	4 19	4 15
Culver Jc.	11 28	11.24 11.28 (sigs)	4 26	4 22
Lewes	11 35	11.35 11.36	4 32	4 32 (sigs)
Palmer	11 44	11 45	4 41	4 41
Kemp Town Jc.	11 49	11 49	4 47	4 47
Brighton	11.52	11.52	4.49	4.53 (3 mins. home signal)

A E Gaylard
H.O. Inspr.

T.W.
22nd September, 1949.

information in the official report.

It would appear that Brighton kept another record of the trials run, and what has survived are details of the tests, timings, delays, etc, that took place on 5, 8, 16, 19 and 20 September 1949. The first two dates are of interest as these were the intended trials to Victoria, so we now have details of the actual running, the problems encountered en route, and the reason why both runs were terminated early – likewise the Crowborough run of 20 September. Each of these three trials was officially regarded as a failure for various reasons. That of 5 September was also covered by the useful and comprehensive report by 'H. O. Inspector' E. Walton, which included the damning sentence, 'Engine berthed in Workshops at Brighton and as far as I am concerned have no desire to see it again.' The full text of the report together with the timings for the runs on the three days were included earlier in the chapter.

But it is what was written by Brighton concerning the runs of 16 and 19 September that really raises questions. In the official report later presented to Riddles all of the five runs mentioned by date were regarded as failures, piling up evidence against 'Leader', part of which was later used to condemn it. Yet, and according to the Brighton report for 16 September, 'Running was satisfactory', and even more so on the 19th: 'The running of the trips from Brighton to Crowborough and back were very satisfactory'.

In view of the importance of these comments, the originals of both days' records are reproduced here.

If the runs of 16 and 19 September were after all successful and not failures, how many more might have been likewise? How many more trips were similarly condemned and used as justification for the project to be cancelled? This is a bold accusation to make, and I do not accuse any person of deliberately manipulating the records. However, Riddles could only form his conclusions on the evidence presented to him, and if that evidence was flawed then perhaps an incorrect decision was arrived at.

Without access to records of all the runs, it is both unsafe and unwise to make further allegations, but is proof that two of the runs at least were not as previously viewed. Those two runs would not on their own have made a difference, and there were some spectacular failures later, so no one can pretend that the difficulties with the sleeve valves, crank axle, weight and firebox lining did not occur. But how many other runs might have been regarded in some quarters as at least satisfactory and in others as failures? Perhaps it depended on which side of the fence the judgement was made, and from which side the report submitted to Riddles was compiled. The Traffic and Chief Mechanical Engineering departments seem to have had different judgemental criteria, which might go some way to explain why the telegrams sent to Bulleid while he was away appeared at variance with the official reports.

What is likewise puzzling is the fact that while these contradictions were occurring – in the autumn of 1949 – Bulleid was still notionally involved. Perhaps the designer himself was being kept away from reality.

[1] Townroe completed more than one book on the classes mentioned, as well as a joint work with Cecil J. Allen on Bulleid's Pacifics (1951 and 1976). All are recommended reading. Townroe was also the author of an authoritative account on bicycle repairing, although this is, perhaps understandably, less familiar to the majority of railway scholars.

CHAPTER FOUR

So was Bulleid Right or Wrong?

No matter what follows in this chapter, there will still be dispute at the end. Slightly more than five decades have passed since the physical conclusion of the 'Leader' project. It is almost six decades since the end of the Southern Railway, and four decades since the end of Southern steam. The problem therefore arises of how to deal with the controversy surrounding a design that today would easily be seen as obsolete from the outset – a design that, with our present-day knowledge, would never have got beyond the drawing-board, probably not even progressed as far as a set of working drawings.

Thus, to answer the question 'Was Bulleid right or wrong?' we must view the circumstances one by one as they existed all those years ago. Comparisons with the present-day railway system will only cloud our judgement.

To start with, let us look at Bulleid himself – a skilled and competent engineer without doubt, but was he one of the great engineers? That is a matter of personal opinion; if you believe that the development of steam by Bulleid with his Pacific and 'Q1' designs was successful, the answer will clearly be in the affirmative. If he is judged by 'Leader' alone, the reverse might be the case.

But Bulleid was not the only Chief Mechanical Engineer to have experimented. Throughout railway history there have been numerous examples of designs that either failed or came close to failure at an early stage, including some promoted by outside builders, as for example the various turbine machines of the 1920s and '30s. Webb, Dean, Drummond, Paget, Gresley, Thompson – they all tried and sometimes failed in one area or another. What often happened was that matters were left to a successor to make the most of his predecessor's designs.

Bulleid did this with some of the Maunsell creations, and Jarvis did it with the Bulleid Pacifics – in terms of efficiency in operation and maintenance. So could something have been made of 'Leader', either by Bulleid or his successor, British Railways?

At this stage we must once again consider the political and economical climate that existed at that time. For some years I was personally of the opinion that had the Southern Railway continued as a private company and nationalisation had not occurred, 'Leader' would either have been made to succeed or, as actually happened, it would have dragged its designer to similar oblivion. But other designers had got it wrong in the past without incurring such drastic retribution – although in terms of private companies, shareholders' money was at stake – while the order for an additional 31 engines from November 1947 would no doubt have been confirmed.

Thirty-six failures then? Meanwhile Richards at the Traffic Department was making increasing noises about the failure of the CME to deliver the power he so desperately needed – perhaps Bulleid would indeed have disappeared with his creation.

So the next questions must be, could Bulleid (or for that matter Riddles at BR) have made it work? Could it have worked in its existing form? The second is easier to answer – undoubtedly, albeit unfortunately, no. In answer to the first question, however, it must be yes – but at what cost in redesign?

As regards the cost, that is formally recorded. The project consumed a total of £178,865[1], broken down as follows: £40,783 8s 9d attributable to No 36001, £6,427 18s 1d on repairs and maintenance to the same engine, and the balance, £131,653 18s 2d, on the incomplete Nos 36002-5. 'A.F.C.' is of the opinion that if the whole figure had been available for developing just the one prototype, the story might have been different. That was never likely, however, as the Southern would have been unlikely to sanction such a considerable sum on a single engine. Yet compared with costs for alternative contemporary rail traction, the price for 'Leader' was not excessive. The pair of LMS diesel-electric locomotives introduced in 1947/48 were stated as having cost £156,000, although it is not known if this included development or just production costs. (The breakdown between costs incurred before and after nationalisation is also not known.)

Bulleid had intended his engine to be a go-anywhere, do-anything steam engine. Freed from the constraints of a design specifically for passenger, goods or shunting roles, 'Leader' could in theory accomplish all with equal ease. In some respects the same could be said for any large(ish) design, but the practicalities of a 'Castle', 'Merchant Navy', 'Duchess' or 'A4' performing such roles might be questioned (although it did happen towards the end of steam, when scheduling meant that there was just not enough work for former express designs, which explains why so many specifically designed express classes were retired earlier than 'lesser' engines.)

'Leader' was intended to be a 'maid of all work', yet at the same time Bulleid wanted to improve upon former designs, but combining the two aims was in reality a step too far. Having said that, in some respects Riddles and his team did just that with the '9F', producing a machine capable of several roles, even if more by accident than design! In the '9F' there existed a powerful machine equally at home on passenger and goods trains with small wheels yet achieving recorded speeds of at least 90mph on more than one occasion. But in most respects it was a conventional steam engine, albeit one that did not endear itself to many firemen, as all that power required a fair amount of human muscle to generate it. Had Bulleid just worked on the principle of smaller wheels and total adhesion it might have worked, but as we know, that was not enough for the designer.

Dealing with the mechanics first, the obvious place to start is with the sleeve valves. These did not work. They had not worked on the Paget engine, they did not work on *Hartland Point* and they did not work on 'Leader'. To be brutal, it is to the best of the author's belief that the only time sleeve valves have ever been truly successful is in a stationary engine running at almost constant speed. In aircraft they were less than successful, while in the 1950s sleeve valves were attempted in the engine of a 'Daimler' motor car – and that was a failure as well, the progress of the vehicle identified by a trail of blue smoke indicating excessive burning of oil. (Day-Lewis comments that the 'features in common' between Paget's engine and 'Leader' were 'largely coincidental'. In the opinion of the present author, however, the tremendous similarity between the two, being so radical compared with every other steam design, is surely too much to be mere coincidence. In one area, though, Day-Lewis was absolutely right: commenting on the features in common and the reasons for failure, he cites 'the same abortive result brought about by prejudice and lack of funds'.

Bulleid appeared determined to incorporate sleeve valves, for the mistaken but commendable belief that they would increase efficiency and save space and weight. These were indeed the advantages of the type, but subject to the variations in speed, power requirements and vibration associated with railway operation, it was another story. All credit must be given to Bulleid for attempting to design out the likely disadvantages: the inclusion of axial rotation to the sleeves and the copious oil supply should have reduced the likelihood of failure, but they were still not enough. (A note in the files refers to the sleeve valves as originally to have been chrome-plated, but this was 'Cancelled by CME 10/12/48'. But which 'CME' – Bulleid or Riddles?)

In later years Bulleid appears to have accepted that the axial rotation connected to the sleeves was a bad idea. In correspondence between Bulleid and Reg Curl in 1965, the former wrote: 'The oscillating of the sleeves was abandoned because of a lack of time to do the experimental work needed; another side-effect of nationalisation!' Three years later, again writing to Curl but this time from Malta, Bulleid continued on the same theme: 'No one but those closely concerned could know it was the oscillating of the sleeves which caused so much anxiety and meant so many trials. *I often wish I had not listened to the suggestion of ... that this oscillation would ensure proper lubrication of the sleeves as it had in the "Tempest" aeroplane's sleeve valve engine.*' (The italics are the present author's, while the missing name is probably Sir Harry Ricardo).

The number of failures due to wear and seizure was a warning of what was to come. Possibly, as with the Pacifics, he might ideally have wished to incorporate Poppet or Caprotti valve gear, but at that time, although such mechanisms existed, such opportunities were not available to him.

Using three cylinders per bogie – six on the completed engine – would achieve a wonderfully even torque (allied to the provision of the chain drive). Power transfer would be superb – indeed, when it worked it was, while the acceleration could also be 'electric'. Recall the comment 'effortless' when the start from Eastleigh was witnessed on 17 October 1950.

However, to achieve such a smooth power take-off, a multi-cylindered steam engine was essential, and it was the desire to incorporate this that had led to the use of sleeve valves in the first place. There was simply not enough room to use three full sets of Walschaerts or other valve gear between the frames; the maximum would have been two inside cylinders per bogie. There was even a sketch prepared at one stage for a 'split sleeve', in appearance not dissimilar to a Westinghouse air-pump laid on its side. This would have produced the equivalent of six cylinders per bogie, but it was rejected. (The question of the split sleeve was put by the author to the late John Click, and the response was a gruff 'We rejected that very early on.') Using more conventional valve gear but still retaining at least three cylinders per bogie conjures up a vision of a mixture of outside and inside cylinders – but again this must be conjecture. For Riddles to have cured the cylinder problem, a radical redesign of the cylinders and valve gear would have been necessary.

So far everything has been negative, so now let us turn to one of the successes achieved by Bulleid in the new design. The advantage of having a multi-cylindered steam engine has already been discussed, likewise the versatility of small driving wheels. But to supply steam to the power bogies required flexible steam pipes, which had already been successfully developed before – recall the Gresley 'booster', which, it was said, occasionally resulted in 'fog working'. Here Bulleid was successful, although such successes were often conveniently ignored and, as is human nature, overshadowed by the failures.

Let us now turn to the final drive through the chains, axleboxes, pedestal guides and crank axles. All these contributed to both the actual failure and potential failure of the drive axle. Opinions here are again mixed. Having a final drive by chains meant that, in order to incorporate

As was briefly mentioned before, despite its physical size, the headroom inside the driving cabs of 'Leader' was restricted. A personal report by J. M. Dunn in SLS Journal No 483 entitled 'I saw a Leader', confirmed this; he said that he was 5ft 8in tall and was able to stand upright only in the centre, and even then his hair brushed the ceiling. (The floor of the firing compartment was below the box girders that formed the main frames of the machine, so the headroom there was greater.)
Pursey C. Short

Above: **In its undressed state, No 36003 reveals detail of the final drive and axlebox springing at its No 1 end. J. M. Dunn was 'very forcibly' of the opinion that difficulty would be experienced in changing the laminated bearing springs, one above each axlebox. 'These were placed in what I can best describe as cupboards without doors and fitted so snugly that there appeared to be just enough room to get one's hand under the spring. How they would be lifted out of and into place I do not pretend to know. It was a wonderful machine but even if mechanically successful I do not think that enginemen could ever be persuaded to work it regularly. From the point of view of maintenance it was, like other locomotives I have met, presumably never expected to require repairs between its visits to the Works, but as one who has lived with railway engines for nearly 40 years, I have very grave doubts as to how this would work out in practice' – the views of a practical man rather than an ideological dreamer.** Ken Dobson

chains of sufficient strength, it was not possible to use two separate chains, one driving 'fore' and one 'aft', on each side of each bogie. Consequently the drive on each bogie was split – centre axle to front axle on one side, and centre axle to rear axle on the other. The result was an obvious counter-pull across the centre axle. In a static situation, without the machine being subject to the pounding associated with steel-on-steel contact between wheel and track, allied to the inevitable track irregularities that occur at points, crossings and the like, the result was inevitably

undue stress on the three-throw crank axle. Townroe was of the opinion that the problem was compounded by insufficient vertical movement in the horn guides of the centre axle, which may well have been the case, although there is no formal evidence to support such a view.

A further opinion is given by J. M. Dunn (see the Bibliography), who described himself as a 'running shed man'. He felt that 'a standard gauge axle with three cranks of 7½-inch throw looked strangely weak'. A little later, referring to the unsymmetrical final drive, Dunn continued, 'This seemed to me to be a curiously un-mechanical arrangement, which, apart from causing uneven wear in the opposite axleboxes (which were all provided with roller bearings) of all three pairs of wheels, must have put a terrific strain on what appeared to me to be the already weak crank axle.'

Some who wish to criticise Bulleid for the sake of it – not the present author – have suggested that when pressing the wheels onto the end of the crank axles, the space between the webs was either not packed at all, or insufficiently packed with hard timber as was the normal practice. Suspicions have likewise been raised that there were pre-existing faults within the steel used for the axle. Another suggestion blames torsional vibration as the cause, although as the rotating speed was just 272rpm at 60mph this is perhaps unlikely. Whatever the reason, the result was crank axle failure after less than 6,000 miles of running. We cannot be totally certain as to the cause – perhaps a combination of the above-mentioned factors – and consequently the necessary cure. In any event, here was another necessary major redesign, perhaps incorporating

coupling rods in place of chains, although the advantage of the even torque when starting would then be lost.

We now turn to the boiler, firebox, engine steaming ability and crew conditions. Make no mistake about it, Bulleid was a master at boiler design allied to water circulation. His boiler on the 'Merchant Navy' class was arguably the most efficient at producing steam on any railway locomotive ever built in Britain – with the exception of 'Leader', which was even better! Rugby Testing Plant was never able to reach the limit of evaporation of a 'Merchant Navy' boiler – the un-rebuilt engine being tested, No 35022, deposited so much oil on the rollers of the test house that it was considered unwise to proceed further! We can therefore be certain that in the boiler for 'Leader', Bulleid would have designed a pressure vessel of the highest efficiency. Yet, as reported, on many occasions 'Leader' ran short of steam or was unable to maintain the required steaming rate.

The firebox is the area where the greatest heat is generated and consequently the greatest evaporation of water into steam will occur. But due to its complicated make-up – two sheets held and separated by countless rivets – it was both expensive to construct and to maintain. This was not helped by the variations in

No 36003 was towed back to Brighton from New Cross on 20 May 1951 behind 'WD' 2-8-0 No 90234. Dunn wrote that the design of the 'Leader' was down to Bulleid himself, although that did not mean that the CME himself was occupied in producing the hundreds of necessary drawings, but the ideas were originating from the top and not being suggested by the drawing office itself. Don Broughton collection

temperature to which any such firebox was subjected – one minute a demand for steam would mean an almost incandescent fire, then a lesser demand would reduce the heat. Such variations (and they would be worse in an oil-burning furnace where the rise and fall in temperatures is both far faster and more dramatic) inevitably led to weeping from the firebox stays. In a number of designs the problem was accentuated by the use of copper for the inner firebox compared with steel for the outer firebox.

Left: **By contrast, here are the boiler and firebox of No 36001 after removal for scrap (it is not known if the crack at the base was caused during the salvage operations). Note the distortion to the plain sides, no doubt caused by excess heat. By this stage the 'butterfly' firehole doors have been removed.** B. Curl collection

Below: **A new and unused 'Leader' firebox and boiler. According to J. E. Chacksfield in his biography of Ron Jarvis, the offset boiler of 'Leader' and the consequent firing position 'were there by default' and a throwback to the original concept of oil-firing. This the present author cannot accept: the suggestion for oil-firing is fully discussed in the text, and Bulleid had ample opportunity to alter the design if he had wished. The corridor and firing compartment were included as built by deliberate policy, even though it was very likely that his assistants could already see that such design ideas were fraught with difficulty.** National Railway Museum/J. G. Click

The choice of metal was determined by its efficiency at conducting heat, although both would expand and contract at differing rates according to heat – hence the weep.

This then was the problem with which not only Bulleid but also every steam engine designer was faced. In the 'Merchant Navy' and 'West Country' Pacific designs, steel had been used throughout for both the inner and outer firebox sides, and while there was reduction in heat transference and consequent efficiency, the consequential savings in maintenance were thus considered worthwhile. In an effort to redress this loss of efficiency, Bulleid incorporated two thermic siphons – basically a further water-filled space within the firebox that thus allowed a greater proportion of water jacket to be exposed to the hottest area. No doubt these features assisted in the efficiency of the 'Bulleid boiler'.

In 'Leader' he went one stage further. Instead of a water-filled jacket surrounding the firebox, four siphons were provided, so there was less difference in heating area compared with a jacketed design. The 'crown' of the firebox – the water-filled canopy at the top of the firebox – still existed, and to it were secured the four siphons. Their positioning produced a triangular shape from the crown to the base of the firebox, and afforded an additional advantage in that they supported the crown itself.

In place of water-filled firebox sides, Bulleid instead placed plain welded sheets around both sides and the rear. A series of interlinked firebricks were secured by small protruding hooks, intended to retain both the bricks and consequently the firebox heat as well as afford thermal protection to the crew.

This was a sound theoretical idea, but it did not work under operating conditions for the reasons described above relating to a stationary engine compared with a moving locomotive. What is amazing was the ability of the firebox and boiler to produce such a vast amount of steam even when ultimately restricted by layers of firebrick reducing its volume.

Unfortunately what none of the official records refer to is the evaporation rate of the boiler. This appears not to have been one of the items tested – or if it was, it was not recorded. Was someone concerned that this would show that the 'Leader' boiler was more efficient at producing steam than possibly any other railway engine ever built? It is known that the eventual grate area was reduced by the addition of one or more rows of firebricks to just 25.5sq ft compared with the 43sq ft that had been designed. This grate area was comparable with an 'N' class 2-6-0, but it was smaller than that of a 'Schools', and smaller than a Stanier Class 5. Yet on its very last outing on 2 November 1950, despite this reduced grate area the boiler was able to generate enough steam to lift 480 tons to 50mph on a rising gradient averaging 1 in 250 from a standing start. A poor steamer? Rubbish! Moreover, this was generated by a total heating surface, including the firebox, of 2,387sq ft (compared with a 'Merchant Navy' at 2,451sq ft and a 'West Country'/'Battle of Britain' at 2,122). The basic problem was that most of the time the cylinders were wasting more steam than the boiler could produce.

It appears that at some very late stage the thought occurred to either Bulleid or somebody in the drawing office that it would be a good idea to wrap a water jacket of sorts around the firebox, not to increase steam evaporation so much as to further supplement the insulation for the crew. Perhaps this may even have been when the external shape of the casing was being decided. Whatever, the effect was counter-productive. The heat-insulating ability of the extra water was minimal, and it added little to the available capacity; instead it had a negative effect on the operation of the injectors, which were situated beneath the firing compartment and close to the firebox. This was not an operational problem, as their position was unaffected by heat, but what did occur was that the feed water was heated to the extent that the injectors were, to say the least, less efficient than they might have been. Had the concept of feed-water heating been incorporated in place of water treatment, this would not have been an issue – proof, if it was needed, of how the design evolved piecemeal rather than as a cohesive thought process.

Next we come to the conditions for the crew. It would be unfair to dismiss this as an irrelevance as in the past so much has been made of the topic of heat – particularly for the fireman. But, as already mentioned, there has been misinformation in this area: on the same day as a temperature of 122°F was recorded in the firing cab of 'Leader', 140°F was recorded in the cab of a 'Merchant Navy'. Yes, 'Leader' was hot and it was unpleasant, and the degree of condensation that resulted could sometimes mean that it was more akin to a Turkish bath.

In attempting to produce his ultimate steam engine, with a reasonable degree of crew comfort, Bulleid had unfortunately 'designed in' the heat. It has been suggested elsewhere that firemen had to wear sacking around their legs, and one man even visited his doctor as a result. But who were these men? Not the two regular firemen involved on the trials, Ted Forder at Brighton and Sam Talbot at Eastleigh. Even so, it cannot be pretended that conditions for the crew were ideal, and the driver also suffered from heat problems, particularly at the No 1 (smokebox) end, despite the smokebox door being lagged – hence the later provision of a partition between the smokebox and driving compartment, and Alf Smith's requirement that the load trials be undertaken with the No 2 end leading. Again, redesign would have been necessary.

The union comment that the fireman could be trapped in the event of a roll-over was valid. Bulleid's desire to give the driver an unrestricted view ahead akin to that enjoyed from the front of an electric unit was just not feasible. It had also added complexity in the need to duplicate the regulator, reversing gear and other controls through mechanical linkage between to the two driving compartments. Possibly some of the operational problems with items such as the reversing gear were compounded by this method of operation. The solution would have been a central cab where both men would work, separating the boiler and bunker portions. In other words, another major redesign.

Finally on the subject of the boiler and firebox, we come to the note in Riddles's report concerning the X-ray examination of the boilers. This he had deemed necessary as the boiler barrel on 'Leader' was not riveted, as was normal, but was welded throughout. Here was another departure from tradition and one that was again viewed with suspicion. In Riddles's report, was this an actual suspicion, or just excessive caution? His comment about not letting the remaining engines into service until their boilers had also been tested was perhaps slightly strange. All the boilers for the 'Leader' class would surely have been subjected to hydraulic and steam tests when built at Eastleigh before being shipped to Brighton. Any difficulty (and there is no suggestion that there was one) could then have been dealt with at the Eastleigh boiler shop.

According to Townroe the first 'Leader' boiler was slow to construct as Margraves, the Chief Metallurgist at Eastleigh, wanted every inch of welding X-rayed; however, Bulleid sent for the negatives, saw no faults and told Margraves to desist. This story got around and added to the staff's anxiety about the way a boiler of that shape might behave under the normal stresses of expansion and contraction. There was also no means of examination from the inside, through the openings at the bottom of the barrel, nor did Bulleid envisage the washing out of the boiler and the consequent mess it would make in the cabs.

It has been suggested to the author in the past that there was in fact a problem with the boiler of No 36001 in the area of the welded seam, but this could well have been a rumour perpetuated as a result of the incident referred to above. To suggest otherwise would be to imply that Riddles was sanctioning additional trials involving a steam engine having a 280psi boiler that was suggested as being likely to fail. Many things Riddles may have been – a fool he certainly was not.

We now come to the weight of 'Leader', which was far in excess of that originally projected. Far from being able to work on the majority of the company's lines, the final design could only work on a minority! The basic problem was the offset boiler and the weights that were subsequently added to effect some form of balance. Again as recounted earlier, even this was not enough, and a restriction then had to be imposed on the weight of the two thing that could be easily varied – the amount of coal and water carried on the tests from Eastleigh.

The offset boiler is perhaps one on the most puzzling aspects of the design. By placing the boiler in such a way, the results would have been obvious. Did Bulleid seriously believe that there would be no adverse effect? Did no one

among his staff not advise him? During his time on the LNER he would surely have been aware of the original difficulties with the Gresley corridor tender: overheated bearings and the need for some balancing weights. Bulleid was a gifted and far-sighted engineer, and it has been suggested that he was influenced by contemporary Sentinel designs, particularly in relation to the 'engine' part of the design, and of course the LNER did have Sentinel steam railcars. In so many areas he saw beyond the strait-jacket approach to conventional steam engine thinking. But in the area of the offset boiler, which was provided only so as to afford some means of communication between the crew, he was wrong. A 'dead-man's handle' and duplicated brake controls would have been sufficient. Centralising the boiler would have been a relatively easy step, and could have been achieved at the same time as a central cab where both men would work together.

The other aspects of 'Leader' that have come in for criticism centre around auxiliary items, primarily the reversing gear, smokebox duct, and grate. The reversing gear problems may have been exacerbated by the complicated linkage involved, while the smokebox duct was an early

The close proximity of the smokebox and its associated heat and the No 1 cab can be gauged here. Only the centre cab window could be opened – outwards – and it will be noted there are several views of the engine with the window open. *National Railway Museum/J. G. Click*

135

Above: **Another major and consistent difficulty with the engine was the reversing gear, which just does not seem to have been up to the task required of it. Possibly the difficulty was compounded by the degree of linkage involved, as can be seen here. Additional strain would have been caused whenever the engine stood on curved track.**
National Railway Museum/J. G. Click

attempt at smokebox cleaning. A mesh screen, as developed and fitted to numerous steam designs in BR days, would no doubt have worked. The grate was also perhaps unduly complicated, but the idea was sound – a little more development and it too would have worked perfectly well.

Many of the failings referred to were basic weaknesses in the design, together with complications added without necessary thought as to how each might inter-react with another. There were too many untried features in one design, leading to inevitable failure. But were the failures due to design, manufacture, assembly, or operational failure? Was the crank axle failure due to poor-quality steel? Were the sleeve failures due to haste in considering adequate lubrication in all areas? The questions are almost endless.

So what we are left with is an engine in which the bad aspects seem to outweigh the good. But did 'Leader'

incorporate any advantages? Did the design contribute in any way to the future of steam? The answer to this is undeniably yes. 'Leader' showed that the development of steam was not finished, and Bulleid was right in wanting to take the basic Stephenson locomotive further.
The failure was not in the design, but in the fact that at the time there were more obstacles to surmount than there were benefits to be gained.

Certainly by the late 1940s the future for steam traction not just in Britain but worldwide was limited. In America

wholesale dieselisation was under way, and in France there were plans in place for major electrification. Britain could not stand in isolation. Riddles's remit under BR was to ensure the survival of steam until replacement traction was in place, and this he did by providing a standard range of locomotives, without frills, as a stopgap. Bulleid's designs – the original Pacifics and certainly 'Leader' – just did not fit in. In effect, it mattered not how 'Leader' performed – it was never going to be multiplied. Only if it had been 100% perfect off the drawing-board, perhaps even 110% perfect, would that have happened – but in the history of technological development has there ever been such a machine?

But that does not mean that 'Leader' was a waste of time. The efficiency of the boiler, a locomotive on two powered bogies (a form of sophisticated Kitson-Meyer perhaps), and other aspects of the auxiliary equipment showed that there was still a potential for development. It was the fault of Riddles and his contemporaries for not taking those ideas and either using them as they stood or developing them further. 'Leader' really bequeathed two important legacies: the body-to-bogie mounting, already

The almost complete No 36002 at Brighton, work on which is reported to have really only started shortly before No 36001 had itself been finished, in June 1949. The 'Leader' design might well not have been the first double-bogie steam engine to run in Britain as, according to E. S. Cox, in 1923 the LMS was considering a such a locomotive of the 'Mallet' type for use on its Toton to Brent coal traffic, which, due to operational requirements, was then being double-headed. An engine of the 'Mallet' type, despite finding considerable favour in America, was rejected fairly early on due to unfavourable loading, with the well-known result that the LMS Garrett design eventually appeared.
W. N. J. Jackson

referred to, and the dashpot axlebox damping, which was developed and incorporated into a very successful axlebox design on EMU stock.

What was not used was the design of the 'Leader' braking system. In general terms perfectly satisfactory, it operated akin to the air compressor and reservoirs on a diesel locomotive or large commercial vehicle. With 'Leader' a vacuum was involved, but the principle was the same – when the vacuum dropped to a pre-set level, it was automatically replenished from a 'holding tank'. When the reservoir and holding tank had equalised, the ejector was brought into use automatically. It worked well with only one slight hiccup in that the release valves were slightly slow in operation – not the fault of Bulleid or the design, but of the manufacturer of the valves. It can only be regretted that a similar system was not used on any other UK steam engine.

Just as Paget's design years earlier had failed to affect future steam locomotive design, so the same fate befell Bulleid. Indeed, it is likely that the same arguments and results affected the 'Leader'. It must for ever be an enigma that Bulleid, as a mechanical engineer, felt he could improve on a very similar design of 30-40 years previously, yet went on to make not the same but even more mistakes.

It might seem that so far the purpose of this chapter has been to vilify Bulleid, but that is not the case. Indeed, we now come to an even more contentious subject – whether there may even have been a deliberate policy against the engine. I cannot and will not put into print any formal accusations, and indeed I make none. What I will do instead is to point out the facts.

To start with, when the first engine was under construction a power bogie was deliberately lifted off the ground and supplied with steam at just 8psi from an external source to both test and observe the operation. Everything ran perfectly 'like a sewing machine' – this was probably the time when the film footage was recorded. This test was a perfectly feasible and logical operation – yet while it was actually under way the fitters in charge were instructed by, it was said, the Brighton Works Manager to reverse the engine without stopping it first; this incident was referred to in Chapter 1. Bulleid was advised of the incident by Doug Smith and Joe Hutchinson, and although both men entered the office of the CME with some trepidation, there was no fall-out.

With the majority of the failures affecting the No 1 bogie, why was the opportunity not taken to exchange the complete bogie with that from No 36002 or 36003? It might have made all the difference. It has actually been suggested that No 36001's No 1 bogie may have been changed before the engine went to Eastleigh for its final trials, and likewise that the boiler may even have been changed. Correspondence in 1989 between the author and B. Musgrave, who in 1949 was a draughtsman at Brighton, revealed that the latter was of the opinion that the No 1 bogie was in fact changed together with the boiler from No 36001 (due to damage to the firebox sides), this

allegedly having taken place just prior to the engine's final transfer to Eastleigh in early 1950. However, this is not confirmed from any other source.

As we have seen, information was fed to Bulleid while he was away in Scotland, Ireland and elsewhere from September 1949 onwards. According to Day-Lewis 'a regular supply of telegrams' was sent to Bulleid by Granshaw indicating progress. But the two quoted by Day-Lewis – 'Successful trip of 100 miles on Saturday, taking engine to Eastleigh tomorrow' and 'Successful Brighton to Eastleigh on Sunday, arrived on time, no trouble during trip, reverser much improved' – appear to bear no resemblance to runs actually carried out by the engine; and in so far as the surviving records are concerned, they are believed to be a true and accurate record of every run the engine ever made.

Another question concerns the alleged water consumption for the light engine runs of 14 and 15 August and the load trial on 21 August, no mechanical work affecting the sleeves having been undertaken between

The results of sleeve-valve failure on No 36001 show clearly the abrasion marks. As referred to in the text, the two cylinder blocks for the original engine were noted to have warped slightly after final machining. This may have been due to ineffective relief of welding stresses or localised excess heat during the welding of these to the main frames. The result was that sleeve-valve failures were almost inevitable, and this may well have been one of the reasons it was found necessary to double the clearance in the liners to 0.036in whilst the back ring was also removed. Had the bogies been exchanged at the time of the crank axle failure, the final tests might well have been very different. Where and when this information on the distortion originally came to light is not known. It is referred to in only one other publication, *Bulleid of the Southern*, although if the information was available to the engineers involved with the locomotive's trials, it provides another example of how the engine was hardly given the opportunity to succeed. National Railway Museum

those dates. 'Leader' is supposed to have run out of water running light, yet could then take a load over a greater distance without running out! Somewhere there is grave inconsistency.

Finally, consider the ability of the engine to haul its train on the very last run made. This showed the potential of the engine and especially the design. But it was ignored by Marylebone.

Very shortly after nationalisation Riddles decided that there would be changes in the senior mechanical engineering staff, and for valid reasons. In this way he could gain first-hand and impartial knowledge from a fresh pair of eyes concerning former company practice. Such knowledge would be invaluable in assisting with both the designs and the later constructional sites to be used for the later build of Standard locomotives. But such interchange also meant there was now a direct line to Riddles that had not existed before. Previously Bulleid and his staff may well have tried to keep matters quiet until difficulties had been resolved, but that no longer applied. Everything was in the open.

The question has also been asked whether, despite the failure of 'Leader', there would have been a place for Bulleid working with Riddles, possibly even as an ideas man, albeit, as had been the case before, perhaps held 'in check'. When asked that very question by *Steam World*, Riddles replied:

No 36001 in the course of being dismantled at Eastleigh: the engine was dismembered in the works, then had its various components cut up.

'As a man I liked him and we got on well, but he was an individualist who wanted to do it his own way, and some of what he did was questionable. I couldn't fathom some of his thinking.'

When asked about the decision to scrap 'Leader', he continued:

'It was the only sensible decision to make. The thing was 30 tons overweight, and the boiler so badly balanced it needed $2^{1}/_{2}$ tons of pig-iron on one side to balance it up. Apart from that, the fireman was forced to stand so close to the firebox he was burning himself. The fireman had to lag himself with sandbags to deflect the heat.'

Had there been a job for Bulleid after nationalisation?

'No, how could there be? Having been king of his own dung heap, how could he suddenly come and serve in mine? The surprise to me was that having failed on the Southern, he went to Ireland and failed there too.'

Riddles's last comment was wrong. Bulleid did not fail in Ireland – the 'Turfburner' worked. Yes, a few

At Bognor shed on 1 July 1950 Nos 36002 and 36003 are in store; chocks have been placed beneath the wheels of 36002 at least. Both engines had spent some time prior to this in the electric car shed at Brighton, and Bognor was possibly chosen until it was clear that there was to be no resumption of work. After this, Nos 36002-4 were moved to various points around the Brighton Works complex until Nos 36002/3 ventured further afield. R. C. Riley

modifications were still needed, but the lessons from 'Leader' had been learned. It was the wrong place, and the wrong time. A decade earlier and it could have been a different story.

Day-Lewis is responsible for another oft-quoted misconception. Generally his account of Bulleid, apart from also being the first book on the man and his work, is arguably one of the best overall, but in one area he has missed the point completely. He is referring to the time when the order came through from Headquarters that work was to cease on Nos 36002-5:

'On that date No 36002 was only two days from completion: after a few minor jobs like coupling up pipes and putting in cab windows the locomotive would have been ready for steaming. With the lessons learned from No 36001 she would surely have been a better engine than her older sister.'

Concerning the trials of *Hartland Point*, when on her last outing she fractured a sleeve at St Leonards, Day-Lewis comments, 'And that was the sad end of No 32039 .... though the lessons she taught were invaluable.'

Both statements are simply not true. No 36002 was built to the same design as 36001, and would have displayed exactly the same tendencies. The only possible variation would be in so far as haste in the construction of No 36001 had led to a slight warping of the cylinder blocks. This had not applied to No 36002, so sleeve-valve failures may have been less common, but it is unlikely that they would have been totally non-existent. Likewise time did not allow any of the lessons learned from *Hartland Point* to be incorporated into the design. If they had, the sleeve valves might have been substituted. *Hartland Point* failed to serve the purpose it had been intended for. If it had, work on the design of 'Leader'

role in the survival or otherwise of 'Leader', being promoted to the position of Chief Technical Assistant at Brighton in 1949, which in effect brought the drawing offices of the Southern Region under his direct control; formerly, prior to nationalisation, Bulleid would of course have had these under his own command. Perhaps he was in many respects a throwback to a past era, which, although recent, was rapidly becoming an anachronism.

According to J. E. Chacksfield, in his biography of Jarvis, morale at Brighton at that time (around 1948-50) was slipping, and while the drawing office at Brighton was heavily engaged in work on various modifications to the Pacific, a small section was occupied full-time on similar modifications to 'Leader'. Jarvis was tasked by Riddles with reporting on the ongoing trials of No 36001; indeed, some of the actual words and phrases incorporated by Riddles in his later reports to the Executive originated from the pen of Jarvis. He was similarly charged with overseeing the later tests from Eastleigh.

To all these men Bulleid was perhaps more of an irritation in his persistence in pursuing untried improvements to the steam engine. But Bulleid cannot be said to have been wrong. In terms of the time and the place perhaps he was misguided, but who can blame the man for trying? If 'Leader' had been running perhaps two years earlier, the outcome might well have been different.

To expand on this theme I can do no better than quote a slightly long passage from E. S. Cox's 1966 biography, *Locomotive Panorama* Vol 2, in which the clash of personalities between Bulleid and the new British Railways regime is well described:

'With Bulleid, on the other hand, there was rather a different situation, which merits some description because of its unusual nature. To an extent unknown on other railways, he had been supreme autocrat within his own department, and had been able to impose his will upon a management otherwise pre-occupied with electrification.

In locomotive matters on the former SR it could be said of him, as of Joseph in the Egyptian prison, that "Whatsoever was done therein, he was the doer thereof". An individualist of the deepest dye, he had no sympathy at all with the painstaking improvement of the breed which I have outlined, but wished with brilliant and dramatic improvisations to solve all the remaining problems of steam by quite other means. To him novelty was everything. If it would not work then this could not be the fault of the idea itself, but only of the incapacity of those who tried to carry it out or use it.

The cross which he had to bear was that his developments with conventional practice were successful, sometimes brilliant, whereas his exercises in the bizarre, which he loved dearly as his brain children, often failed. A recent book [Day-Lewis] has described in great detail

would surely not have even commenced until trials with No 2039 were complete.

So, were No 36001 and her sisters stillborn – was the 'Leader' project a triumph or a fiasco? Here personal preference will again play a part. An engineer might admire the Bulleid approach, while an operational or maintenance man might well take a differing viewpoint. This is borne out in the strong feelings displayed by the late John Click, an engineer by profession who was apprenticed to Bulleid at Waterloo and was later seconded from BR in the 1950s to assist in the development of the 'Turfburner' on the CIE. Bulleid was a very strong personality, with considerable charisma. It was these characteristics that no doubt enabled him to convince, perhaps 'carry', others. Throughout all this, Bulleid's former Waterloo ally, Missenden, then at the Railway Executive, was strangely silent – could it be that even he recognised a step too far?

More objective viewpoints were perhaps displayed by other professional engineers – Bond, Cox, Jarvis and Riddles – all of whom held senior positions on BR at the same time. Ron Jarvis would be destined to play a pivotal

the fascinating personality and the ideas, achievements and failures of this enigmatical man. He knew in advance that we were bound to introduce practice which was alien to his own thought processes, and to divert the activities of his assistants from frantically trying to solve the impossible into more normal channels. I recollect my first official contact with him after my new appointment when he assembled all his principal technical staff for lunch at the Old Ship Hotel at Brighton to meet me. His charm and tact eased a confrontation which could have been difficult, and he offered then, and loyally upheld later, every assistance from his people in what we wanted to do. He did not disguise his attitude, however, and expressed in an extremely gentlemanly way that he had cast his pearls before swine, and that if we found nothing to learn from his "Merchant Navy" and "Leader", so much the

worse for us. It intrigues the imagination to consider what policy would have been followed and what locomotive designs would have been produced had any of the above-mentioned men either taken Riddles's place or held the post of CME if the four individual railways had carried on exactly as before.

In this context I must refer to a matter which caused the acutest embarrassment to Riddles and his officers at the time, and which it is difficult to write about objectively even after this lapse of years. I refer again to Bulleid's "Leader" class locomotive and the following are the facts of the case. Towards the end of the war the Southern Railway was considering a new design of tank engine, to handle cross-London freight traffic according to Bulleid's son in his book *Master Builders of Steam*, but, in our own records, for the purpose of replacing the M7 Class 0-4-4 Tanks which would cover a slightly different kind of duty. Whatever may have been the true original need, the sight of Raworth's C-C electric locomotive fired Bulleid with the idea that its outstanding advantage of being a "total adhesion" machine ought to be equally applicable to steam traction. This was no new thought as witness Holden's "Decapods" and various "Fairly" designs through history, but these all operated at low speed. With characteristic

Out of sight and out of mind: No 36002 at New Cross shed on 23 June 1951, the day before she was towed back to Brighton for dismantling. No 36002 lasted longer than any of her sisters, albeit by just a matter of weeks. As with No 36001, the roller-bearings from the axles were salvaged for possible reuse, but in the end, with everything else from the project, they were consigned to scrap. This was the nearest a 'Leader' would ever come to London. *Brian Morrison*

enthusiasm, Bulleid now enlarged the proposal and
persuaded his management that what they really needed
was an all-purpose, go-anywhere locomotive capable of
hauling 480 tons passenger or 1,200 tons freight, and of
attaining 90mph. Accordingly, five of these unknowns
were authorised by the SR on its 1947 programme, and
anticipating success, 31 more were proposed for 1948.
The newly formed Railway Executive approved the former
and included them in its own 1948 programme, but having
regard to their untried nature, cancelled the 31. Bulleid
disclosed some particulars about the project in his
Presidential Address to the Institution of Mechanical
Engineers in October 1946. He listed therein ten
objectives, all of which were above reproach in the
advancement of steam traction, and nearly all of which
were capable of attack by more than one method. When we
became responsible for technical matters throughout
British Railways in 1948 we found this design almost
completed at Brighton, and at once encountered an
approach and a process of thought so alien to that of our
own, with our different background, that our standards of
judgement tended to flounder. The solution of the problem
of designing a high-speed double-bogie steam engine
seemed a task of some magnitude in itself, and we could
not but be somewhat dazed to see that other novel and
untried features were also crowded into the same
framework, to wit sleeve valve cylinders, driving wheels
coupled by chains and an offset boiler having for a firebox
a row of thermic siphons encased in a firebrick lining
without external water legs. We accepted untouched,
however, what this original mind was producing and on
June 21st, 1949, No 36001 was competed, with two others

No 36002 in its last days: Bulleid himself commented, 'The tragedy was
that it ['Leader'] was built two years too late.' Day-Lewis succinctly
added, 'His own ingenuity was needed to solve the problems that it
raised.' Peter Dunk

coming up strongly behind in the erecting shop at
Brighton. Then followed trial running through to October
1950, on 90 days of which tests were carried out including
two series of dynamometer car tests, but as is well known,
there were continual failures and the engine was never
able to enter revenue service.

Some day and in another place, it may be possible for
somebody else to give a full engineering account of all that
happened in this period, but the engine encountered
trouble after trouble in all of its unusual features.
Successive modifications were made and, to give these the
best chance of success, Bulleid was specially retained for
six months after his retirement in September 1949 in
order to give advice and supervise the alterations. But all
to no avail. Reliable running proved unattainable, and
even in the final best condition to which the locomotive
could be brought, its coal and water consumptions were
respectively 68 and 47 more per dbhp-hour than that of a
Southern U class 2-6-0 tested under identical
circumstances, this excess being due amongst other
things to steam leakage past the 192 piston rings
associated with the sleeve valves. Further, the
temperature conditions in the boiler compartment
amidships were insupportable, and there was only one
hero amongst the firemen on the Southern who was
prepared to tolerate them even for test running only.
I think that Bulleid believed to the end that with more

143

No 36002 and the incomplete yet movable 36003 are seen at New Cross. While it may be understandable to try and glorify certain of the achievements of No 36001, they must be put in the context of steam development elsewhere. What Bulleid had attempted was in many ways paltry compared with the work of André Chapelon, whose No 242A.1 achieved 3,500-4,000dbhp on level track at a constant speed with a train of 664 tons – such achievements showed that there was a future for steam. Indeed, Chapelon had himself indicated as much in his original 1938 work *La Locomotive à Vapeur*, although this was produced some years before 242A.1 was achieving such phenomenal outputs. It has been suggested that none other than the GWR Board of Directors had suggested to its own CME, C. B. Collett, that he should study Chapelon's work, no doubt with the intention of revitalising Swindon! Bulleid might well have done likewise, and aimed for improved efficiency rather than developing novelty. The last opportunity for change was with Riddles, but as with the others the opportunity thus presented went unheeded. Ken Dobson

drastic modifications success was just round the corner, but for Riddles and the RE enough was enough. Although regretting the outcome they could have no remorse that they had not given this novel attempt every reasonable chance to prove itself. At the end of 1950 it was decided to scrap the engine and the uncompleted chassis and finished components for the other four. As the engine remained unnamed, we shall probably never know who

the Leader was to be who would provide the type name for this breakaway from convention had it fulfilled the hopes of its protagonist.'

Cox continued later with a brief description of the 'Turfburner', which for completeness is also included. Fittingly, the brief comment made by him on the Irish connection was right at the end of his book:

'...we visited Eire, where Bulleid, then Chief Mechanical Engineer of the railways there, showed us much hospitality and laid on a display of motive power for us at Inchicore. There we saw the last fitful gleam of steam development in the British Isles. Nothing daunted by the fate of the "Leader" class on the Southern Region, this indefatigable enthusiast presented to us a reconstituted "Leader" having many of the same features, but with the added complexity of seeking to burn peat. For a long time previously one had seen occasional photographs of Irish locomotives of conventional design, looped with writhing external pipes curling in all directions, a veritable Laocoon of motive power. These were the guinea pigs upon which the attempt was made to solve the immense problem of reducing the high natural moisture content of this fuel. Bulleid took Bob

Arbuthnot, President Elect, and myself a half-dozen miles up the main line and back on this Irish "Leader" in its final shape. The locomotive certainly went and was clearly without some of the worst disabilities of its predecessor, but to the best of my knowledge, it never entered revenue service...'

The reference to the limited time available for steam after nationalisation needs to be taken further. The development of other forms of motive power – diesel (with varying forms of transmission and control gear, electric, mechanical, hydraulic, etc), electric, gas-turbine – indicated that the way forward was the abolition of steam, and progress for steam could only be made in the remaining years by simplifying maintenance and minor improvements to deal with ever-changing socio-economic conditions.

The late Stephen Townroe recounted his own experiences of 'Leader' to the author in correspondence dated July 1984, in what can only be described as a masterly form of understatement. Describing the project in engineering terms, first he recounted some of the practical difficulties that were encountered: 'There were other little difficulties, such as breakage of the oil-pump drive, so that to get home without motion seizure the crew had to pour oil down through the cab floor... Riding in 36001 might be imagined as sharing the inside of a small submarine with a hot boiler and smokebox, and sundry live steam pipes. The heat and humidity were almost unbearable...'

He continued, 'At the time of the dynamometer tests Bulleid was installed as CME in Ireland. I had hoped that he might pay us at least one visit to get first-hand information and to say a few words about his intentions, but he stayed away. He must have known by then that the Leader was a dead duck because he set about building a turf-burning version at Inchicore using piston not sleeve valves and with an external driving cab. The late R. C. Bond, at the time Riddles's deputy, told me later of the interview at Marylebone at which Bulleid was told of the reasons why the Leader was not a practical proposition, care being taken to have every word taken down in shorthand!'

A later note to the present author from Townroe expanded on the autumn 1949 meeting between Riddles and Bulleid slightly further, recalling that Bond advised him of the 'rather difficult' discussion that had taken place between Riddles and Bulleid and 'about the impossibility of further progress and Riddles had to firmly insist that no more money could be spent'. This would have been around the time the order was given for work to cease on Nos 36002-5.

Townroe wrote of Bulleid as follows, and for obvious reasons this was not included in the original works:

'Bulleid soon left BR to become CME of CIE in Ireland. It was a revelation of Bulleid's ways of thinking that he proceeded to repeat his mistakes with a similar design to

No 36002 is back at Brighton. Note that none of the modifications made to No 36001 have been undertaken on the No 2 end of 36002, the only subsequent work of any sort carried out to this and No 36003 after November 1949 being to dismantle the connecting rods, which were then placed within the cabs so as to make both engines fit for towing. *National Railway Museum/J. G. Click*

One last look at No 36002 inside Brighton Works on 25 June 1951. She had remained in this limbo-like state for some 17 months. Meanwhile No 36004 was a main frame and boiler temporarily fitted onto a pair of coach bogies, while 36005 was a 'kit of parts'. It is likely that components destined for both Nos 36004 and 36005 were salvaged to keep 36001 running. But there were also some other parts, as a full-size wooden mock-up of the 'Leader' main frames had been constructed at Brighton. Another model, to quarter-scale, showed the 'figure of eight' sleeve motion, and was used successfully to test valve events. This latter item was reported to have been handed over to BR Archives, although since then its location has never been established. *Don Broughton collection*

No 36001, except that this time he put the enginemen in a separate cab. It was an experiment which the Irish railways could not afford and it, too, had to be scrapped without earning a penny or a punt. Such blindness to reality was/is inexplicable.

Those who worked on Bulleid's personal staff on the Southern found him an enigma. When approached for decisions on routine matters, they would receive the most illogical answers, and after years of contact they had to admit that they did not know what to make of him. He was a dreamer; certainly inventive and an originator (innovator) but lacking in hard common-sense. When he went into retirement, he was restless, and changed his residence at least five times.'

Townroe was nothing short of abrupt when referring to the former CME:

'Bulleid was clever, self-centred, conceited, ingenious, charming with equals but inconsiderate and supercilious towards his underlings ... he was a cold fish, he was erratic. Even his personal clerk often didn't know his whereabouts. He would tell his car driver to be ready to leave for Eastleigh at 9.00am, leave him waiting until after his lunch and then tell him to drive to Ashford...

The last days for No 36003 are recorded on 22 May 1951. It may appear that criticism and questioning of Bulleid's designs is a recent phenomenon, but more than half a century ago, in 1952, A. F. Cook produced an article for that year's *Trains Annual* entitled 'A challenge to orthodoxy: Bulleid designs of the Southern'. *Don Broughton collection*

Right: **On the following day No 36003 entered the works for scrapping. However, she seemed reluctant to succumb to her fate as the leading bogie became derailed during the shunt move, stopping just short of the coastway running lines. It was but a brief interruption, as once inside the works the engine was quickly disposed of.** Don Broughton collection

Below: **What might have been: Bulleid was naïve enough to envisage that all the motive power requirements on the Southern could be handled purely by machines of his own design. The 'Merchant Navy' and 'West Country' Pacifics were two elements of this, with the 'Q1' a third. He also proposed two versions of 'Leader' – and No 36001 was the** *small* **version! (It is not believed that any work was ever carried out on this large 'Leader'.) Like Bulleid, Riddles was essentially a steam man, although with a choice of the conventional compared with the radical he veered towards the former. In fact, he had no choice, his remit being to continue with steam until more modern motive power was available. In theory this could have been achieved by the straightforward continuation of any number of pre-nationalisation designs, although he knew that these were unlikely to be well received outside their original home territory. Thus by providing a 'Standard' design he was attempting to incorporate the best ideas and best practice in a type of machine that would be accepted by all. That he did not always succeed was certainly not through want of trying, while also having to walk the political tightrope of not favouring any one former company. In this latter aspect he did fail: the LMS influence was all too obvious. But what other choice was there? The GWR had nothing new to offer, was far too entrenched and was generally anti-nationalisation, the LNER had a new Pacific, the 'A1', but otherwise its designs were problematical or unlikely to find favour, and on the Southern there was Bulleid. A fleet of Bulleid Pacifics and 'Q1s' for the whole of the nationalised railway? Hardly likely – although some Bulleid locos did venture on to Great Eastern lines, albeit without any great success. If Bulleid had been left to provide a fleet of standard designs, one might envisage a fleet of 'Leaders' from Penzance to Wick – now there is an interesting thought…**

His deputy, E. A. W. Turbett, was left to try and keep order in the CME Department affairs and kept clear of involvement in design...

Bulleid was in Workshops all his life. He had no first-hand outdoor experience as a District Traffic or Motive Power Officer. He did not discuss his design ideas with the users ... hence nobody warned him that the inside of the Leader would be unbearable.'

Bulleid did not like people with practical experience and I am convinced that was why he did not talk about the MN design with my Chief in 1939, nor about the Bleeder in 1946.

Now that he has passed away, I think that the truth about him can be written without any offence, and of course without malice.'

Returning to the standard of engineering on BR in the 1950s, it might be said that innovation was limited, with the result that design stagnated – much the same way perhaps as at Swindon after 1930 (again, I await the brick-bats!). It took too long for items such as high-degree superheat, roller-bearings, differing exhaust systems (Kylchap/Lemaitre), etc, to be accepted as able to improve reliability and performance without major engineering change. Even alterations to valve gear operation – Caprotti in particular – may have improved steam performance and enabled standards of output to be maintained as all the while coal quality decreased.

Digressing slightly, it should not be forgotten that BR *did* in fact carry out one major steam experiment in the 1950s, which related to the fitting of a batch of the new Riddles '9F' type with the Italian design of Crosti boiler. This was in effect a long pre-heating tube placed under the main boiler barrel into which was directed what would otherwise be waste heat from the exhaust, thus improving thermal efficiency. The manufacturers had promised something like a 20% increase in efficiency and commensurate reduction in coal consumption. Unfortunately such results were not achieved and there followed a long and at times acrimonious discourse between BR and the Italian owners of the patent over payment of royalties.

Improvements had been seen on the Italian railways, but as far as is known only on certain classes of steam engine. In the main these were old and, compared with more modern types, relatively inefficient designs. Clearly the Crosti variant was able to improve thermal efficiency to a

It appears that Bulleid's creation has spread far and wide, albeit with an interesting colour scheme of yellow ends...

far greater degree on a steam engine of greater age than on a 1954-designed '9F'.

The failure of the Crosti boiler to perform to expectations in the UK was only one of a long line of attempts over the years to improve steam engine efficiency that never quite reached the intended goal. But like the 'Leader' project there certainly existed a genuine belief that improvement could be made. Bulleid had designed and built a machine that in theory at least should have showed considerable advantages in a number of areas. Unfortunately any advantage gained was more than overshadowed by the deficiencies that were only too apparent. What is perhaps the most surprising is how a man with the obvious design capabilities of Bulleid persisted in the pursuit of ideas that had either never worked in a railway or other environment or had clearly been proven not to. By all means experiment, for that is how development occurs. But learn also from others. Failure to do so leads to that cliché of 'reinventing the wheel'.

Bulleid was right to try, but he was perhaps wrong in his final approach. British Railways was likewise right to scrap the 'Leader', but wrong not to use the ideas it suggested.

[1] Allowing for inflation, the original figure of £178,865 5s equates to £3,990,834.41 at 2004 values, £1 in 1950 having increased in proportionate terms to £22.31 over the period.

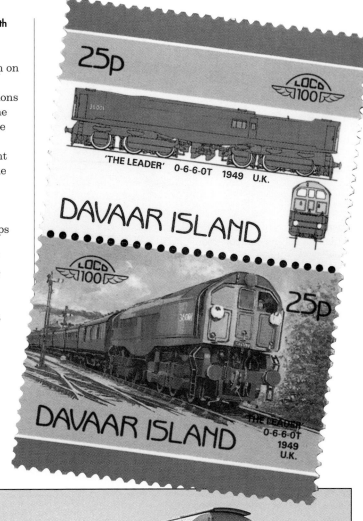

No 36001 appears to be in almost a silver grey livery outside the front of Eastleigh Works on what is either 26 or 27 June 1949. At this stage she was awaiting number and BR insignia decals and inspection by 'the great and the good'. S. C. Townroe/Colour-Rail

CHAPTER FIVE

Bulleid Vindicated?

In the preceding chapters, the impression may have been given that the intention was to criticise the designer as much as the design. If that appears to have been the case, I will at once apologise. There was never any intention or desire to criticise Bulleid the man, or his memory.

But is it perhaps just possible that Bulleid was right? Possible that circumstances – and circumstances over which he had no control – conspired to effectively kill 'Leader' even before an objective assessment had been made? I admit that I am coming around to that conclusion as a distinct possibility, as explained in this final brief assessment.

We already know that the period during which 'Leader' was conceived and built was far from ideal for such a project, and something over which Bulleid had no control. Yet ever since 1941, when the first of his Pacifics appeared, there seems almost to have been a concerted effort to discredit the design, criticising the faults rather than promoting the benefits. However, this is not the place to embark on a general discussion of the Pacific type; much has been written by others on this score, some good, some bad, some well-reasoned, and some nothing short of scandalous. One aspect on which the critics do seem to agree is the chain-driven valve gear, which was an example of inferior design, principally due to the chains stretching after only a short period in use, with consequential effect upon the valve timing. Indeed, this was one of the reasons given to prove the need for rebuilding.

This opinion appears to have been rarely if at all challenged in print in the past, yet almost 40 years since the end of steam in daily service it might be possible to put the record straight, primarily as a result of a comment in the book *Engine Sheds in Camera* by David Hucknall (Sutton Publishing, 2005). This work centres around the photographs and recollections of former Salisbury Shed Master George Harrison, who recalls a conversation with Bulleid over the allegation of chain stretch. The response in a letter from Bulleid to Harrison was as follows:

'Mr Smith, in his letter, spoke of chain-stretch and I think this must be a confusion with what I believe to be correct, namely that the links bed down onto the pins and it is this that results in the sag of the chain. It would require very high forces indeed to stretch the links themselves. I feel sure I told you that when the Eastleigh Works Manager reported to me this sagging, the makers asked me to tell him to hang up, side-by-side, from an overhead crane, the chain complained about and a new one and then let me know the difference. He did, and found none.'

Indeed, while from an engineering perspective the links might very well wear, the likelihood of the chains stretching must be remote. Vindication at last, then, for the original Pacific design, and in so far as the valve gear on 'Leader' was similarly driven, it might undermine allegations that chain stretching was responsible for the various sleeve-valve failures.

Regarding the sleeve-valves on 'Leader', a recent conversation between the author and a third party threw up what can only be described as an alarming accusation. It was suggested that, while on trial at Brighton, there were occasions when deliberate sabotage took place to prevent test runs being successful. This is of course both a dangerous and insidious accusation to make, and it must at once be qualified. It was alleged that one of the crews working on 'Leader' from Brighton would deliberately introduce sand into the sleeve valves to promote failure, the reason being that the men were paid a daily rate for a complete test, so if the run could be terminated early they would finish their shift early, yet still receive the same pay. I must say that I do not believe that this would have been done by the regular test crew mentioned earlier. So was it possible, and could it have happened? Was it a spontaneous act or was it done with the connived blessing of a senior source?

It would indeed be possible to introduce a foreign substance into the valve areas. With various engineers and technical men being present on the engine, for many of the trials conversation was inevitable. The crews would probably have gleaned the how and why of both the design and its weaknesses very early on. (Given the position of the oil pumps on *Hartland Point*, could such sabotage have occurred on earlier occasions?) Many questions then, but few answers.

There is certainly no positive evidence to support any of these hypotheses, yet there is circumstantial evidence. Why did 'Leader' fail sometimes and not others? Why on one test in the autumn of 1949, with Bulleid on the footplate, did the engine perform faultlessly in the morning, then on a repeat run in the afternoon, without the designer present, did it fail? Perhaps just coincidence. Yet consider also the seeming reduction in sleeve-valve failures after the engine was transferred to Eastleigh.

Any allegation of this type is easy to make, but very hard to prove or disprove, but was made to the present author without encouragement, even before the correspondent knew of the present intention to reassess the whole project. There was certainly nothing to be gained from such a comment.

Finally, let us look at the almost absolute way in which the design, with all its faults, was portrayed to BR Headquarters as a failure. The positive aspects of the engine – the total adhesion, the boiler's ability to raise steam, the braking system – are conspicuous by the absence of praise in the official reports. It is almost as if there was a fear of admitting that the engine did in fact show potential. Certainly it could never have survived in its original form, but surely it did not deserve to be condemned out of hand. Those at Brighton in positions of power were the ones who had the future of the steam engine in their hands, but conservatism would eventually hold sway. To speculate on the alternatives would be to go beyond both the remit and intention of the present work, although the whole subject of the potential for steam on Britain's railways is one that would make for a lively debate. Perhaps we might have seen an engine numbered 37001 emerge – a Mk 2 'Leader' with the errors put right, and incorporating the lessons of the past century learned both at home and overseas.

One final point worth mentioning is simply that Bulleid may have been portrayed as 'The Last Giant of Steam' (to quote Sean Day-Lewis), but he was certainly not 'The Last Man of Steam'. If we talk of giants, head and shoulders above the rest must be André Chapelon. But in many ways Bulleid was not far behind. He had the vision and would probably have gone a lot further – and succeeded – if time had allowed. Where the likes of Chapelon and Bulleid paved the way, others followed, even if their names are not perhaps so well known. Engineers such as L. D. Porta, David Wardale, Phil Girdlestone, Shaun McMahon, Nigel Day and Roger Waller come to mind. None has attempted to redesign 'Leader' – so far at least – but each has indeed achieved with steam, and shown that Bulleid was right to innovate. It was not really Bulleid who failed in 1950, but fate that contrived to fail him.

The final photograph in this book depicts No 36001 at the end of the departure road from Eastleigh running shed and no doubt pending a trial run. The fact that the loco is 'light' – without the dynamometer car, yet with the hole cut in the cab of No 1 end through which the cables were passed – means that it could possibly be one of the final runs referred to in the text, October or November 1950 (the photographer's record has not survived). Potentially such a scene might just have become commonplace. Perhaps then the class would have been renamed 'Perseverance'.

Below: **An already doomed outing for No 36001. She was destined never to haul as revenue-earning train, whilst her reputation, along with that of her designer, has continually been tainted by incorrect accusations and statements.** John Bailey

Appendix

Chronology of No 2039

12.05-2.06	Built by Kitson & Co. Given number '39' by LBSCR.
12.08	Steam heating fitted.
6.13	Named *La France*.
1.26	Renumbered and renamed by SR to No 2039 *Hartland Point*.
7.47	To Brighton Works for conversion.
5.11.47	Ex-Works from Brighton.
3.12.47	Yard trial at Brighton in presence of Bulleid and Ivatt.
15.12.47	Light engine together with 'E5' No 2404 to Lewes.
1.1.48	Worked three-coach set, Brighton-Eastbourne.
1.48	Daily test train, Brighton-Groombridge via Lewes. Light engine runs, Brighton-Three Bridges. 'K' class 2-6-0 propelled to Three Bridges and return.
2.48	Works visits. Trip(s) to Eastleigh.
3.48-mid 7.48	Test train on coastway line, Brighton to Lewes or Cowden. Three-coach set, Brighton-Tunbridge Wells West and return. Similar load to Hastings and return.
Mid 7.48-8.48	Works visits?
9.48	Train of bogie utility vans. Works visit.
12.48	Light engine trials to Hastings. Failed at St Leonards with broken valve rod on 19.12.48.
1-2.49	Works. Trials?
14.3.49	Public passenger train, Brighton-Redhill and return.
16.3.49	Trial with three coaches, Brighton-Redhill. Failed at Earlswood.
4-6.49	Special to Ashford with Bulleid on footplate. Stock trains, Lancing Carriage Works-Eastleigh. Works visits and storage.
14.6.49-3.9.49	Brighton Works, overhaul.
9.49	Stored at Brighton.
17.2.51	Towed from Brighton to Eastleigh.
24.2.51	Withdrawn from Eastleigh.
28.2.51	Breaking-up order No 958 issued.
3.51	Scrapped at Eastleigh Works.

Complete list of 'Leader' workings compiled from official sources

Date	Working	Official result
22.6.49	Initial trial trip	Failed
25.6.49	Light engine with 'E4' tank to Falmer and Groombridge	
26.6.49	Light engine with 'K' class 2-6-0 to Eastleigh	
29.6.49	Light, Eastleigh-Brighton	Failed
7.7.49	Light to Falmer and Crowborough	
8.7.49	Light to Falmer and Crowborough	
12.7.49	Light to Falmer and Crowborough	
14.7.49	Light to Crowborough twice	Failed

Date	Working	Official result
23.7.49	Light to Crowborough	
24.7.49	Light to Seaford	Failed
12.8.49	Light to Crowborough, Seaford and Lewes	Failed
13.8.49	Light to Crowborough, Seaford and Lewes	
14.8.49	Light to Crowborough, Seaford and Lewes	Failed
15.8.49	Light to Crowborough, Seaford and Lewes	Failed
16.8.49	Light to Crowborough, Seaford and Lewes	Failed
17.8.49	Light to Crowborough, Seaford and Lewes	Failed
18.8.49	Trial to Eastleigh with 248 tons	Failed
20.8.49	Light, Eastleigh-Brighton	Failed
30.8.49	Light to Crowborough	
31.8.49	Light to Crowborough	
1.9.49	Light to Crowborough	
2.9.49	Light to Crowborough	
5.9.49	Intended trial to Victoria with 260 tons	Failed
8.9.49	Intended trial to Victoria with 260 tons	Failed
16.9.49	Trial to Crowborough with between 180 and 271 tons	Failed
19.9.49	Trial to Crowborough with between 180 and 271 tons	Failed
20.9.49	Trial to Crowborough with between 180 and 271 tons	Failed
23.9.49	Trial to Crowborough	
24.9.49	Trial to Crowborough	
25.9.49	Trial to Crowborough	Failed
27.9.49	Trials to Oxted, Crowborough and Lewes with 150 tons	Failed
28.9.49	Trials to Oxted, Crowborough and Lewes with 150 tons	Failed
29.9.49	Trials to Oxted, Crowborough and Lewes with 150 tons	Failed
30.9.49	Trials to Oxted, Crowborough and Lewes with 150 tons	Failed
3.10.49	Trials to Crowborough with 150 tons	Failed
4.10.49	Trials to Crowborough with 150 tons	Failed
9.10.49	Trials to Crowborough with 150 tons	Failed
22.10.49	Trials to Oxted and Crowborough with 150 tons	
23.10.49	Trials to Oxted and Crowborough with 150 tons	
24.10.49	Trials to Oxted and Crowborough with 150 tons	Failed
29.10.49	Light to Crowborough and Tunbridge Wells	Failed
30.10.49	Light to Crowborough and Tunbridge Wells	
31.10.49	Trial to Crowborough with 161 tons	
1.11.49	Trials to Oxted and Crowborough with 153-255 tons	Failed
2.11.49	Trials to Oxted and Crowborough with 153-255 tons	
3.11.49	Trials to Oxted and Crowborough with 153-255 tons	
4.11.49	Trials to Oxted and Crowborough with 153-255 tons	
7.11.49	Trials to Oxted, Polegate and Crowborough with 153-255 tons	
8.11.49	Trials to Oxted, Polegate and Crowborough with 153-255 tons	
9.11.49	Trials to Oxted, Polegate and Crowborough with 153-255 tons	
10.11.49	Trials to Oxted, Polegate and Crowborough with 153-255 tons	

Date	Working	Official result
11.11.49	Trials to Oxted, Polegate and Crowborough with 153-255 tons	
16.11.49	Trial to Oxted with 255 tons	Failed
21.11.49	Trials to Oxted and Polegate with 153-255 tons	
22.11.49	Trials to Oxted and Polegate with 153-255 tons	
23.11.49	Trials to Oxted and Polegate with 153-255 tons	
24.11.49	Trials to Oxted and Polegate with 153-255 tons	
25.11.49	Trials to Oxted and Polegate with 153-255 tons	Failed
29.11.49	Trial to Polegate with 153 tons	Failed
1.12.49	Trials to Polegate, Oxted, Tunbridge Wells and Groombridge with 153-255 tons	
2.12.49	Trials to Polegate, Oxted, Tunbridge Wells and Groombridge with 153-255 tons	
3.12.49	Trials to Polegate, Oxted, Tunbridge Wells and Groombridge with 153-255 tons	
4.12.49	Trials to Polegate, Oxted, Tunbridge Wells and Groombridge with 153-255 tons	
5.12.49	Trials to Polegate, Oxted, Tunbridge Wells and Groombridge with 153-255 tons	
6.12.49	Trials to Polegate, Oxted, Tunbridge Wells and Groombridge with 153-255 tons	Failed
12.12.49	Trials to Crowborough and Oxted with 153-255 tons	
13.12.49	Trials to Crowborough and Oxted with 153-255 tons	Failed
16.12.49	Light to Eastleigh and return	
27.1.50	Light to Tunbridge Wells	
2.2.50	Light to Eastleigh and return	
13.4.50	Light to Eastleigh	
6.6.50	Eastleigh-Fratton and return with 332 tons	
7.6.50	Eastleigh-Fratton and return with 332 tons	
8.6.50	Eastleigh-Fratton and return with 332 tons	
12.6.50	Eastleigh-Woking and return with 337 tons	
15.6.50	Eastleigh-Woking and return with 320 tons	Failed
29.6.50	Intended Eastleigh-Woking trial with approx 240 tons	Failed
15.8.50	Light, Eastleigh-Botley and return	
15.8.50	Light, Eastleigh-Botley and return	
18.8.50	Light, Eastleigh-Fratton and return	
21.8.50	Trial, Eastleigh-Woking-Guildford and return with 231^1/$_2$ tons	
23.8.50	Trial, Eastleigh-Woking-Guildford and return with 264 tons	
24.8.50	Trial, Eastleigh-Woking-Guildford and return with 290^1/$_2$ tons	
21.9.50	Light, Eastleigh-Fratton and return	
25.9.50	Trial, Eastleigh-Woking-Guildford and return with 241^1/$_2$ tons	
26.9.50	Trial, Eastleigh-Woking-Guildford and return with 275 tons	
27.9.50	Trial, Eastleigh-Woking-Guildford and return with 294^1/$_2$ tons	
28.9.50	Trial, Eastleigh-Woking-Guildford and return with 325^1/$_2$ tons	
14.10.50	Light, Eastleigh-Cosham and return	
17.10.50	Trial, Eastleigh-Woking-Guildford and return with 430 tons	
2.11.50	Intended trial, Eastleigh-Woking-Guildford and return with 480 tons, terminated at Basingstoke, engine returned light	Failed

The statistical information contained in these tables should be read only in conjunction with the text and not taken as a full and accurate assessment.

Place	Booked time (pm)	Actual time (pm)	Boiler pressure	Steam chest pressure	% cut-off	Water in glass (in) (F = 6½in)	Smokebox vacuum (in of water)	Temp °F, large tubes	Temp °F, small tubes	Remarks
Eastleigh	6.45	6.45	260	145	67	Full				
				140	15	Full				
Allbrook Junc		6.51¼	250	200	30	Full	4½	620	600	Engine worked very lightly to Allbrook Junc and mainly due to this 5 min lost to Winchester Junction
			260	230	30		8	700	630	
			245	230	15		6½	700	630	
Shawford		6.57	240	230	18	5	8	700	640	
Shawford Junc			225	220	18		8	710	635	
St Cross Tunnel			225	220			8½	710	635	
Winchester		7.1¼	230	225	20	4	9	740	680	Shower of sparks from chimney, about 20% being alight on reaching ground
Winchester Junc			235	225			9	760	730	15mph pws
Wallers Ash Box			250	240	20	2½	4	660	620	
Weston Box			240	235		2	7	720	680	
Micheldever		7.14½	220	205		2	8	720	685	BP and water in glass not maintained
Litchfield Tunnel			185	160		2	6	715	675	
Worting Junc	7.19	7.23	200	60		2½				
Basingstoke	7.24	7.32	260	130	67	2	4	630	580	6 min taken to get engine set for water
	7.32		255	160	15					
Hook		7.46½	240	135	15	1½	5	670	630	
Winchfield		7.49	230	120	15	1¼	4	665	625	
Fleet		7.55¼	230	120	15	1¼	5	650	610	
Farnborough		7.55¼	230	120	15	1¾	5	645	600	
Brookwood		8.1	210	200	15					
Woking	8.5	8.3¼								To local line. Sig checks

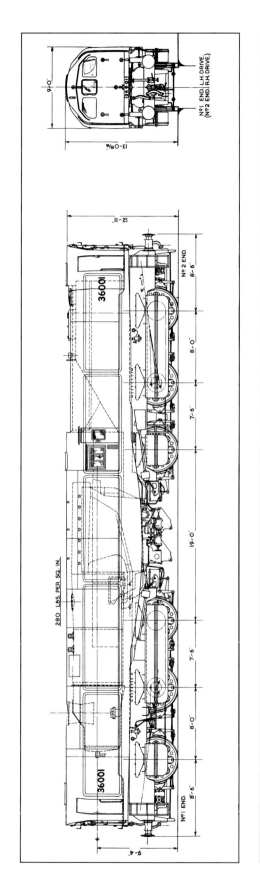

280 LBS. PER SQ. IN.

36001

No 1 END

No 2 END

No 1 END: L.H. DRIVE.
(No 2 END: R.H. DRIVE.)

'Leader' test of 2 November 1950

Place	Booked time (pm)	Actual time (pm)	Boiler pressure	Steam chest pressure	% cut-off	Water in glass (in) (F = 6½in)	Smokebox vacuum (in of water)	Temp °F, large tubes	Temp °F, small tubes	Remarks
Eastleigh	6.40	6.40	260	240	67	Full	1	500	500	Started without difficulty
			270	130	25		1.75			
Allbrook Junc	6.45	6.45½	245	240	10	Full	2½	650	620	Pricker and dart used
			260	255	38		4	680	630	
Shawford		6.53½	230	225	18	Full	6½	730	680	
Shawford Junc			220	210	18	Full	7	730	660	Pricker used
St Cross Tunnel			220	210	18	Full	7	730	660	
Winchester		6.58¼	245	240	18	Full	9	750	700	Pricker used
Winchester Junc	6.59	7.13¾	255	225	18	Full	10½	760	710	
Wallers Ash Box		7.5	245	220	18	Full	10½	750	700	Pricker and dart used
Weston Box		7.7	240	225	18	Full	10	750	720	
Micheldever		7.9½	250	235	18	5½	10	785	750	
			260	250	20	5	13.5	800	780	
Litchfield Tunnel		7.12½	255	240	20	4	13½	820	800	
Worting Junc	7.19	7.18½								Pricker used
Basingstoke	7.24	7.26								Sig stop 1½ min

Comparative performance of 'U' No 31630 and 'Leader' No 36001

	17 October 1950	2 November 1950
Load (tons)	430	480
Coal (total cwt)	52¹/₂	22 (Eastleigh-Basingstoke only)
lb/mile	59.6	-
lb/mile	86.0	94.8
lb/dbhp hr	6.5	6.4
lb/sq ft grate/hr	125	130 (Eastleigh-Basingstoke only)
Water (total) gall	3,570	1,834
gall/mile	37.4	-
gall/mile (Eastleigh-Basingstoke only)	55.0	70.5
lb/dbhp hr	41.0	51.0
lb/hr (Eastleigh-Basingstoke only)	19,000	24,500

Comparative performance based on average results obtained

	'U' class No 31630	'Leader' class No 36001	Difference ('U' class = 100%)
Boiler pressure (psi)	187	240	+28.3
Steam chest pressure (psi)	167	135	-19.2
Exhaust pressure (psi)	1.81	7.3	+403
Smokebox vacuum (in of water)	2.34	4.00	+71
Inlet steam temp (°F)	478	546	+14
Exhaust steam temp (°F)	220	285	+29.5
Smokebox A temp (°F)	570	574	+0.7
Smokebox B temp (° F)	578	620	+7.26
Trip, coal (lb)	1,455	2,457	+68.8
lb/mile	29.75	50.17	+68.7
lb ton/mile (inc engine)	0.0818	0.121	+48.0
lb/hour (running time)	1,125	1,830	+62.7
lb/sq ft grate/hour	45	71.8	+59.6
lb/dbhp hour	4.01	6.727	+67.6
Water, gallons	1,245	1,850	+48.6
gals/mile	25.44	37.78	+48.5
lb/hour (running time)	9,621	13,790	+43.3
lb/dbhp hour	34.34	50.66	+47.55
lb/sq ft evap heating	6.334	5.777	-8.8
lb/ton mile (inc engine)	0.702	0.912	+30.0
Evaporation (lb water/lb coal)	8.554	7.532	+12.0
Boiler efficiency	78.29	71.22	-9.0
BThUs/dbhp hour	53,893	90,262	+67.5
Overall efficiency (%)	4.72	2.82	-40.25

Index